TO
HELL
AND
BACK

TO HELL AND BACK

AUDIE MURPHY

FOREWORD BY TOM BROKAW

A HOLT PAPERBACK

HENRY HOLT AND COMPANY | NEW YORK

Henry Holt and Company
Publishers since 1866
120 Broadway
New York, New York 10271

www.henryholt.com

A Holt Paperback® and ⓗ® are registered trademarks of Macmillan Publishing, LLC.

Library of Congress Cataloging-in-Publication Data
Murphy, Audie, 1924–1971.
To hell and back / Audie Murphy ; foreword by Tom Brokaw.
p. cm.
Originally published: New York : H. Holt, 1949.
ISBN 0-8050-7086-9 (pbk.)
1. Murphy, Audie, 1924–1971. 2. World War, 1939–1945—Personal
narratives, American. 3. Soldiers—United States—Biography. 4. World War,
1939–1945—Europe. I. Title.
D811 .M87 2002
940.54'8173—dc21   2002017232

Henry Holt books are available for special promotions and
premiums. For details contact: Director, Special Markets.

First published in hardcover in 1949 by Holt, Rinehart and Winston

First Holt Paperbacks Edition 2023

Printed in the United States of America
40 39 38 37 36

Foreword

Audie Murphy was such a quintessential American hero it was as if someone had invented him. The Texas poor boy with the baby face and the sharpshooter aim personified all of the great symbols of this country: he was a gunfighter from the American West defending freedom and justice against great odds. He was personally modest and handsome as a movie star.

As you will learn in *To Hell and Back*, the story of his World War II combat experiences, that title is not hyperbole. In all of the research I've done on World War II combat veterans I cannot recall another story that involves so much up close and personal fighting. He was a brilliant and courageous warrior with deep feelings about his fellow fighting men, their safety, and their common mission.

For three years he was almost constantly on the front lines in North Africa, Italy, and Northern Europe. For much of that time he was out front, leading scouting patrols into hostile territory or putting himself in harm's way when fierce fighting was expected. I am still astonished that he survived so much firepower directed at him day after day, month after month.

In this era of high tech combat, with laser guided missiles and remote controlled battlefields, Murphy's exploits are all the more inspirational. It was his personal courage, cunning, and instincts that converted him into the most lethal one-man weapon the Army had on the ground against the Fascist forces.

But this is more than a book about fighting. It is most of all a story of the kinship formed in military units fighting for a great cause and personal survival. Murphy's buddies came alive for me as he described their bravery and idiosyncrasies, their wounds, and their heart-breaking deaths. You will come to know that other enduring American trait: the tough guy with the tender heart.

I was first aware of Murphy as a war hero; he was on the cover of *Life* magazine when I was a youngster. Later he was a regular part of my Saturday afternoons as he starred in the matinees at the small-town movie theaters where I lived.

I was always drawn to his laconic, confident style as an actor and I now realize those were the same qualities that made him such a popular leader of men during the war.

Not long before his untimely death in an airplane accident I was working in California when Audie Murphy came back into the news. A woman friend of his had sent her dog to a trainer and she wasn't happy with the results. As I recall, she asked Audie to intervene. He visited the dog trainer who then complained to the police that Murphy had shot at him.

The local police brought Murphy in for questioning. By then his acting career was in decline and unfortunately his World War II heroism was pushed into the background by concerns over the widening war in Vietnam.

Nonetheless when Murphy was released without charges a large number of reporters were outside the police station. Murphy agreed to take a few questions. One of the reporters asked, "Audie, did you shoot at that guy?"

Audie Murphy, the most decorated combat veteran of World War II, stared at his interrogator for a moment and then said in that familiar Texas voice, "If I had, do you think I would have missed?"

I loved that moment and all that Audie Murphy stood for as a citizen, a soldier, and a hero.

—Tom Brokaw

TO HELL AND BACK

1

ON a hill just inland from the invasion beaches of Sicily, a soldier sits on a rock. His helmet is off; and the hot sunshine glints through his coppery hair. With the sleeve of his shirt he wipes the sweat from his face; then with chin in palm he leans forward in thought.

The company is taking a break. We sprawl upon the slope, loosen the straps of our gear, and gaze at the blue sky. It is my first day of combat; and so far the action of the unit has been undramatic and disappointingly slow.

Just trust the army to get things fouled up. If the landing schedule had not gone snafu, we would have come ashore with the assault waves. That was what I wanted. I had primed myself for the big moment. Then the timing got snarled in the predawn confusion; and we came in late, chugging ashore like a bunch of clucks in a ferryboat.

The assault troops had already taken the beach. The battle had moved inland. So for several hours we have tramped over fields and hills without direct contact with the enemy.

It is true that the landing was not exactly an excursion. There was some big stuff smashing about; and from various points came the rattle of small arms. But we soon got used to that.

Used to it!

A shell crashes on a nearby hill; the earth quivers; and the black smoke boils. A man, imitating Jack Benny's Rochester, shouts, "Hey, boss. A cahgo of crap just landed on Pigtail Ridge." A ripple of laughter follows the announcement. "Hey, boss. Change that name to No-Tail Ridge. The tail go with the cahgo."

The second shell is different. Something terrible and immediate about its whistle makes my scalp start prickling. I grab my helmet and flip over on my stomach. The explosion is thunderous. Steel fragments whine, and the ground seems to jump up and hit me in the face.

Silence again. I raise my head. The sour fumes of powder have caused an epidemic of coughing.

"Hey, boss. The cahgo—"

The voice snaps. We all see it. The redheaded soldier has tumbled from the rock. Blood trickles from his mouth and nose.

Beltsky, a veteran of the fighting in North Africa, is the first to reach him. One glance from his professional eye is sufficient. Turning to a man, he says, "Get his ammo. He won't be needing it. You will."

"Who me? I got plenty of ammo."

"Get the ammo. Don't argue."

Snuffy Jones does not like the idea at all. A frown crawls over his sallow face; and beneath a receding chin, his Adam's apple bobs nervously. With shaky fingers he removes the ammunition from the cartridge belt. One would think he was trying to neutralize a booby trap.

"Who is he?" asks Brandon.

"He *was* a guy named Griffin," Kerrigan answers. "I got likkered up with him once in Africa. Told me he was married and had a couple kids."

"That's rough." Brandon's eyes are suddenly deep and thoughtful.

"He could have stayed out, I guess. But he volunteered. Had to get into the big show."

Novak, the Pole, has been listening with mouth agape. Now his lips curl savagely. "The sonsabeeches!" he growls to nobody in particular.

Unfolding a gas cape, Beltsky covers the body with it.

"That'll do him a lot of good now," says Brandon.

"It's to keep the flies from blowing him," explains Horse-Face

Johnson soberly. "Flies go to work on 'em right away. Fellow from the last war told me they swell up like balloons. Used 'em for pillows out in No-Man's Land. Soft enough but they wouldn't keep quiet. They was always losing wind in the dead of the night. Such sighing and whistling you never heard."

"For chrisake, shut up," says Kerrigan.

Johnson's blue eyes twinkle sardonically. His long, lean face stretches into a grin. And his laugh is like the soft whinny of of a horse.

"Don't let it get you down, son. Used to be skittish myself till I worked as an undertaker's assistant out in Minnesota. Took my baths in embalming fluid. Slept in coffins during the slack hours. Grave error. Damned nigh got buried one day when I got mistook for the late departed."

"Shut up!"

"It's the dying truth, son."

"Then why didn't you get hooked up with a body-snatching outfit? You look like a natural for the buzzard detail."

"Why, you know, son, the army wouldn't be guilty of giving a man a job he knowed anything about. Got tired of the racket anyhow. Couldn't argue with the late departeds. Whatever I said they was always dead right."

"Oh, for chrisake," mutters Kerrigan pleadingly.

"Whee-he-he-he."

"Okay, men," says Beltsky. "You've seen how it happens. Maybe you know now this game is played for keeps. Everybody on your feet. All right there, what's the matter with you?"

"Me?" drawls Snuffy. "I'm gittin' up. Just give me time. Snapped-to once so fast that I mislocated my backbone."

"Would you like to be carried on a stretcher?"

"Stretch who?"

"Okay. Okay. Let's move across Sicily."

"He was just sitting there on the rock," says Steiner, his face filled with awe. "I was looking at him just a minute before."

"So what?" snaps Antonio irritably. "He shouldn'ta been

makin' like a pigeon. He oughta kept his head down." He taps himself on the chest. "You didn't see me givin' out wit the coos, did you?"

"How could he know it was coming?"

"Aw nuts! You could hear it comin' a mile."

As we plod over the hills in sweat-soaked clothes, the uneasiness passes from my stomach to my mind. So it happens as easily as that. You sit on a quiet slope with chin in hand. In the distance a gun slams; and the next minute you are dead.

Maybe my notions about war were all cockeyed. How do you pit skill against skill if you cannot even see the enemy? Where is the glamour in blistered feet and a growling stomach? And where is the expected adventure? Well, whatever comes, it was my own idea. I had asked for it. I had always wanted to be a soldier.

The years roll back; and in my mind, I see a pair of hands. Calloused and streaked with dirt, they looked like claws; and they shook as they cupped around the match flame. He puffed on the cigarette. And as I waited, all ears, he bent over in a fit of coughing.

"It's that gas," he explained. "Nearly eighteen years, and it's still hangin' on."

"But you knowed where they were," I said.

From the shade of the tree, he gazed over the cotton fields.

"Of course, I knowed where they was," he said. "Any ijiot would have. It was still early mornin'; and when they crawled through the field, they shook the dew off the wheat. So every blessed one of 'em left a dark streak behind. That give their positions away."

"So what did you do?"

"What would you done? I lined up my sights on the machine gun and waited."

"A machine gun?"

"Yeah. It's the devil's own weepon. When they got to the edge of the patch, I could see 'em plain. There was nothin' to it. I just pulled the trigger and let 'em have it."

Fascinated, I glanced at the hands again, picking out the trigger finger. "You killed 'em?"

"I didn't do 'em any good."

"Did they shoot at you?"

"Now what do you think? This was war. But I kept my head down and got along all right until that night they thowed over the gas. We didn't get the alarm until I'd already breathed a lungful."

"What was they like?"

"The Germans? I never took time to ast 'em. They was shootin' at us; so we shot at them."

"But you whipped 'em."

"We whopped 'em all right, but it wasn't easy. They was hard fighters. Don't ever kid yourself about that."

"Some day I aim to be a soldier."

"A sojer?" he said disgustedly. "What fer?"

"I don't know."

"If you want to fight, start fightin' these weeds." He coughed again, spat out a gob of phlegm, and muttered, "A sojer." He was still shaking his head when he gripped the plow handles and said, "Giddap," to the mules.

A soldier.

Steiner is a soldier, but you would never see his kind on the recruiting posters. Short and pudgy, he has the round, innocent face of a baby and a voice as gentle as a child's. He cannot get the knack of the army, though he tries hard. His gear is forever fouled up. It drips from his body like junk. Now he stumbles and falls. It is the third time he has tripped today; and Olsen, a huge, blond sergeant, is fresh out of patience.

"What's a-matter? What's a-matter?" he snarls. "Pick up your dogs."

"It's the legging strings. They keep coming unlaced."

"For chrisake, paste 'em on if you ain't got enough sense to lace 'em. Aw right, come on. Snap to it."

"Gotohell."

"What's that?"

"Whyn't you let him alone?" says Antonio. "De kid can't help it."

"Keep your big nose outa this."

"Okay. Break it up," says Beltsky. "You'll soon have a belly full of fighting."

No, it was not the least bit like the dream I had as a child. That afternoon in Texas I had followed the veteran of World War I into the field. The sun beat down and the rows of cotton seemed endless. But I soon forgot both the heat and the labor.

The weeds became the enemy, and my hoe, a mysterious weapon. I was on a faraway battlefield, where bugles blew, banners streamed, and men charged gallantly across flaming hills; where the temperature always stood at eighty and our side was always victorious; where the dying were but impersonal shadows and the wounded never cried; where enemy bullets always miraculously missed me, and my trusty rifle forever hit home.

I was only twelve years old; and the dream was my one escape from a grimly realistic world.

We were share-crop farmers. And to say that the family was poor would be an understatement. Poverty dogged our every step. Year after year the babies had come until there were nine of us children living, and two dead. Getting food for our stomachs and clothes for our backs was an ever-present problem. As soon as we grew old enough to handle a plow, an ax, or a hoe, we were thrown into the struggle for existence.

My mother, a sad-eyed, silent woman, toiled eternally. As a baby, I sat strapped like a papoose in a yard swing while she fought the weeds in a nearby field.

Our situation is not to be blamed on the social structure. If my father had exercised more foresight, undoubtedly his family would have fared much better. He was not lazy, but he had a genius for not considering the future.

One day he gave up. He simply walked out of our lives, and we never heard from him again.

My mother, attempting to keep her brood together, worked harder than ever. But illness overtook her. Gradually she grew weaker and sadder. And when I was sixteen she died.

Except for a married sister, who was unable to support us, there was no family nucleus left. The three youngest children were placed in an orphanage. The rest of us scattered, going our individual ways. Boarding out, I worked for a while in a filling station; then I became a flunky in a radio repair shop.

God knows where my pride came from, but I had it. And it was constantly getting me into trouble. My temper was explosive. And my moods, typically Irish, swung from the heights to the depths. At school, I had fought a great deal. Perhaps I was trying to level with my fists what I assumed fate had put above me.

I was never so happy as when alone. In solitude, my dreams made sense. Nobody was there to dispute or destroy them.

After the death of my mother, I was more than ever determined to enter military service. When the Japanese hit Pearl Harbor, I was half-wild with frustration. Here was a war itself; and I was too young to enlist. I was sure that it would all be over in a few months and I would be robbed of the great adventure that had haunted my imagination.

On my eighteenth birthday, I hurried to a marine corps recruiting station. This branch seemed the toughest of the lot; and I was looking for trouble. Unfortunately, the corps was looking for men, men italicized. A sergeant glanced over my skinny physique. My weight did not measure up to Leatherneck standards.

Leaving the office in a blaze of unreasonable anger, I tried the paratroops. This was a new branch of service, lacking the legendary color of the marines, but it sounded rough. There was another point in its favor: paratroopers wore such handsome boots.

That office was more sympathetic. The recruiting sergeant did not turn me down cold. He suggested that I load up on bananas and milk before weighing in. My pride was taking an awful beating. The sergeant was the first on a long list of uniformed authorities that I requested to go to the devil.

The infantry finally accepted me. I was not overjoyed. The infantry was too commonplace for my ambition. The months would teach me the spirit of this unglamorous, greathearted fighting machine. But at that time I had other plans. After my basic training, I would get a transfer. I would become a glider pilot.

Thus, with a pocket full of holes, a head full of dreams, and an ignorance beyond my years, I boarded a bus for the induction center. Previously I had never been over a hundred miles from home.

Nor had I reckoned with realistic army training. During my first session of close-order drill, I, the late candidate for the marines and the paratroops, passed out cold. I quickly picked up the nickname of "Baby." My commanding officer tried to shove me into a cook and baker's school, where the going would be less rough.

That was the supreme humiliation. To reach for the stars and end up stirring a pot of C-rations. I would not do it. I swore that I would take the guardhouse first. My stubborn attitude paid off. I was allowed to keep my combat classification; and the army was spared the disaster of having another fourth-class cook in its ranks.

But I still had to get overseas; and my youthful appearance continued to cause much shaking of heads. At Fort Meade, where we had our final phase of training in America, I was almost transferred to the camp's permanent cadre. An officer, kindly attempting to save me from combat, got me a position as a clerk in the post exchange.

Fuming, I stuck to my guns; and in early 1943, I landed in North Africa as a replacement for an infantry company. The war in this sector was about over. Instead of combat, we were given another long, monotonous period of training.

Finally the great news came. We were to go into action in the Tunis area. We oiled our guns, double-checked our gear; and prayed or cursed according to our natures. But before we could move out, the order was canceled. The Germans in the area had surrendered.

I took no part in the general sigh of relief. Perhaps now I would react differently.

At this moment, the fluttering roll of an enemy machine gun is causing my flesh to creep. "The devil's own weapon," the veteran had said. "And, of course, I knowed where they was."

Does the enemy know where we are. He could. Easily. We are stretched in an open field; and the cover is something less than adequate. Before us lies a railroad track along which the machine-gun crew has dug in.

The gun has suddenly become quiet. I hear the labored breathing of our men; see Beltsky's worried face; feel my heart churning against the ribs. "What would you have done?" the veteran had said. "I lined up my sights and waited." He had no corner on that little game. It too could be the enemy's.

The order comes down the line.

"Spread out. We're going over the track."

Olsen's mouth sags; and the fear in his eyes is sickening. My jaws clamp; my heart slows down. I have seen the face of a coward and found it loathsome.

The secondary order is passed along in hoarse whispers.

"When you get the signal, make a run for it. Stop for nothing until you find cover on the other side of the track."

Beltsky studies his wrist watch. His hand goes up in a wave. We scramble to our feet and take off.

Brrrrrp.

From the corner of my eye, I see two men in the center platoon reel backward and fall. Then I hear the crackle of rifles; the blast of a grenade. I leap the track. Johnson passes me. "Son," he calls, "get the lead out of your shoes. Them krauts have started a shooting war."

I find a gully, drop into it, and sprawl out. A body thuds on top of me. It is Novak.

"By gah, you excuse," he says. "I see nahthin' when I jump."

"You were coming too fast to take in the scenery."

He has an odd, crooked smile; his nose is bent; and a mop of oily black hair tumbles over his forehead. Carefully breaking a cigarette in two, he hands me a half.

"I don't smoke."

"Nah? You gotta smoke to stay happy. You try it."

"No, thanks. Did they get the machine gun?"

"They get it." His eyes burn fiercely. "But the sonsabecches knocked over two of our men."

"I saw them."

"When they tear up Poland, that is bad enough. But when they shoot our men, it is too much. From now on, Mike Novak is not to be soft, no chicken heart. He uses his gun."

The following day I am ahead of the company with a group of scouts. We flush a couple of Italian officers. They should have surrendered. Instead they mount two magnificent white horses and gallop madly away. My act is instinctive. Dropping to one knee, I fire twice. The men tumble from the horses, roll over and lie still.

"Now why did you do that?" asks a lieutenant.

"What should I have done? Stood here with egg on my face, waving them goodbye?"

"You shouldn't have fired."

"That's our job, isn't it? They would have killed us if they'd had the chance. That's their job. Or have I been wrongly informed?"

"To hell with it. I guess you did the right thing."

I later discover that such mental confusion is common among new men. In the training areas we talked toughly, thought toughly; and finally we believed we really were tough. But it is not easy to shed the idea that human life is sacred. The lieutenant has not yet accepted the fact that we have been put into the field to deal out death.

I have. If there were any doubt in my mind, it began to vanish in the shell explosion that killed Griffin; and it disappeared altogether when I saw the two men crumple by the railroad track.

Now I have shed my first blood. I feel no qualms; no pride; no remorse. There is only a weary indifference that will follow me throughout the war.

Again my youth catches up with me. My company commander, looking at my thin frame and cursed baby face, decides that the front is no place for me. He has me transferred to headquarters to serve as a runner. I should be grateful, but I am not. I am constantly sneaking off with patrols and scouting parties.

The company commander finally calls me on the carpet.

"I hear you can't stay away from the front, Murphy."

"Yessir."

"What's wrong with you? You want to get killed?"

"Nosir."

"I tried to do you a favor. Most men would have appreciated it."

"Yessir."

"Now I'm going to do myself a favor. I'm putting you back in the lines; and you'll stay there until you're so sick of action you'll want to vomit."

"Yessir."

"And, incidentally," he grins, "you've been made a corporal. You may have to take over a squad. Now get up there and give 'em hell."

I did not only want to vomit, I did. Not long after I returned to the front, the enemy defenses began to collapse; and speed on our part became urgent. The march toward Palermo became virtually a foot race. We had to average from twenty-five to thirty miles a day over rugged terrain.

Dust lay over the highways like a smoke screen; not a cloud appeared in the sky. Often we could not stop even to eat. We gulped our rations as we walked.

My brain swam; and my internal organs rumbled. Finally I could take it no longer. I fell out of the ranks, lay down on the roadside, and heaved until I thought I would lose my stomach.

A major paused in his jeep. "What's wrong?" he asked. "Are you sick, soldier?"

"Nosir. I'm just spilling my guts for the hell of it."

"Maybe you'd better report to the medics."

"Yessir."

But I did not. I rose to my feet and staggered up the road, cursing the war in detail.

The next day I black out completely. When I regain consciousness, I hear voices; but they seem to be coming through a thick wall. I open my eyes, and the bright sunshine dazzles me. This is odd weather indeed. Despite the sweat rolling from my face, I am shivering.

A face bends over me. "Something wrong with you, soldier?" a voice asks.

"No. I'm perfectly all right. Where am I?"

"At an aid station. How do you feel?"

"I feel like hell. I'm cold."

"You look like hell. Must be malaria."

It is. Darkness blots out my mind again; and I awake in a field hospital.

A week later I am marked fit for duty. As we pass through Palermo on the way to the front, the streets swarm with our men. The natives gape, and supply trucks speed through the town. Lines of soldiers, with their weapons slung on their shoulders, stand before brothels, patiently awaiting their turn. Individual dignity has been transformed to fit the nature of war.

The regiment reaches the west bank of the Furiano river on its drive toward Messina in the final phase of the Sicilian campaign. Across a narrow strip of water from Messina lies the Italian mainland itself.

The Furiano area, including the stream bed itself, is heavily mined. The eastern terrain slopes down to the river; and on the west bank is a series of hills rolling toward rugged Mount Fratello, which dominates the area. The enemy is entrenched and determined.

On our approach to the stream, we are caught in a concentration of artillery and mortar fire. The earth shudders; and the screaming of shells intermingles with the screaming of men. We fall back, reorganize, and again storm forward. For a second time the barrage hits us. Again we withdraw.

Olsen is the first to crack up. He throws his arms around the company commander, crying hysterically, "I can't take any more." The harassed captain tries to calm him, but Olsen will not stop bawling. So he is sent to the rear, and we watch him go with hatred in our eyes.

"If I ever throw a whingding like that, shoot me," says Kerrigan.

"Gladly," I reply. "In North Africa, I thought he was one tough boy."

"Yeah. He threw his weight around plenty."

"He seemed to be everything the War Department was looking for. He was my idea of a real soldier. Then one night that little Italian, Corrego, came in drunk; and Olsen beat him up."

"He should have been shot right then."

"It was against regulations."

"At least, we should've mauled hell out of him."

"Yeah. I'll never judge a man by his appearance again."

"Nor women either," says Kerrigan, thoughtfully scratching his groin. "I thought that dame in Palermo was perfectly okay until I woke up with the mechanized dandruff."

"Maybe you got them from a latrine."

"No. Army regulations say that only officers can catch the bugs there. I've been fighting them with gasoline and my skin is blistered. I ought to have introduced Johnson to that girl."

"Sure. That's what you get for holding out on a pal."

"Think I'll plant a few of the bugs in his breeches anyhow. He drawed a blank in Palermo and won't know where in hell they came from."

"Why make it a few?"

"That'll be enough. They spread faster than a rumor."

Part of the regiment crosses the river under the cover of a smoke screen. I remain behind to help guard a machine-gun emplacement. The assignment suits me. I now see that the fighting will not run out. There will be plenty of war for everybody. While the battle grows in violence, I lie in a vineyard, eating grapes and watching the fight.

Our men are pinned down on a slope. They cannot advance; and they cannot retreat, because the Germans have laid a curtain of fire between them and the river. Our company commander is among those killed before they can withdraw during the night.

A co-ordinated attack consisting of a surprise landing at the enemy's rear, thrusts its way around Mount Fratello, and a direct assault on the hills themselves finally reduces the German defenses.

I contributed little to the battle; gained much. I acquired a healthy respect for the Germans as fighters; an insight into the fury of mass combat; and a bad case of diarrhea. I had eaten too many grapes.

2

THE Sicilian campaign has taken the vinegar out of my spirit. I have seen war as it actually is, and I do not like it. But I will go on fighting, even as Brandon, Steiner, Kerrigan, Johnson, and Jones will go on fighting. Experience has seasoned us, made us battlewise and intensely practical. But we still have much to learn.

We land with undue optimism on the Italian mainland near Salerno. The beachhead, bought dearly with the blood and guts of the men who preceded us, is secure. The Italian government has surrendered. We are prepared for a quick dash to Rome.

The dash soon slows to a walk, however; and the walk, to a push. Right now we are not moving at all. We sit in a ditch near a road northeast of Salerno. Ahead a bridge over a shallow stream has been blown; and just beyond the ruins is an enemy machine-gun emplacement. We have heard its sputter; spotted its position.

Kerrigan is irritated. He flings off his helmet and mops a sweating brow.

"If those krauts don't stop monkeying with those guns," says he, "somebody's going to get hurt."

"A-feudin' and a-fightin'. Hot damn. I've had it all my life," remarks Snuffy Jones as he shifts a cud of tobacco in his cheek.

"Bitch, bitch, bitch," says Kerrigan mincingly. "You scrambled-eyed hillbilly from Croaking Hollow, you never had it

better." The Irishman does not speak a language so much as
he spits it.

"Steiner," says Horse-Face, "you damned nigh broke my back
when you tumbled in that hole on top of me. Get tripped up in
your cartridge belt?"

"I'm sorry. If there was a hole around, I might have known
you'd be at the bottom of it."

"If this was a horizontal war, you'd win it singlehanded."

"I don't go around reaching for splinters. I'm not bucking for
the Purple Heart."

"Speaking of Purple Hearts," says Horse-Face, "I seen a couple truck loads coming up from the rear. Must be expecting
some heavy scrapping ahead."

"There's going to be a little scrap right away," I say. "That
gun has got to be knocked out."

"Wait for the tanks," suggests Kerrigan.

"And let those kraut-headed babies get dug in further up?
Huh uh."

"Okay," says Steiner, putting on his helmet. "Let's go."

"I thought you wasn't the Purple Heart kid. Stay here, son.
I'll go."

"Nope. Afraid I'll catch cold in this ditch."

"You done got it. Your teeth are chattering like a katydid."

"Like a katydone, you illiterate rumhead."

"I go," says Novak. "I itch to bump up some krauts."

"It's the lice," remarks Brandon; "just scratch yourself and
wait. Somebody loan me a couple grenades."

"You got two."

"Here," says Snuffy. "Take my two aigs, and don't say I never
give you nothing."

"Eggs. Looks like you've been carrying them around so long
they're about hatched."

"That's what makes him so chicken."

"They'll be hatched in a few minutes," says Brandon quietly
as he buckles on the grenades.

I check my watch. "It's nine twenty. In fifteen minutes start laying down your blast, and keep the lead high. We don't want to walk into it."

"Fer chrisake," says Antonio. "If you miss, the krauts will have us zeroed. How we going to git out?"

"Ring for a bellhop."

"Yeah. Room service," says Kerrigan. "Make plenty of room between you and them goose-stepping bastards."

"Aw shadup. You always got to be the wise guy."

"Ready?"

"I'm okay. How about you, Steiner?"

"I've been ready so long I'm about to get unready."

I would rather have any other two men in the squad to accompany me. It is not because they lack courage. But Brandon takes too many chances; and Steiner is apt to stumble.

We crawl in a wide arc through the weeds to reach the stream. It is almost dry. The banks are lined with brush. We can advance up the bed in a crouching walk.

I slip forward while Brandon covers me; then Steiner passes me, while I cover him; Brandon jumps us both; and I go again. It is like a grim game of checkers. If lead flies ahead, the man in the forward position will get it.

We are nearing the bridge when Steiner reaches an open space in the bushes. The Germans have anticipated such a maneuver as ours and cut the brush away for the fire path. For a moment Steiner hesitates on the edge of the clearing; then he runs for the bridge. The machine gun blurts. Steiner pitches forward and lies with his flesh quivering. Our men in the ditch lay down their blast, but the bullets are snapping too high to keep the Germans down.

It is Brandon's move.

Suddenly a picture pops into my mind. It is that of his nine-year-old daughter. I see the eyes, eager with life; her pert freckled nose; her pigtails with bows of ribbon at the ends. And the letters scrawled on rough tablet paper: "Deer daddy i am in school but the teecher is not looking . . . when are you coming home i miss you."

Let the war wait. I signal for Brandon to remain where he is, but I may just as well try directing the wind. He thumbs his nose at my gesture and moves up. I part the bushes quickly, spot the machine-gun emplacement, and dig into it with a hail of lead from my tommy gun. Brandon rapidly scuttles over Steiner's body, and I shift to a new position.

A head pokes warily out of a foxhole to the rear of the gun emplacement. I give it a burst and drop to my knees. Brandon has reached the bridge ruins. Now he jerks the pin from a grenade, holds it briefly while the fuse sputters, hurls it. Before the smoke can clear from the explosion, he has thrown two more.

A kraut staggers out of the machine-gun nest with a pistol in his hand. I send a burst into him, and he topples to the ground.

Brandon crawls up the bank, rises, and starts walking with the last grenade in his hand.

"Keep down. Keep down. Are you nuts?" I yell. He pays not the slightest attention. Suddenly he wheels, lobs the grenade to the opposite side of the road, and falls. From the muffled sound of the explosion, I guess that the grenade has hit another foxhole. I scramble out of the stream bed. The five Germans are dead. Brandon surveys the scene with a frown on his face.

"Jesus," he says. And from the manner of his speaking, I cannot tell whether the word is meant as an oath or a prayer.

I shout for the squad to move up. We carry Steiner's body to the highway, where it will be easily found. In death, he still bears the look of innocent wonder. He could not have lived long after tumbling. The bullet ripped an artery in his throat.

The heat of summer has passed, and a sharpness is in the air. It is October. When we pause on our marches, Novak gazes over the earth, sniffing strangely. He must be thinking of the season and harvest. He grew up on a farm in Poland and has a feeling for land.

In his squat, gnarled body, one can see the record of toil. His knotted muscles bulge through his clothes. The long, hairy arms dangle like an ape's; the hands are large and calloused. In his eyes is a strange, broken light which heightens the habitual sadness of his features.

We all like him. He is a top-notch soldier, seldom complaining and fearing little. He has a great love for coffee and cigarettes, of which he can never get enough. They must have been scarce items in his former days. When drafted, he had been in America only five years; so he has not got used to the idea of plenty. He is forever scrounging; and his pack is crammed with extra rations. But there is nothing selfish about Novak. He would divide his last drop of blood with a comrade; or his last bit of lead with the enemy.

To him all Germans, dead, living, or wounded, fall into one class: "Sonsabeeches." He hates them personally and passionately.

"They ruin Poland; they ruin America," he says one night when we are holed up together. "Is a good country, America. By gah, I know. Is to eat, is to speak, is to drink as you will. Is America. Is to work, to save, to buy a farm maybe; and nobody take it from you."

"You want a farm?"

"Sure. A lil farm; few babies. I write to the girl and say, 'Mike's coming back. You wait. Few years in the steel mill; then the farm. You wait.'"

"And what did she say?"

"She don't answer yet. She's busy working too. You got a girl?"

"No."

"Thass bad. Everybody should have girl."

"I know it."

"My Alice speak good English. By gah, she teach the babies

speak without accent. You wait. You like her. Blue eyes, yellow hair, and built like a smokestack."

"Smokestack?"

"Yeah. Round. Tall."

"Sounds okay. How long have you known her?"

"Few months. Few dates. But she wait. I write her."

"When?"

"Africa, I think."

"So that's why you've always got your nose poked in the mail bag."

"Sure. Why not? Some day she write. Planty time."

"Yeah. She'll write."

"She's wan popular girl, but I sue her up."

"Sue her up?"

"Sure. Give her lotsa things. Beads. Ring. Hat. Clock with a bird on it. By gah, she don't forget Mike."

"No. It's in the bag."

"She's no bag."

"I didn't mean that. It's another way of saying she's all sowed up."

"In the bag, hey. It's a good English?"

"It's bad English. Slang. Was it a cuckoo clock?"

"Coocoo. Boocoo. Elgin. What's the differance. It's a fine clock. Fifteen dollars and ninety-eight cents, with tax."

"What did she give you?"

"She give me planty when I go home. You wait."

"You ever figure on not going home?"

"Who me? Naw. I go home. Sonsabeeches don't get me, you betcha."

"I'll bet we're in for a soaking. Clouds are getting lower than Kerrigan's mind."

"Sure. I smell it. So what? We get a bat."

We got more than a bath. The good weather is temporarily over. But the drive does not let up. As we plod through the country, seeking contact with the enemy, the rain slashes down, wetting us to the skins.

Some are also wet internally. The natives, whether from fear or friendliness, have been slipping the men bottles of wine as we pass through the villages.

Snuffy is drunk. Reeling through the mud, he sings, "Glory, glory, halleluja, for I am marchin' on." His voice is about as musical as a crow's.

"That guy claims to've been a bootlegger," snorts Kerrigan. "Be like a rabbit running a lettuce market."

"Probably invented the blind staggers and the seven-day hangover."

"Yeah. The smoke from the Smoky Mountains got in his brain."

"A little wine is good for the stomach," declares Snuffy, his eyes beginning to flame. "But cussin' is a bombernation. Repent and mend your ways, Kerrigan. Hell yawns for an Arshman."

"If you pass out, we're going to drag you to the front and throw you to the krauts."

"Repent, brother. Been aimin' to talk to you about your language. There's time yet for salvation."

We stop for a break in a deserted house. Snuffy strips down to his underwear and falls asleep in a large box. When we are ready to leave, he answers our pleas with snores. Kerrigan and I drag the box out into the rain. Snuffy awakes with a mighty oath.

At dusk, we halt in a grove, with orders to dig in. Novak's prowling eyes discover a strawstack.

"We sleep tonight like a hotel," he says. "Soft like a goose feather."

"Yeah. Complete with running water."

"We fix that too. You wait."

As we load our arms with straw, voices sound on the opposite side of the stack, but we pay no attention to them. There is plenty of straw for us all.

"We make a roof too. Weave. I show you. We get dry, you betcha."

"We'd better get some sack-time in tonight. Tomorrow things are liable to start popping."

"Sure. We get it easy too long."

As we prepare to leave, two straw-laden figures round the stack.

"You build a cover too. Is easy. You weave," says Novak.

"Gott im Himmel."

"Sonsabeeches."

For an instant, the four of us stand stupidly sharing a mutual paralysis of surprise. Then, still clutching our straw, we take off.

If those two Germans ran any faster than we, they must have broken some track records.

3

THE RAIN still falls in a steady drizzle when we reach the banks of the Volturno river. It is early night when we creep up to a dugout built by the enemy. It is supposed to be abandoned. But Kerrigan is not sure. He is a stickler for front-line courtesy. Before entering strange places, he first sends in his favorite calling card, a sputtering grenade.

We crouch on the slope while he sneaks up to the mouth of the tunnel leading into the cave. At the sound of the explosion, we dive for the dugout entrance, rolling over a wall of sandbags. The krauts may be just curious enough about the noise to send up a flare.

The interior of the cave is as dark as a bat's wing; and the bit-ing fumes of powder linger in the damp air. There is another smell too. The sour stench of decaying food and moldy clothing tells us that the Germans have been up to their usual job of bad housekeeping.

Striking matches, we carefully search for booby traps. Even Snuffy Jones bestirs himself to the task.

The place is evidently safe. Mentally we each mark off a few square feet of the earthen floor and unload our equipment. There is no way of knowing how long we will be here. Our orders are to hold the dugout until we are relieved.

Swope, a Cherokee Indian, volunteers for the first watch. He has nerves of iron, a fine eye for targets, and a weakness for automatic weapons.

Novak digs into his pack, hauls out a fat, squat candle, and lights it. Kerrigan sniffs at the procedure. "By the gods above us," says he, "a holy candle. Our pal has been robbing churches."

"I find it in ruins," Novak explains. "I burn it for you; and may the saints have mercy. Soon in hell you burn like the candle."

"Amen," adds Snuffy. "The sinful sonofabitch."

"Fer chrisake," snarls Antonio, "ain't you guys got no respect fer nuttin'."

"Respect," says Kerrigan, spreading his hands out pleadingly. "The boy talks about respect. For what? The ignoramus has been shooting up churches from here to hell-and-gone. Now he speaks of respect."

"Aw shadup," the Italian replies, "you got diarreah of the mout. Out of the whole army, I had the bad luck of gettin' tied up wit an outfit like this. You're nuts. Every one of you. Nuts."

"Nuts?" Snuffy echoes. "He calls us nuts. Why the guy musta had a pull wit the draft board even to git in the army. They take one look at him and say, 'This guy ain't got a brain in his head. But he might make a good officer in the air corps.' 'But, no,' says he, 'please let me be a dogface. I'm a fightin' fool jus' foamin' to go.' They say, 'We ain't doubtin' the fool part; but it 'pears to us that the only thing you ever fought was a bowl of macaroni.'"

It is Kerrigan's turn to say, "Amen. Keep right on talking, Reverend Jones."

"Yep," Snuffy continues, "they soak him in a barrel of cresote to de-louse him. Then they send him to school to build up his brain till he can tell the hay-foot from straw-foot. Can he learn? No.

"They give him an intelligent test to see if he's got enough sense to come out of the rain. He ain't. They have him try pouring water out of a boot. He don't know how. 'Jus' one thing left,' they say. 'Kin he or kin he not pee a hole in the snow?' They fill him with beer and stake him out in a blizzard. Dog saves him. Comes by and cocks a leg on Antonio, makin' the purtiest hole you ever see. That done it. Draft board says that man ain't quite dumb enough for the air corps. Figure he was infantry material when he didn't know enough to come in out of the rain."

"So they give him a gun," cuts in Kerrigan; "and ever since he's been trying to hand that rifle back."

"Why don't you shadup," says Antonio. "Why don't you all please step to hell and roast."

I crawl through the tunnel to check our position. Swope, with a Browning automatic between his knees, sits quietly behind the sandbag wall.

"What's all the noise about inside?" he asks.

"They're kidding Antonio. He thinks we've lost our sense of respect."

"That guy thinks the army's picking on him."

"Yeah. He makes it rough on himself."

Across the river a machine gun chatters. A grenade explodes; and we know from the sounds that one of our patrols has been discovered.

With his gun in readiness, Swope peers through a firing slot in the sandbag wall. If the Germans shoot again, they may reveal their position. But evidently they are too cautious for that. In the quietness we hear only the murmur of the men inside the cave and the gurgle of the river below us.

The Indian relaxes. "Boy, they're close," he says. "That gun couldn't have been over two hundred yards away."

"They're probably closer than that. They're supposed to be."

"Is the river big?"

"I don't think so. But the bridges are all out, and the krauts are dug in like gophers on the other side."

"They've probably got this joint pin-pointed."

"That, I think, is also according to plan. The krauts think we're going to attack in this area. As I get it, that's what they're supposed to think. Our job is to keep them busy while another outfit crosses upstream and hits them from the rear."

"So we're pigeons? The damned decoy?"

"I guess you could call us that."

The Cherokee leans back on his elbow. "Suits me," he says. "At least we ain't going wading, and we're not in the rain."

If there is an element of fear in his make-up, I have never seen it.

When I awake next morning, the artillery is firing sporadically. It is a routine, harassing action, which means that no full-scale attack can be expected immediately. I go out to check the terrain.

Across the river there is no sign of life. Rain still falls on the shell-battered trees. One tall poplar shimmers goldenly above the muddy water of the river.

The opposite slope is covered with rock and scrub. If the Germans are there, they are well camouflaged.

"I heard them talking just before daylight," says Kerrigan who has been on guard. "I just hope they don't bring in armor. Heavy stuff would cave in this rat trap."

I see a curious shrub in a thicket. Its leaves seem to be turned the wrong way. Borrowing Kerrigan's Garand, I take a few pot shots at the thicket. From two sides of it comes sniper fire. The bullets plunk into our sandbag wall.

"Zero and crossfire. If we're not in a helluva trap, I'll be a cross-eyed Armenian."

Pulling up his trouser legs, Kerrigan scratches circles of bumps about his ankles.

"What do you suppose is eating on me now?" he asks. "Since hitting this country, I've been bit by everything but a mule and a mad dog."

"You've probably got fleas. I've been itching myself."

"That's it. I'll bet that cave is jumping with fleas."

"And lice."

"I don't worry about lice. They'll all make for Antonio."

Inside Novak is heating coffee on a little gasoline stove, which, next to his rifle, is his most precious possession. No matter how long the march or how heavy his equipment, that stove finds a place on his belt. Now its blue, purring flame sounds as cheerful as a cat in a sunny window.

"Is good our spot here?" asks Novak.

"Good as a graveyard. Looks like we're in a trap."

"No? You make some coffee."

"The krauts are just across the river."

"That's a fine. We eat some breakfast and go kill 'em."

Pouring water for my coffee, I notice that my canteen is light.

"How's your water holding out, Mike?"

"It's about gone. We get some."

"Where?"

"I hear it runnin' from a pipe on the road last night."

"If the krauts have got us pegged, we can't get out."

"We get out. We shoot hell out of 'em."

During the day we have nothing to do but pull our shifts at guard and fight insects. Kerrigan's guess was right. The cave is hopping with fleas.

Time drags. Snuffy rattles a pair of worn dice in Kerrigan's face.

"Go ahead. I'll fade you," says the Irishman.

"On credit?"

"Hell, no. Cold cash. Ten lira."

"Okay. Dice, show this low-down stumblebum what you can do for a real man. Wham. Bam. Thank you, ma'am."

Snuffy rolls a twelve. "Hot damn. Midnight. A mighty hard point but I think I can make it."

"You horse's patoot, pass over my dough."

"Where I come from twelve is a winner."

"Where I come from it's a crap-out. Give me the folding stuff."

"Put it on the war debt."

"Do I get my do-re-mi, or do I take it out of your hide?"

Snuffy reluctantly fishes out the money. Then he gets an inspiration.

"Kerrigan, I always figure you're the lousiest guy I ever met. So I'm givin' you a break. I've got another twenty that says I got more fleas on me than you have."

"Under ordinary circumstances, you'd be a dead cinch on that proposition. But the bugs have got me hemmed here. It's a deal; and you've got to catch the fleas before they hop."

"Play the lice wild."

"Just the fleas, man."

They shed their clothes and search industriously. I make a side bet on Kerrigan and win ten lira from Horse-Face.

"Mighta knowed it," drawls Snuffy. "Them Arshmen draw fleas like the sun draws water."

Antonio is glummer than usual. He lacks patience with our situation.

"All my life I wait to come to Italy," he says. "And here I am buried like a goddam mole. I write my old man that the country stinks. 'Wait'll you get to Rome,' he says. 'Wait'll you see your grandfather's place. Then you'll see the real Italy.'"

His voice rises jeeringly. "The real Italy. Rome. In a pig's eye. We ain't goin' nowhere but to another sonofabitchin' mudhole crawlin' with lice."

"Is no vacation," declares Novak. "We come here to fight."

"Yeah?" Antonio says. "We fight. And fer what? I'm askin' you: Fer what?"

"Plenty," Kerrigan replies. "For sixty bucks a month and a few dog biscuits. For the privilege of living in a nice cool dump like this."

"And such other punishment as the court martial may direct," adds Horse-Face."

"For the opportunity of associating with such a bunch of genteel, clean-cut, Christian gentlemen as you find here."

"And such other punishment."

"For excitement. For adventure." His voice lowers reverently. "For the cause, my boy. For the cause. If you keep your bowels open and your mouth shut; your head down and your chin up, you too may become a civilian."

We have heard the story of Antonio's grandfather many times. But we still regard it with a cynical tolerance. In the army, life is a bog of monotony marked by moments of excitement. We are used to repetition. So if a man wants to retell his story, well and good. It is a way of passing the time.

The Italian stares at his boots. "Yeah," he says, "in a pig's eye. I've seen all I want of the country; and you can have it. But it woulda been nice. I was goin' to get myself a pass. Maybe a furlough."

"Whee-he-he-he," laughs Horse-Face.

"So what?" snaps Antonio. "A man's got a right to a furlough. It says in the regulations."

"Whee-he-he-he."

"Let him alone. This is getting good," says Kerrigan. "Tell us about the cousins."

Antonio glares, but resumes his tale. "There are eight girls, all living near the old man."

"You introduce me?" asks Novak.

"Huh uh. Remember that dame back home."

"She wait. She know nahthin'."

"Sure," says Antonio, magnanimous with self-importance. "I'll introduce you all. We'll have a party. But no monkey business. These are my kinfolks, see."

Kerrigan yawns and stretches himself. "I can see it now. Family reunion. Tony kicks open a door, tosses a grenade, and counts ten before entering the old homestead."

"By gah, yeah. He do that," cackles Novak.

Kerrigan nods. "Certainly. Cousins and all—bologna."

Antonio's mood shifts. "There ain't a one of you comin' along," he decides. "Fer chrisake, I wouldn't take you to a dog funeral."

That night the artillery fire is stepped up. The cave rocks; I cannot sleep. So I go out to the tunnel mouth, where Brandon is on watch. One always feels a gentle strength in his presence.

This tall, quiet man from the hills of Kentucky is closer to me than a brother. We have shared much in silence. He is as solid as the earth, a sticker. If the gates of hell burst open, Brandon would stick to his position.

The quality of stubbornness is in that square-cut jaw. His eyes, as deep and dark as mountain lakes, betray nothing. Only in odd moments, such as when he passes those letters from his daughter around, do we get a glimpse of the sentiment in him. He has his moods, but he does not inflict them on others.

Tonight I sense immediately that his spirits are low. That can mean but one thing. He has been thinking about home again; and that is bad indeed.

"Do you want to hit the sack? I can't sleep, so I may as well take over."

"No," he says. "I'm wide awake."

"Anything been stirring?"

"Nothing but the artillery, and a little small-arms stuff downstream."

"Don't you want to go in for a cigarette?"

"No. I've smoked till my throat's raw."

"It's none of my business. But have you got something on your mind?"

"Nothing but water, I guess."

"Drain it off."

"Oh, I've been thinking too much maybe."

"About the little girl?"

"Yeah. And about the ex-wife. Sometimes I think the old torch has burned out; then it comes back."

"You're still in love with her?"

"I don't know. I shouldn't be. If there's anything I hate in the world, it's a quitter. But I don't know. Maybe it was my fault."

"To hell with her."

"You can't say to hell with a girl that you've been in love with from the time you were twelve. It's not that easy."

"I wouldn't know. I never had the chance to fall in love. Too damned proud to let a girl see the patches on my pants."

He laughs quietly. "I know what you mean. But we grew up together; and I see her all over again in my daughter. She was like a child too. Restless and full of mischief."

"You ought've spanked her maybe."

"No. You can't spank a child. You would've understood if you'd known Mary. She wasn't mean. We got married too young. And the big things I'd planned didn't pan out. I wanted to be an electrical engineer. But the baby came; and I ended up working in a brick yard."

"You can study engineering by mail."

"I know. I was going to get around to that. Then Mary got unhappy. Things were in a mess. We were trying to pay for a home and a car; and I don't suppose she had much fun."

"Neither did you."

"That's where you're wrong. I was blind happy. Maybe it was this other guy all the time; and I couldn't see him. Anyhow she married again. And that was it. I'd had it."

We sit in silence. Then from over the river comes a clattering sound, followed by laughter. A German must have fallen in a hole and his comrades are amused at his clumsiness.

"I hope he broke his neck."

"Not a jerry," says Brandon. "Their necks are as thick as a bull's."

The noise seems to have caused the front to stir in its sleep.

A German shouts in English, "Sleep, swine. We kill you all before breakfast."

From a dugout below us, a voice yells, "Go to hell, you kraut-heads." The plea is punctuated by a blast from a Browning automatic.

It is the third day. The yellow, sputtering flame of the candle sends shadows skipping over the bearded faces of the men. In the flickering light, their strained, red eyes gleam like the eyes of caged animals.

The last of our water disappeared last night. Now thirst begins to torture our bodies. Lips crack; brains grow dizzy; talk becomes an effort.

We still have rations, but we dare not eat lest the food increase our thirst. Nerves stand on edge. We growl at one another and quarrel over trifles. Johnson's face is longer than usual; Kerrigan has lost his bubble; Snuffy cannot sleep; and Novak is out of coffee.

Gun duels have broken out. Swope has been exchanging fire with a German machine gunner, who has our range to perfection. The slope to the river is as deadly as a gas chamber. No matter. Tonight somebody has to go out. We must have water.

As the hours wear on, I say without belief, "Relief will come today. Headquarters knows our situation."

Antonio turns upon me with glittering eyes. "Nuts! They're all a bunch of bat-brains."

"Remember the Articles of War," Kerrigan warns. "You'll not show disrespect for your superior officers by word or deed."

"To hell with my superior officers."

"Careful of your language. I carry a picture of my wife in my pocket," says Horse-Face.

"Shove it."

"Your grandfather," Novak suggests anxiously.

But Antonio will not be diverted. He licks his parched lips; stares at the dim wash of light through the tunnel, and says, "You can take Italy and ram it. To hell with it. To hell with everything."

"Brother," says Kerrigan, "the boy's got some original ideas."

"Whee-he-he-he."

The spurt of energy exhausts us. We sink to the floor; the talk ceases. The artillery is drumming furiously.

Despite the noise I doze. I dream that I stand in an open field surrounded by a forest in which birds sing. Then a dark shadow swoops over the earth; and all becomes expectantly, fearfully still. My feet seem rooted to the earth. I struggle to free them.

Brrrrrp.

I awake like an animal, instantly visualizing the picture. Novak beats me to the tunnel. Nobody is on watch. We drop to our knees and gaze through the slit.

The burst of fire has knocked Antonio down. I shout, "Come back, you crazy fool. Come back," and seize the BAR to cover him.

He scrambles from the ground, still clutching his canteen. Pure terror stands on his face. He takes a step and his right lower leg bends double. The bone thrusts through the flesh; and he tries to walk on the stump. I cannot locate the enemy gunner, but he either has ammunition to waste or is bored with the lack of targets. His second burst is long and unhurried. The lead eats through Antonio's mid-parts, like a saw chewing through wood. The kraut is a butcher.

Little Mike screams, "Gah damn sonsabeeches," and starts around the sandbag wall. I drop the gun and grab him. He kicks me flat. I recover and seize him again. He beats me with his fist; and I throw a hard punch to his stomach. He doubles up. I get a headlock on him and yell for Brandon and Kerrigan.

The Irishman shakes and curses Novak back to sanity, while I sit on the ground and wipe a bleeding nose.

Swope joins us. "I should have known he'd popped his topper," he says. "I oughtn't to let him take over."

"It wasn't your fault. He was bound to get it that way sooner or later."

"I didn't notice the canteen. Said he just wanted a little air." The Cherokee picks up the BAR, thrusts its barrel through the slot; and murder is in his eyes.

I go inside to see Novak. He is stretched on the ground with his face in his arms. The little candle sputters; the men breathe heavily. And thick veins bulge at the Polack's temples.

"Mike."

He makes no response.

"Goddammit, man, it would have been no use. Antonio was already dead."

He still does not move. So I rejoin Swope and Kerrigan. The Indian has his gaze fixed on the opposite bank. Kerrigan drums on his knees with his fingers.

I peep through the slot. Antonio lies in the mud with his leg doubled beneath him. He has come home to the soil that gave his parents birth.

Within a few hours a furious fire fight is raging across the river. And we know that our men have broken through the German lines. The pressure is off. Our relief arrives with rations, water, and ammunition. The next morning we cross the river on a bridge and join the drive toward our next major objective, the communications center of Mignano.

4

MIGNANO lies in a broad valley through which run an important railroad and the famed arterial Highway Six. North of the town, steep, brush-covered Mount Lungo splits the flatlands like a spur. On the eastern side of the valley is oval-shaped Mount Rotondo. At its base is a rocky elevation, known on the military maps simply as Hill 193. The highway curves around it like a horseshoe and winds onward toward Cassino and Rome.

On both the mountains the Germans are strongly entrenched, with their guns dominating the valley. The area forms a powerful outpost for the lines that the enemy has prepared for his winter defensive. Cassino, which will soon have the eyes of the world turned upon it, is now but a focal point in the German lines.

Our strategy is to by-pass Mignano and strike directly against the mountains protecting the city. The terrain over which we advance is a nightmare for offensive troops. The narrow trails, frequently on the edge of sheer cliffs and deep gorges, are so treacherous that pack mules often lose their footing and tumble to their death. Sometimes the mules cannot make it at all. Supplies have to be dragged up the slope by men inching their way on all fours.

The Germans, holed-up among the rocks, are difficult to locate until we are upon them. The ground is slippery with mud; and visibility is cut drastically by a heavy autumn mist that lies over the land.

Beneath the mist my squad moves cautiously forward on a reconnaissance mission. A German tank waits at the edge of a grove, but it is so expertly camouflaged that we overlook it. We are walking straight toward the tank when Novak stops abruptly. He cocks his ear to the right and left. His worried eyes dart all about.

"Somewhere here are the sonsabeeches," he whispers.

"You're dreaming things, Mike. You're battle whacky."

"Naw. Naw. Smell 'em."

"That's Snuffy's feet. They get washed only during landings."

"Good gah, look! There!"

The snout of the cannon is being quietly lowered upon us. Our minds freeze. Like birds fascinated by the eyes of a snake, we stand motionless. The krauts jerk the camouflage net from the tank. The engine starts. Our minds snap free of the spell.

"Head," says Horse-Face, "stay with me. Feet don't let me down." He is off.

I follow Novak's churning short legs. Speed is the one essential. No adequate cover is at hand. The first shell screams overhead, smacks into the earth, and explodes just ahead of us. Horse-Face pivots to the right, and we follow him.

"Wait! Wait!" cries a terrified voice. "I've busted my goddam leg."

We pause, turn. It is Capehart, who came in as a replacement for Antonio. He is floundering forwards on hands and knees, still dragging his rifle by the sling. Kerrigan and Brandon dash toward him. Seizing him by the shoulders of his canvas jacket, they drag him along like a sled.

The tank has lurched out of its hiding place. Another shell cracks. We slide into a gully. Capehart has gone into a panic.

"Oh, jeezus. Don't leave me. Don't leave me. It's broke."

"Take it easy, son," says Horse-Face. "Nobody's pulling out on you." He peers over the gully's edge. "It's coming all right. Somebody's got to pull a Samson. You, Kerrigan. You're the only one that's got the jawbone of an ass."

"It's not funny," spits the Irishman. "I've been in worse spots, but I can't say just when."

Novak whistles and motions us to a far end of the ditch. He has discovered a clump of bushes. We crawl toward it flat on our bellies; and in this maneuver Capehart is the most energetic of us all.

The tank has stopped. A crew member pokes his head out of the hatch and sweeps the terrain with field glasses.

"Six inches of armor; and the bastards are still scared of the open," says Kerrigan.

"I hope they stay scared," adds Horse-Face. "I got a skin that's allergic to lead."

"You got a skin like an alligator."

"Reminds me of an old girl I knowed once. Worked in a circus in summer and wintered in Baltimore. Says, 'Colonel—'"

The hatch door on the tank closes. The engine starts.

"Says, 'Colonel—'"

"For chrisake, shut up."

The nose of the tank swings toward us.

"Had a hide like a real alligator. Says, 'Colonel—'"

"Shut up."

The tank turns completely around and rumbles back toward the grove.

"A fraidy-cat," says Snuffy.

"Fraidy, hell. Where've you been?"

"I been rat here."

"You been so quiet I thought you'd died."

"I was savin' my breath for the rat race."

Capehart's ankle has swollen badly. We have to cut off his shoe before carrying him on down the slope.

In the valley the battle grows in intensity. Several times we try storming up the southern side of Mount Rotondo and are stopped cold. A ruse finally does the trick. While elements of our regiment attack from the south and southwest to divert the Germans, a battalion of the 30th strikes from the flank and rear, taking the enemy by surprise. The mountain falls into our hands. But counteraction is immediate and sudden. Barrages of artillery and mortar fire are thrown upon us. Groups are isolated. Lines become confused.

As dusk falls, we wait for the company to assemble at the bottom of Hill 193, which our battalion is to take over. The clump of boots causes me to prick up my ears. It is time that the rest of the men were showing up. When the dark shapes appear on the road, I shout to give them the direction.

The shapes halt; and I hear the growl of a German. It is too late to warn the men. I throw my rifle into position and start firing. The krauts fall back. But they know where we are now, and there is no time to waste. We start scrambling up the slope of the hill; and we do not stop until we find an abandoned quarry, which we slip into for the night.

Now the light of the new day is streaking the sky, beneath which the enemy is creeping.

A combat patrol.

Seven gray-coated and helmeted forms emerging like ghosts from the mist of an Italian dawn. Beneath the uniforms, seven men. The warm blood throbs through their veins; their chests heave. And one casts an anxious eye toward the light that blooms in the sky.

Seven soldiers seeking us out. Grenades swing from their belts; their rifles are ready; and the ears are bent for the slightest sound that will give our position away. Trained to kill without an instant's hesitation or an atom of mercy, they want only the opportunity to blow us into mincemeat.

We accept the facts coolly; remove the safety locks on our

rifles; and lie as still as the rocks among which we hide at the edge of the quarry.

My mouth goes dry; muscles tighten, the heart beats in slow, steady pulsations.

Quietly, rapidly Swope checks his machine gun. He chooses his range, gauges his sights, and freezes into position. It is his job. If he fails, we must think and act quickly; otherwise we may think and act no more. But we have every confidence in that calm trigger finger and piercing blackness of eye.

The Germans labor up a draw that cuts the slope like a wrinkle in a fat man's stomach. Despite all care, their boots slip on the stony soil; and at each small sound the men start nervously.

The leader is obviously an old-timer. I can see from his actions that he does not like the situation at all. The route he has chosen is dangerous indeed, but is the best that the area offers. On two sides, he has at least partial concealment.

But what of the forward end of the draw? A greenhorn should know that would be covered. Evidently the German knows too. He halts, waves his men down, and moves forward a few yards alone.

He pauses and gazes straight in our direction. I glance at Swope. He has the tense, sensitive, motionless appearance of a bird dog at point.

Apparently the German has not spotted us, but still he is not satisfied. Again he advances, stops, and scans the terrain. Then he shrugs his shoulders and motions for his men to join him.

We know when they are in effective range of the gun. Still Swope waits. With his cold Indian cunning, he is letting them come dangerously close.

"What's the Chief going to do?" whispers Kerrigan irritably. "Shake hands with the krauts before he shoots them?"

The bronzed head snaps forward. Rat-ta-ta-ta . . . Twenty rounds. No more. Swope is not one to waste ammunition.

"Okay," he says, without turning his head. "They're yours."

We spring to our feet, fingering the triggers of our rifles. Long ago we learned the wisdom of a stock army saying: "The only safe Germans are dead ones."

Four of the krauts, with weaponless hands hoisted, register stunned surprise. No matter how much you expect it, you're always surprised when it comes. Their comrades lie on the earth. Already the blood wells from their middle-parts. Swope aims not too high, not too low. He seldom misses the vital organs.

From the ripped bodies comes only the sound of gasping. Shock for the instant stifles the pain that will soon stab through the flesh like thrusts from a red-hot sword.

Brandon, for all of his experience, has never learned to accept such sights. He turns his head from the bleeding men, muttering, "Belly wounds."

Snuffy is different. His pale watery eyes view the scene placidly. Plopping to the ground, he hauls out a plug of tobacco, bites off a hunk, and chews. Thoughtlessly he spits into the wind. His face is spattered with tobacco juice. He wipes it off with the back of his hand. "Looks lak them three done drawed their rations," he says.

Novak is ignoring the wounded. Jabbering fiercely, he frisks the four captives. "So you go hunting, hey? You kill us, we kill you. To turn about is fair play." The Germans do not understand the language, but the attitude is obvious. They regard the angry little Polack with alarm.

"Don't scare 'em any more, Mike," says Horse-Face. "We'll have a sanitation problem on our hands."

A single German cannon opens up on Mount Lungo. The noise of the projectile grows to the roar of a freight train as the hills throw back the echo. The shell is not intended for us. It goes overhead and crashes on Rotondo.

"Reveille," says Kerrigan.

"Sonsabeeches."

The gray light washes about us, and mist is curling from the hill.

Horse-Face is assigned to escort the prisoners back to company headquarters and notify the medics of the wounded. Looking over the bushy terrain, he grins sardonically. "If them guys were only jerry WACs or nurses," he suggests. "For just once why can't we capture some women?"

"Women?" says Snuffy. "If I ever git married, gonna marry a cow. Somepin' I can milk, love, and plow."

Far down the slope mortars begin to cough, but their firing is not in rhythm. The gunners are perhaps not yet fully awake.

Horse-Face studies the terrain professionally. Suddenly he is all business. "I'll see you joes in the graveyard," he says. "Hell's goin' to hop on this hill."

He arranges the Germans in a single file, and with the tip of his rifle gooses the rear one. The German wheels indignantly about. Horse-Face guffaws and waves him forward.

We turn our attention to the wounded. They are all still conscious. One has the embarrassed expression of a man suddenly exposed while answering a call of nature. He appears too old to be gadding about with a gun. His face is shriveled; and his uniform fits like a sack.

His lips peel back in a yellow grin. It is the forced smile of an unwilling loser. Or maybe he wishes to be friendly. He coughs. Red froth bubbles from his mouth. He ceases pretending. Fear and shame pass from his eyes. He must know now that he is dying and we can harm him no further.

The other two are not so sure. They are young, hardly over twenty; and from the freshness of their uniforms, we guess they are newcomers to the lines. They cringe and snarl defiantly, doubtless not knowing how badly they are wounded.

I glance at the sky. On the eastern horizon, a lone shaft of sunlight knifes through a mass of dark clouds. The enemy artillery on Mount Lungo is limbering up in earnest. We can now see the bursting of the shells. The direction of fire is steadily drifting our way.

The wounded must be got under cover. The peculiar ethics of war condone our riddling the bodies with lead. But then they were soldiers. Swope's gun transformed them into human beings again; and the rules say that we cannot leave them unprotected against a barrage of their own artillery.

"Let's get them into the quarry," I say.

"They die and start stinking," argues Little Mike. "Is no good living with dead men."

"I'll stay with them till the medics come," offers Brandon. "It won't be long."

"Yeah?" snorts Kerrigan. "That Cherokee's gun has probably telegraphed our position to every kraut in this neck of the woods."

He may be right. The mortar fire has come so close that we can hear the whistling fragments.

"Grab the men and get going."

"Is that an order, sir?" asks Kerrigan.

"It's an order."

"Please do me the courtesy of shoving it, sir."

Grinning, he seizes the largest German by the shoulders, while Brandon takes the feet. The man whines fearfully.

"Do your bitching to the Chief," says Kerrigan. "He handed you that lead, not me."

The Irishman notices that Snuffy still remains seated, speculatively squirting tobacco juice. He lets go of the German, picks up a rock, and throws it at Jones.

"Okay, gourd-head. Get that cotton-picking butt off the ground and give us a hand."

"Sich language," Snuffy replies, as he creaks lazily to his feet. " 'Y god, are we supposed to kill 'em or cure 'em?"

Kerrigan reaches for another rock.

"Okay. Okay," says Snuffy. "Don't get your bowels in a uproar."

He and Novak lift the old fellow frowningly. A pool of blood has collected in his pants. It now pours in a stream from his sagging posterior.

I remain with the third man until Brandon returns. The youngster stares at the sky, breathing laboriously. I loosen his collar, and he mutters, *"Danke."* As we carry him up the slope, an enemy machine gunner spots us. He gives us a burst, but his distance is too great for accuracy. The bullets walk to our left, angrily kicking up gravel.

Swope, sitting stolidly behind that gun of his, has lit a cigarette. He does not take even a professional interest in his targets.

Kerrigan says, "Next time, Chief, shoot only the little ones. That one I had must've weighed a ton."

The Indian shrugs. He has done his work without hatred, pride, or compassion. Now he relaxes.

The artillery fire grows into a heavy barrage, but in our rocky hole we feel secure enough. If the mortars do not get our range, we are relatively safe. The chance of a direct hit or an air burst by the big guns is small. However, twice 88-millimeter shells explode close enough to send showers of dirt and stone into the quarry.

The shock is passing from the Germans; and as the pain awakes in the flesh, their dignity and manhood as soldiers vanish. One of the youngsters is openly weeping.

We have broken open first-aid packets and started dressing their wounds. It is a habit. No more. We are all aware that a battalion of doctors could not undo the work of Swope's gun. But through instinct and training we are compelled to act.

Kerrigan has unbuttoned the old fellow's shirt, baring a bony, shrunken chest. One bullet has pierced the left lung.

"Superman," says the Irishman quietly, "you should have been home with your grandchildren."

The German, seeing that Kerrigan is not angry, attempts a feeble smile. Then he closes his eyes, muttering, "*Wasser.*"

But three of the bullets have punctured his stomach. Blood clots around the ugly little holes. And a man with belly wounds must not drink water.

"*Wasser.*"

Kerrigan attempts to explain. He rubs his own stomach, shakes his head, and says, "No water. It's bad for you."

"*Wasser.*"

"*Wasser verboten,* goddammit."

"*Wasser.*"

"Give him the water," says Brandon.

"You give it to him. Or shoot him right through the head. It's the same thing, only quicker."

"Is thirsty?" asks Novak. "Give him coffee."

"For chrisake, what's the difference?"

"Aw, let him have a drink," drawls Snuffy. "He's gonna die anyhow."

Kerrigan jerks a canteen from his belt and hurls it at Snuffy. "By god, there's the water. Give him the drink yourself."

"What you gettin' sore about. All I said is that he'll die anyhow."

"No," says Kerrigan. "He's in good shape. All he needs is an oxygen tent, a new lung, eight quarts of blood plasma, and seventeen feet of unpunctured gut."

"Aw, go jump in a lake and pull the water up over you."

Says Kerrigan, "I wish to Christ I could."

As the morning passes, the clouds move inland; and rain, that persistent plague of the foot soldier, sets in. I bend over the wounded Germans. The old fellow and one of the youngsters are unconscious. The third puckers his lips and fumbles with a coat pocket. It is a smoke that he is doubtless after. I search through his clothes and draw forth a package of American cigarettes. Anger flares inside me as I wonder whether he got them from a corpse or a prisoner.

He reads my thoughts, flinches, and starts vomiting. Suddenly I feel ashamed. I wipe off his mouth, thrust a cigarette between his lips, and strike him a light. He smiles gratefully and sucks weakly at the tobacco. I remove my own slicker and cover him against the rain.

In the late afternoon, we hear the sputter of automatic fire. Novak, who is manning our machine gun, yells, "Our man. Hurry!" Then he squeezes his trigger so long that I fear he will burn out the gun barrel.

We snatch our weapons and disperse among the rocks at the top of the quarry. Our man lies in spread-eagle fashion. The bullets rip the ground about him. I shout for him to start crawling.

He moves; and we lay a cover of fire overhead. That must give the kraut something to think about. His gun is silent as our man snakes his way up the slope.

We pull him into the hole. He is too weak to stand. Brandon hands him a canteen. He takes a slug of water and lies breathing like a terrified horse.

"Jeezus!" he finally says.

"You bring mail?" asks Novak.

"Jeezus!"

"What's up?"

"Let me get my breath. You're to stick here. The old man's been hit."

"Bad?"

"Nearly bled to death. Dillon finally got through for some plasma. It was all that saved the old man."

"Is he out?"

"His mind comes and goes. But you don't put his kind out unless you kill them. When he's conscious, he's yelling orders.

44

And when he's unconscious, he raves them. Between times he's cussing the krauts."

"What about the medics for these jerries here?"

"They won't get up until morning. Maybe not then. They're up to their elbows with our own men. And they couldn't get through anyhow."

"Dillon got through."

"With his luck he could get through the Siegfried Line on skis. He wears horseshoes around his shoulders and shamrocks in his shoes."

"No mail?" Novak asks again.

"Mail! Now, good god, man, do I look like a postman? The old man says to keep on the alert for a big counterattack. We're expecting it. If it doesn't come, we'll attack ourselves."

"Sounds just perfectly lovely," says Kerrigan. "We got about as much future as Snuffy's got sense."

"You'll probably get a lot of artillery."

"What the hell we been getting? Birthday greetings?"

"The old man says if the krauts think they're going to have to pull out, they'll likely throw all their surplus at us first."

"You got any good news?"

"Yeah. You won't be eating C-rations much longer. If some supplies don't soon get through, you won't be eating any rations a-tall."

The rain falls harder. The Germans mutter feverishly. Pools of water have gathered about their bodies, but there is nothing we can do about that. Brandon tucks the covers about them. "The poor bastards," he says softly. "What is death waiting for?"

He understands the necessity of killing men when they advance upon him with arms, and in combat he is ferocious. But he does not comprehend the purpose of this drawn-out agony of dying. He does not approve of it. Yet he will do everything within his power to keep breath in these shattered bodies.

So would we others. But we are all realists. Since there is

no hope for life, we wish these men would die quickly. If they go into deliriums, it will be bad for our nerves tonight. And the noise of their raving may attract another enemy patrol.

I sit down beside Kerrigan. My eyeballs burn; my bones ache; and my muscles twitch from exhaustion. Oh, to sleep and never awaken. The war is without beginning, without end. It goes on forever.

Snuffy is unconcerned. Stretched in the mud with his helmet pulled over his eyes, he snores loudly.

"That," says Kerrigan, "is how the South lost the war. All the Confederate soldiers ate a big 'possum dinner and fell asleep. The Yankees found them and beat out their brains, such as they were, with stovewood."

The blue eyes snap. The nostrils quiver. The loose grin spreads over his face.

"He told me once that he was born 'tard,' and never got rested. Said he comes from so far back in the hills that he had to swing into home on grapevines. Used to think there were just two kinds of people in the world: the whisky-making kind and the 'revenooers.' First letter he ever got was from the draft board. Sees 'War Department' on the envelope; and thinks right off it was from the 'revenooers.' They were the War Department as far as he was concerned, and he wanted 'no part or passel' of it. Damned near got chucked in jail for not reporting."

"I'd liked to've seen him during his basic."

"Got gigged every day, he said. Couldn't get the hang of the spit and polish. He usually spit and ended up polishing."

Scooping up a handful of gravel, Kerrigan hurls it at the sleeping man's helmet. Snuffy pops up like a jack-in-the-box. Glaring wildly about, he grabs for his rifle.

"Damn you," he says, seeing the Irishman's broad smile; "cain't a man have a little peace?"

"Peace, he says. And Patton wanting to see him. With a skull thick as his, the general thinks he can use him as a tank."

Snuffy's neck seems abnormally long. At its top is a knoblike head from which the large ears stick out like flaps. His thin lips stretch into a grin, revealing short, stained teeth and too much gum.

"Kerrigan," he says, "I's jest dreamin' that you was eat up with crud and corruption and enjoyin' myself no end. The buzzards was peckin' out your eyeballs and talkin' among themselves. One buzzard said, 'Times is gettin' mighty tough when we get low-down enough to eat an Arshman.' Another buzzard pukes. 'Don't mention an Arshman while I'm eatin',' says he. 'It makes me sick to my stomach.'"

He stretches again in the mud, pulls his helmet over his eyes, and resumes his nap.

For a while Kerrigan sits silently with his eyes roaming over the dismal prospects of our quarry. Finally he says, "You wouldn't know where I could get a blonde, two gallons of whisky, and a six-months pass."

"Write your congressman, Rumhead."

Sergeant Emmet J. Kerrigan. He sits in his rain-soaked clothes, four thousand miles from his native New England. Three men are dying before us; and we ourselves may not last the night.

He runs a hand through his sandy hair; scratches an ear pensively. "Do you think," asks he, "that there'll be any beer left in America. I'm making my postwar plans."

"You can limit those plans to one mattress cover and six feet of dirt in a military cemetery. I can see it now," I reply. "The headlines: 'Sergeant Emmet J. Kerrigan Gives Life For His Country.' Fell down the steps of an Italian cellar and broke his blasted neck. All cat houses south of the firing lines will be closed for one day of mourning."

"Murph," he spits, "you get the gawdamndest ideas. When

I was tapped for the draft, I was about to become a family man."

"Some girl in trouble?"

"Why hellsfire, no. Nice girl. A proofreader in the printshop where I worked."

"Sounds cozy."

"It was, Scramble-brain."

"Why didn't you marry her then?"

"Duck under some woman's skirts to get out of the service?"

"You'd been out of the draft all right, unless . . ."

"Don't say it. We're talking about Rachael. I didn't know what the war was all about. I still don't know."

"Who does?"

"Novak, maybe. And he may be all cockeyed. Anyhow I felt it coming. And I didn't want to be saddled by a dame on this long, long trail a-winding. And I didn't want her to be stuck with me."

"I can hardly stand it. You got a conscience."

"Conscience? Man, in my youth I was a choir boy."

"So that's what happened to religion?"

"And that's not all. If somebody had given me a shove, I might have become a priest."

Darkness closes in, the rain still falls, but a weird dull light remains in the quarry. Somewhere above the clouds, the moon shines. In our sodden clothes, we shiver like dogs. The runner has returned to headquarters. The artillery still pounds, but the mortar fire has let up.

The elder German is delirious. For periods, he lies quietly; then, as if seized by some sudden horror, he tries to get up, jabbering excitedly. We have lashed his arms together with a belt to prevent his clawing the bandages.

As the hours wear on, he is joined in his raving by one of the younger men. In the night, they seem to be carrying on some ghostly conversation.

"They kill us too. By gah, you wait," says Novak, as if trying to salve our consciences. It is unnecessary. Remorse does not bother us. The men had to be shot. Swope should have aimed a bit higher.

When dawn breaks, two of the Germans are dead. Their eyes stare glassily. Their mouths are open, and the old man's swollen tongue protrudes between his teeth.

"Looks like he left us a Bronx cheer," says Kerrigan. "Who the hell is this joke on anyhow?"

"Is no joke if they stink," says Novak.

"I'd rather smell them than Snuffy."

"You go to hell."

"Gladly. Just give me the address."

The third German has a rattling sound in his throat. And the feverish red of his face is becoming mottled with white. I remove the slicker from the corpse and add it to his covering. The act is useless. The man would not know if he lay in ten feet of feathers.

We heat water for our coffee in canteen cups, using wax strips torn from K-ration packages for fuel. It is a trick that Novak taught us, a tedious, but smokeless process, handy when hiding from the enemy.

The clouds scatter, and the sun appears. Steam rises from our uniforms. We check our gear, cleanse our weapons of mud, and wait for orders.

They do not come. Instead we receive another barrage of artillery. It is far worse than the one thrown at us yesterday. The whole hill trembles. We huddle among the rocks, pulling our helmeted heads into our shoulders like frightened turtles.

Swope is back on the gun. Concussion from a nearby blast sends his helmet spinning. I clamber up to him. Blood runs from his nose. He cannot hear. Otherwise he is unharmed, and refuses to leave the gun.

In the afternoon the last German dies. He takes a long, gasping breath, exhales with a sigh; and it is all over. I remove my raincoat from the body and spread it on a rock to dry.

That night we all feel better. The clouds are gone. The moon washes the earth with a silvery light, lessening the probability of enemy patrols.

In the light the faces of the dead seem green and unearthly. That is bad for the morale, as it makes a man reflect upon what his own life may come to. Brandon finally turns the bodies face downward. We should have thought of that in the first place.

"If the people at home could only see this," says Kerrigan.

"Home?" echoes Novak.

"Yeah. Home is the place where they send you when you lose an arm or a leg. I've read all about it in the papers. You ride in a hospital train, with beautiful nurses and Red Cross dames drooling all over you. With newspapers writing how you gave your all for your country. With the train stopping at little towns, where the people are waiting at the depots to cheer. You look out of the windows and see the sweet little shacks around the railroad tracks, and say, 'It won't be long now.'"

"The hell you do," says Snuffy.

"That's what the papers say," continues Kerrigan.

"Oh, tell us more," I say with sarcasm.

"Sure. Just like a picture. Your mama cries and calls in the neighbors to see her hero. You sit around the old store with your chest full of ribbons, and tell the people about the war. You say, 'It wasn't so bad; and we're beating the hell out of the krauts.'"

"No! I can't stand it."

"You get your picture taken; and the home-town paper gives you a headline: 'Local Boy Says Nazis Not So Tough.'"

"Yeah. They're a big bunch of sissies."

"You forget about nights like this. All you do is eat hot dogs and drink coca-colas, the absence of which has mostly occupied your mind in the field.

"Then you're discharged. Think of that. Discharged. For a while you miss the old gang. And you feel like a fish out of the water in civvies. You won't have to go back clerking in a grocery store, because the good old army has trained you for a better job."

"Come again."

"Sure. You've learned a lot of useful things. You can pick off a man at three hundred yards with an M-1. You can toss a grenade further than anybody else in town. You can sleep among corpses, bathe in ditch water without any complaint a-tall. As civilians we'll be in great demand."

"Horse manure," says Snuffy.

The next day breaks quietly. The enemy is strangely silent. Then our own artillery starts whamming. The whizzing of the shells overhead grows into a mighty roar.

"Whoopee!" yells Snuffy. "Hitler, start counting your boys." If there is one thing a dogface loves, it is artillery—his own.

Horse-Face comes up from headquarters. "Sling on your gear, and get the lead out of your pants, I got great news for you sad sacks," says he. "We attack."

5

CRAWLING with filth and sodden with weariness, we are pulled out of the lines in mid-November. The valley is clear of the enemy. Mount Lungo has fallen. From its heights we can see Cassino.

The war drags north, its roar receding in the distance. In a short while, Hill 193 will be but another small rise in Italy's rugged terrain. Already burial squads scurry like ants over its slopes seeking the bodies of men to whom the last order of "Forward" has been given.

Looking back upon the bloody valley, Snuffy says, "What was all the shootin' about? I wouldn't give one turnip patch in Tennessee fer the whole damned country, and Sicily thowed in fer good measure."

As we straggle on foot down a shell-torn road, we become giddy at the prospect of living. Despite the lateness of the year, it is a pleasant sunny day. A light breeze whispers in the trees; the earth is solid and friendly.

The clump of our boots is like stirring music. Our veins swell to the rhythm; and we regard one another with foolish affectionate grins. It is as simple as that. An order comes through; and you are handed back life on a platter.

Kerrigan is sure that there has been some mistake. Otherwise we have been reprieved merely to be checked for venereal disease.

"All they'll find on me," says he, "is mudsores."

Our derision is turned on Horse-Face Johnson. In a newspaper his wife has seen the picture of a G.I. vigorously embracing two Italian girls. She is sure that Horse-Face is up to the same mischief. That is why she has not heard from him in three weeks.

We halt for a rest by a clear stream. Brown leaves fall in the water and spin in the eddies. Novak, the cautious, removes his shoes and bathes his feet in the cool water. He doubts the official word that we are to walk only six miles. The army has a way of changing its mind; and the six miles may grow into thirty.

A group of replacements on the way to the front falls out on the opposite side of the road. The men are clean shaven and newly outfitted, as if prepared for inspection. All are subdued; a few are plainly white-faced, dry-mouthed with fear. They finger their weapons, pull at their canteens, and glance nervously in the direction from which come the dull, angry sounds of combat. Their leader, a leathery sergeant, lies on his back in the grass and puffs a cigarette. From his relaxed attitude, we know he has been in the lines before, perhaps many times.

Kerrigan is elated by the scene. He flips his head toward the replacements and in a loud sardonic voice asks, "Has anyone ever seen a nicer pack of fresh meat?"

The sergeant's eyes twinkle. "Still rough going up there?"

"Rough," says Snuffy. "Out of the whole damned battalion here's all that's left. We're being sent back, because the gravediggers run out of mattress covers."

The replacements grin at us without mirth. The wind curls through the grasses; the stream gurgles cheerfully.

The sergeant grinds his cigarette into the ground and gets up. "All right," he says, "let's go."

The men fall in quietly, squaring their shoulders to their packs. We regard them with casual interest. Pity is a luxury we cannot afford. We have survived our stretch at the front. Now it is up to them to save their hides also. As they plod up the road, Kerrigan shouts, "Cannon fodder. Don't get those nice uniforms dirty."

A man in the rear turns and thumbs his nose at the Irishman.

At headquarters, we are ordered to strip and report to the medics for a checkup. The air nips at our skin; our teeth chatter lightly. In uniform we feel the strength of our union and manhood; naked we are all individuals, seeming suddenly alone and ridiculous.

Kerrigan was partially right. We have seen no women for weeks. For days we have been in the lines. But army routine is immutable. The first phase of our examination is a short arm.

A young corporal glances at our organs perfunctorily. His cursory attitude brings an admonishment from Horse-Face.

"Careful there, son," he says. "My wife thinks I've had half the women in Italy."

"He's eat up with the gonorrhea," adds Kerrigan.

The corporal casts a bitter glance at the two. "Why don't you go to hell?" he asks. "This ain't my idea of fightin' the war either."

The mystery deepens. We are not returned to the lines, but instead are sent to a swampy terrain near Naples for a period of rigorous training. Twice daily we have hot chow, and we sleep on cots in pyramidal tents. Weariness drains from our flesh. We kick up our heels at discipline.

Snuffy is called on the carpet for not shaving. His stubbly chin might have gone unnoticed, but he also looked straight into the eyes of a natty headquarters lieutenant and failed to salute. The officer, bristling like a young Airedale, ordered him to snap to. By a mighty effort of will Snuffy opened both eyes and straightened a shoulder, which was his idea of standing at attention.

"Get that belly in and those shoulders back," says the wrathful lieutenant. "You're in the army."

"Yessir," replies Snuffy.

"And front-line slovenliness, either in appearance or action, will not be tolerated in this area."

"Come again," says Snuffy.

The face of the officer purples. "No wisecracks, soldier. Get those whiskers off immediately; and don't let me catch you failing in your military courtesy again."

"Yessir." Snuffy turns on his heel.

"Goddammit," says the lieutenant, "come back here. When being dismissed by an officer, you're supposed to salute."

"Yessir." He throws a hand to his forehead.

"Dismissed. This time I won't report you. But watch yourself. You're not in the lines, you know."

"Yessir."

Unperturbed, Snuffy ambles into our tent. "I got news for you guys," says he. "We're not in the lines. In all your life did you ever hear such horse manure?" He studies his chin in a mirror. "What's wrong with that sonofabitch?" he asks. "I jest shaved day before yisstidy."

Kerrigan gets drunk. He has paid an outrageous price for a pint of grain alcohol which a medic stole from the infirmary. The fiery liquid was cut with grapefruit juice; and now the Irishman sits in our tent, solemnly sharing a canteen cup of the mixture with Novak.

As the liquor disappears, the Irishman's brain is aswarm with great plans. "When I get out of this man's army," he announces, "I'm going to buy me a place in the woods. A whole damned summer resort. There'll be cabins by the dozen, and a trout stream right in the middle."

"Listen to that," says Snuffy. "If brick houses was selling for a quarter apiece, he couldn't buy a one-hole privy."

"Quiet," Kerrigan orders. "Have a drink."

"Can't. I'm in trouble enough already."

"Then be quiet, and let a man drink in peace." His mind snaps into focus, and again the dream flourishes. "Yep," he continues, "I'll have a lodge to take care of the overflow guests. It'll have one big room with a fireplace at the end and a clock on the mantel that strikes bong, bong for them that cares what time it is. I won't. There'll be a bar two hundred feet long, all made of polished oak."

His face brightens with a new idea. "Say, I'll be needing a lot of help about that place. Who wants to work for me?"

"Get me out of this army, and I'll settle for a hard-tailed mule and some stumpy new ground," says Snuffy.

"You give me a job?" It is Novak that speaks.

"Why hell, yes," Kerrigan assures him. "I'll make you the head bartender. A hundred and fifty a week. No, that's too damned much as a starter. How's a hundred a week?"

"Suits me."

"Then you're hired."

"By gah, I never make so much money in the steel mills. In the old country, I farm seven years to get wahn ticket to America. Kerrigan, you are my fran. I never have such a fran before."

The Irishman is touched. He passes the cup to the Polack. "Friend," says he, "drink. Drink it all."

"To my fran."

A formation whistle blows. We pull Kerrigan to his feet; and he reels to his place in the company line.

We are detailed to erect tents. Gone is the wonderful vision. Sweat pours down Kerrigan's face, as he pounds stakes in the ground with a sledge. The exercise sobers him.

To Novak, he says, "I talk a lot of bologna. That place in the woods is a pipe dream. I hired you; now I fire you, just to get things straight."

"It is no difference," the Polack replies, "you are my fran."

One afternoon Brandon and I are walking down a road when we spot a chicken pecking in a field. It raises its head and struts stiffly about in alarm.

"At this distance," says Brandon, "it would be a damned crime. But . . ."

His carbine cracks, and the fowl is a flopping mass of feathers. I vault over the wall encircling the field and scoop it up in my arms. It is an old hen with a bald neck. Evidently she has been molting out of season. We crouch behind the wall, hastily plucking and gutting the carcass. Then we wrap the dressed flesh in a field jacket and hide it in a clump of grass.

In combat, we can destroy whole towns and be patted on the back for our efforts. But here in the rear, the theft of a chicken is a serious offense indeed. Army regulations say, "No looting." If anyone questions us about the shot, we will swear that the gun fired accidentally.

I am in favor of broiling the fowl over an open fire. But Brandon insists that we must be sensible about the matter. He is certain that the flame will be seen. Taking the chicken to a farmhouse would be safer.

"If," I say, "it is not the farm to which the hen belonged."

"Oh, the hell with that," he replies. "We'll say we swiped it from our kitchen."

We select a likely looking house; and at dusk we recover our chicken and sneak across the fields, walking gingerly. While our brains do not concern themselves with mines, our legs are instinctively cautious.

It is an old house, with the yard reeking of manure. And we hear the soft moo of a cow.

A burly, fat man opens the door. As he stands against the candlelight, he seems almost gigantic. His voice has the arrogant weariness of one who has seen too many soldiers.

"No wine," he says.

Brandon dangles the chicken by the legs. The man peers at us suspiciously.

"No wine," he repeats.

"The hell with the wine," says Brandon. "We eat. *Mangiare.*"

"Ah!" the Italian exclaims. "You honger."

"Damned honger," Brandon assures him, weighing the fowl temptingly in his hand.

"Damned honger. You enter," says the man, carefully fumbling for English.

His wife is as dark as a gypsy. Her hair is plaited into a stringy long braid. In her ears are large, golden rings. She scrutinizes the chicken and speaks to her husband. He answers with an impatient volley of Italian. She shrugs her shoulders and thrusts a bundle of twigs into the stove. The flames leap, crackling. In their light, the woman's face seems ancient and lonely.

We still clutch our carbines, but our host appears not to notice the weapons. Perhaps he has learned from experience that it is wise not to suggest that soldiers disarm themselves. Many disapprove of the courtesy.

We seat ourselves at a table. Brandon passes his cigarettes. The woman takes one, says, "Thank you," and puts it on a shelf. In a war-torn country nobody refuses anything offered. Even G.I. contraceptives have become a shameless medium of exchange.

The man inhales expansively, then blows volumes of smoke out of his nostrils. His mood grows genial. He opens a cupboard and brings out a bottle of red wine, which he sets with three glasses on the table.

"I thought the guy said he had no wine," remarks Brandon.

If our host understands, he gives no sign. He fills the glasses, passes us two, and says, "You drink. Is good wine."

We lean our carbines against the wall and toss our cartridge belts into a corner.

The chicken bubbles in an iron pot. The smell of garlic and peppers fills the room. A second bottle of wine appears on the table.

"New York?" asks our host.

"New York," Brandon nods. With our ignorance of the Italian language, attempting to explain the existence of a state called Kentucky is not worth the effort.

"Your freen? New York?"

"New York," I reply, hoping the news never gets back to Texas.

"I have in New York a cousin. Pietro Dominico," says the Italian.

Brandon gulps down a half-glass of wine, vigorously exhales, and rubs his stomach.

"I know Pietro Dominico," he declares.

The Italian gapes in astonishment.

"Pietro Dominico, you know."

"My friend" answers Brandon, holding two fingers closely together. "Pietro and me are like that."

The man speaks excitedly to his wife. Her eyes widen. She rattles a string of Italian in my comrade's direction.

His imagination soars. He raps himself on the chest and turns to me half-belligerently. "Do I know Pietro?" he snaps. "He asks me if I know Pietro Dominico."

"Well, do you?"

Brandon slams a fist on the table; the wine glasses dance. "Of course. He owns a macaroni joint on Fifth Avenue; and he leads a gray kitten about with a rope. His wife is named Ruby. She's half Swede, three-fourths Chinese, and the other part Navajo Indian. She cooks her catfish with a sweet potato dressing, and tells fortunes while she rests. Am I right?"

"Right."

The Italian bends anxiously forward. "I no understand what you speak."

Brandon is exasperated with the limitations of language, but suddenly he has an inspiration. He raises his glass. "To Pietro Dominico, who's been better to me than my own brother. Saloot and santee."

"Ah," the Italian sighs, "it is Pietro." He drinks deeply. The little kitchen has become rosy with friendship. The stove purrs; and the candlelight grows in its richness. We no longer have the feeling of strangers.

The major portion of the chicken is put on our plates. It is so spiced with pepper that tears roll from our eyes as we chew. But we eat the last shred of it and mop up the gravy with chunks of dry bread.

Then the magic dies.

A roach crawls over the table. It pauses to twiddle its long antennae. The Italian crushes it with his hand, wiping the messy remains on his pants. The fire goes out in the stove. The room becomes stuffy and sordid.

The enchanted bottles are drained. Talk ceases. The Italians regard us impatiently. We sink back into our old indifference. Our eyes grow heavy. We buckle on our cartridge belts and pick up our carbines.

"*Buona sera.*"

"*Buona sera, amici. Addio.*"

Outside the night is so clear that the stars seem liquid. To the north, we can see the flash of artillery fire, but we are too far away for the noise. We walk through the fields alert for the challenge of guards.

"This Pietro Dominico," I say.

Brandon laughs. "You didn't for a minute believe that he had a cousin in New York," he replies.

Discipline tightens. Night and day, we spend hours executing new tactics against a supposed enemy. In full battle gear, we wade to our hips in sea water and crawl through the marshes on our bellies. Our clothes are crusted with mud and salt, and we think longingly of the heat of Sicily.

The men are in a dark mood. They are certain we are being prepared for slaughter. We pick fights with rear echelon troops. Tempers snap; and fists fly among old comrades at little provocation. Even Kerrigan is depressed. He becomes so dispirited that one day he even decides to write home.

Rumors buzz. We are to spearhead an assault on a new beachhead. We are to invade southern France. We are to be sent to England for a cross-channel D-Day. And despite the amphibious training, some say we are to lead an all-out drive on Rome.

Drago, a native Italian, has joined our company as a camp follower. The brass has not discovered him, and the men do not care. He is a born soldier of fortune, sliding from one uniform into another with little effort and no conscience. He avoids work with an artistry, whistles a great deal, and makes many jokes.

Novak does not trust him; nor do I. I try to avoid him, but he cottons to me like a brother.

There is a new rumor. Kerrigan swears he got the news from a headquarters clerk who heard a captain confirming it. We are to get overnight passes to Naples.

Drago becomes suddenly popular. He has lived in Naples, knows the town, and has promised to get girls for half the men in the company.

The idea of an actual girl sets my brain afire. As I lie in my blankets at night, she comes to me from the darkness. A tiny brunette with chestnut hair tumbling to her shoulders. She is delicate as a flower, and beautiful as June; and God knows what she sees in me. But for some reason I am an exception.

She is a virgin who has somehow escaped the rot and evil of war. No soldier has ever touched her. She has lips the color of cherries, and laughter is in her eyes.

She is eighteen. The curves of her body show through her dress. It is a long gown of black velvet, with a ribbon to match at the throat. Her shoes are absurdly small with bows of red ribbon on the tops.

An only child, she lives with her parents on a broad, clean street in Naples. Two tall poplars stand in the yard; and in the house a caged bird sings.

Her name is Maria. The introduction is superfluous. We feel that we have known each other forever. Have we not? She has lived in my dreams for years. So what is the need of Drago's introduction. A matter of form. Okay. He performs it and bids us a hasty good night.

Her parents, sensing that we wish to be alone, start yawning. They are sorry to be such dull company. But after all, it has been a hard day. And they have to get up early tomorrow. So *Buona sera, amico.*

We lie on a thick, woolen rug by a stove on which a kettle bubbles tunefully. The fire crackles, and there is a good smell of wood smoke. Maria laughs at the canary because it is annoyed. With beady, resentful eyes fixed upon us, it chirps sleepily.

"He's unhappy because of the light," she says.

"Well, turn it out."

"Oh, no."

"Oh, yes."

"Okay."

At the touch of her fingers, the fever of war disappears. Weariness goes from the body, and hope comes again to the heart. Tomorrow becomes a golden word.

Tomorrow.

The girl snuggles to me hungrily, with her warm flesh filling all the hollows of my body. The brain does not think. Time does not move. We grow together; and for the moment there is only one identity. We.

This is the absurd dream that I fashion in the heart of night, when a man can be so much alone.

Abruptly comes the terrified cry, "Tanks, tanks!"

Instinctively I bolt to a sitting position. But it is only Martinez and his nightmare again. Kerrigan thrusts out a leg and tumbles over the Mexican's cot.

In the dim light, Martinez stares stupidly about as he rubs the sleep from his eyes.

"Jesus," he finally says, "where are we?"

"El Paso, Texas," Kerrigan replies. "You've been drunk for three days."

The six occupants of the tent are all awake. Canteens clink, and flames spurt as cigarettes are lighted. I squint at the luminous dial of my watch. It is one o'clock in the morning.

For a while we lie without speaking. We have been together so long and closely that there seems not a detail of one another's lives with which we are not familiar. Nothing remains to talk about.

Horse-Face smokes his second cigarette. Cupping his chin in his hand, he leans on his elbow. "That Martinez would have to scare up his tanks just as I was about to get places with an old girl," says he. "Blonde I met in Ohio. Saw her in a beer joint. Introduced myself. Asked her to dance. She said, 'Get away, soldier. I know what you're lookin' for, and I ain't that kind of a girl.' 'For chrisake,' says I, 'who said I was lookin' for what? I'm a lonesome dogface just wantin' a little fun before I take off for parts unknown to fight for the likes of you.' 'Oh, yeah?' says she. 'You're damned tootin',' says I.

"Finally broke her down. Bought her a beer. She histed her glass and said, 'Here's to it.' Spent all my money gettin' her drunk. Then she rubbed herself all over me. Had boobs as big as punkins. 'Honey,' says I, 'what're we waitin' for?' Says she, 'My husband.' 'You're kiddin',' says I. 'You'll see,' says she.

"Husband comes in lookin' like a damned gorilla. 'Have a beer,' says I. 'Okay,' says he, 'you sonofabitch, I'll take splat.' With that he gives me a punch in the jaw. Splat! I get up off the floor and say, 'Like a beer myself. I'll take crash.' Pick up a chair, bust it over his head. Crash! Then I take off like a bat out of hell. Didn't have bus fare back to camp. Had to walk seven miles.

"A few nights later, saw the girl again. Says she—"

"For the love of god," snarls Brandon, "shut up and let a man get some sleep."

The cots creak as we twist our bodies into the taut canvas. Silence again. But the dream is broken. Maria does not return. Burning tobacco glows from Brandon's bunk. When he pulls on his cigarette, a red light falls on his face. His eyes are wide open.

(Deer daddy i am in school but the teecher is not looking. she is a good teecher but gets awaful mad sometimes. i ride my bicikel to school. it rained yesterday and i made 100 in arithmetik but i did not make 100 in speling. when

are you coming home. granny says the war is abot over.
i hope so becaus i miss you. mama come to see me sunday
and granny woud not talk to her. she brot me a new dress
and took me walking. we met her new husban at the drug-
store and he bought me some ice cream. but i was not
hungry. when are you coming home? well i will close
with love from your daughter Marion. we don't have to
go to school thankgivin. uncle jim fell off a horse and
brok his arm.)

I hear the changing of the guard and know that it is four o'clock. Still I cannot sleep. I pull on my shoes and walk to the latrine in my underwear. A yawning sentry, who has just finished his watch, is relieving himself at the urine trough. We do not speak. To the south, ack-ack shells are bursting in the sky, and tracer bullets stream upwards. Naples is having an air raid.

6

THE PENDULUM swings with a loud tick-tock. The clock's hands stand at three. A sprinkle of chimes spills over Naples. Slanting, yellow light from a winter sun crawls up the sides of the buildings. It is January.

At a corner table in the café, an American paratrooper sleeps. His head, nestled in his folded arms, rests on the marble top. He breathes heavily. A waiter, who has the mincing movements of a girl, removes two empty bottles and wipes off the table. He shakes the slumbering soldier, but the man does not stir.

The waiter shrugs his shoulders. *"Ubriaco,"* he says to us. "He ees dronk."

"Then let him alone. He's bothering nobody," Kerrigan replies.

"Sì, *signore*. He ees a freend?"

"He is a soldier."

"Eet ees obvious," says the waiter indignantly. He tosses his chin up and flutters over to the bar.

"You have hurt his feelings," Brandon observes.

"He is a butterfly," says Kerrigan.

"A butterfly?"

"A flutter-bug. To hell with him." He glances at the stupefied G.I. "What a way to spend a pass. Folded up like an accordion."

"What's wrong with it?" Brandon asks. "At least, he's unconscious."

"Why don't you loosen up?" says Horse-Face. "We ain't got much time in this burg."

"I've got the blue, screaming willies; and I can't shake 'em. This wine must be watered."

"I've drunk worse," says Snuffy. "But if we jest had a quart of Carolina corn like my uncle used to make."

Kerrigan is slightly sarcastic. "Your uncle? He ever shoot any revenooers?"

"Why shore. But Uncle Ephe was too soft for his own good. Used bird shot instead of buck. Had a still in a laurel thicket. Run the stove pipe up a holler tree to hide the smoke. Set the tree on far. Revenooers happened to be in the neighborhood; seen the smoke; come up to see what goes on.

"Uncle Ephe lets go with a double-barreled shotgun. But them bird shot just sting the revenooers; makes 'em mad. As I said, he shoulda used buck; but uncle weren't no blood thirsty man. Them revenooers mow him down like a rabbit.

"Then somethin' moves in the bushes. Revenooers blaze away agin. Kill my uncle's cow. It was a sad day. People from all over come to my uncle's funeral. Never seen such a turnout. People said, 'There goes the best damned moonshiner in these hills. Never bothered nobody. Allers give full measure; and his whisky was smooth as a snake's hips.' My aunt shore took it hard. Almost went nuts. Sich weepin' and wailin' you never heard the like. She shore thought a lot of that cow."

Tick-tock. Tick-tock. Tick-tock. Time, precious time, flows by.

Three British soldiers in heavy, frayed uniforms enter. They are husky men with blithe, red faces. One leads a terrier on a leash. They seat themselves near us. The dog hops into a chair, puts paws on the table, and perks up its ears.

The waiter is distressed. "No dogs," he says. "Ees forbeeden."

"Ay?" replies the Britisher who holds the leash. "The dog? No, no. 'E's a good bloke." Turning gravely to the terrier, he adds, "There is no beer. But if it's wine you want, speak, lad."

The dog barks joyfully.

"Ees forbeeden," the waiter repeats angrily.

"Oh, get a move on, mon. A bottle of wine and four glasses. 'Urry."

"Sì, *signore*, bot—"

The soldier half-rises. "On your way, mon."

"Sì, *signore*. Foor glasses."

The dog gingerly laps the wine from the tumbler, pausing frequently to lick the red drops from his chops.

Snuffy is intrigued. He goes over and pats the dog on his head.

"What's his name?"

"Cornwall," is the reply. " 'E's a bloomin' sot."

"Had a dog myself once," says Snuffy. "Named Lily. Smartest hound in the whole Smoky Mountains. Done everything but speak English. Could've learned that too, but she quit school at the age of six months. Didn't like the 'rithmetic teacher. I taken her to town and got her a job playing shortstop on a baseball team. Never missed a fly; never missed a grounder. Caught the ball in her mouth and run like hell with it to the baseman. Fastest thing on four feet. Circus man seen her and offered to swap me an elephant for her. I said, 'No. Be like tradin' off my own flesh and blood.' "

"Ay?" one of the Britishers interjects. "A dog, you say."

"Shore," Snuffy continues. "Old Lily. She kept my family in rations for years. Best hunter any man ever seen. I worked out a system with her. Tacked different sized possum hides on boards. Say we had one person comin' for dinner. I'd hang the littlest hide on the back porch. Lily'd get the measure, go out into the woods, and fetch back a 'possum the same size. Say we had three people comin'. All I done was hang out a bigger hide. Lily never missed. She was a stickler for rightness."

He pauses dramatically. The British are fascinated. "What 'appened to her?" asks one.

"A sad thing. One day a man wearin' a coonskin coat visited us. Hung the coat on the back porch. Poor Lily. I can see exactly what took place. She took the measure of that coat and said to herself, 'Couldn't be.' But she was a dog that knowed her duty. She took off into a woods and never come back. She's still out lookin' for a 'possum big as that coat."

The faces of the Britishers register blank astonishment; then hearing our laughter, they turn to us grinning good-naturedly.

"I say, Yanks, we should breed Old Lily to Cornwall 'ere," suggests one. "We'd get the damndest set of pups in the bleedin' combined armies."

Says Snuffy, "She'd never take to that wino." He glances at the glass in his own hand. "I'm scared to death she'll find out I've been hittin' the stuff myself."

The shadows spread in the street. The paratrooper has aroused himself and staggered through the door. It is Snuffy who is napping now. Brandon stares into space. Kerrigan and Horse-Face are bleary. They sing one of our ribald marching songs, keeping time, to the annoyance of the waiter, by tapping their glasses on the table. It is a ballad of endless verses that chronicle the mournful story of a G.I. who has lost a very private and potent part of his anatomy.

I do not drink, but if the wine helps my comrades to a few hours of forgetfulness, well and good. I have my own form of intoxication. The dream of a girl. At six o'clock I am to meet Drago at the military parking lot and be taken to meet Maria. She's a nice girl, not one of your trollops that falls in with anything wearing khaki.

Horse-Face perks up. He gives Kerrigan the elbow, and the Irishman squints his eyes into focus. Two women have entered the café. Their dark eyes boldly, swiftly case the room. They see our stares and suddenly assume dignity.

It is an old ruse. They are obvious prostitutes, but, begging our pardon, they would have us to know they are ladies. I notice that they are more pertly dressed than the usual Italians. Doubtless they have bought their clothes from the black market.

They seat themselves near us and address the waiter in Italian. His attitude is respectful, almost fawning. He goes to a room in the rear and returns with two tall, slender glasses of green liqueur. One reaches into a huge artificial leather bag and fishes out a bundle of "occupation" money. She tosses some bills on the table. The waiter bows. *Grazie, signora.*

At close range, they appear to be in worn middle-twenties. A caking of powder on their olive skin makes their faces look dirty. Their lips are full and scarlet. One of the women has a scar in the middle of her forehead. The other has two gold teeth which gleam when she smiles. But for all that they are still women with their feminine bodies, provocative, mysterious, and ready. I feel nervous and uncomfortable.

Kerrigan pulls himself to his feet and goes to their table.

"Come sit with us," he says. "I wish to introduce you to the most eminent set of sonsabitches that you'll ever have the pleasure of meeting."

Gold-Teeth regards him with haughtiness. "No speak English," she declares.

"Neither do I," says the Irishman. "The language I speak is bed."

"What you mean? Is bed?"

"Is bed. *Letto*."

"Ah, *letto*. You are a bed boy." She heartily laughs at her own pun.

"Now will you come to our table?"

"Sì, why not? You buy us a drink?"

"I'll buy you two drinks; and they'll be bed for you," says the Irishman significantly.

"Ah, you are foney."

"What you mean phony?"

"Foney. You make me to laugh."

"I'll make you all right," says Kerrigan, pleased at the compliment.

Introducing us, he uses the names of our company commander, platoon officer, and first sergeant. It is a precaution against possible aftermath. If names are mentioned, let the men who own them do the explaining to headquarters.

Gold-Teeth eyes me intently; then she runs her fingers through my hair. "He is a babee," she says. "He is too yong for soldier."

I grow cold inside and fling her hand off, growling, "Get away before I break your neck." I cannot explain the attitude. My scalp feels tingly and dirty.

Horse-Face guffaws. "Be damned sure he don't get you in a corner. He'll babee you. He's the champion tomcat of east Texas and parts of Oklahoma. To get him in the army, recruiting officers set a bear trap and baited it with a woman."

"He is a babee," Gold-Teeth insists. "I teach him."

"Let him alone," says Kerrigan. "I'll teach you—plenty." He grabs her knee, and she lets out a yell of surprise.

The waiter rushes over, alarmed. "*Signori,* the *polizia militare.* The café weel be off leemets."

"Okay. Okay," says Kerrigan. "Don't bust a blood vessel."

"Where'd you learn English?" Horse-Face asks Gold-Teeth.

"In school. From my boy friend too. He is a sergeant in the antitanks. Very rich. When the war is ended, he comes back to Napoli. We marry and live in America. California."

Kerrigan howls.

"It is true," she declares in the manner of one mortally offended.

"It is posteef," adds her companion.

Brandon rises in disgust. "I'm blowing," he snarls. "You guys can have these bags."

"A bag. Whosa bag?" Gold-Teeth's ears are tuned for slander.

"Who do you think?"

"Aw, take a walk, boy. Take a walk. The fresh air'll do you good," says Horse-Face.

"After this, I think I need a bath—a lysol bath."

Outside he pauses on the sidewalk, undecidedly. Loneliness sits on his face. He wheels and walks briskly away.

"What's wrong with that character?" asks Horse-Face. "Every time, he's a wet blanket."

At Kerrigan's shake, Snuffy raises his head, blinking sleepily.

"This," says the Irishman, "is a hillbilly who claims to be a soldier. But I've used more ink signing G.I. payrolls than he's drunk army coffee."

Snuffy glares at the women; then his head flops back to the table.

"No ambition," Kerrigan explains. "Take me. When I was his age, I'd already won fourteen loving cups and six medals for sexual prowess. I was pursued by women far and wide. Blondes, brunettes, red heads. Got so many dames on my hands, I had to hire a secretary to keep books on my dates. She quit after two months. Nervous breakdown from overwork."

Gold-Teeth fails to follow the speech. "What you say?"

70

"He claims he's hell on wheels with women," explains Horse-Face. "Knows all the ropes."

"You wanta a woman?" Gold-Teeth suddenly becomes professional.

"Sure, *one* will do for a starter," says Kerrigan. "But drink up. Hey, waiter, wine. More wine."

Dusk is gathering in the streets as I stroll toward the parking lot.

"Hssss. Hey, Joe, you wanta fried eggs?"

"No."

"You wanta scramble eggs?"

"No."

"You wanta beefsteck?"

"No."

"You wanta nice girl?"

"No."

"Fine type girl. Seexteen."

I turn upon the ragamuffin boy who trails me. He darts back and pauses at a safe distance.

"Hey, Joe, you gotta ceegarette?"

"Come here."

"What you want?"

"Come here, I say."

He approaches with the timidity of a wild animal wondering how far it can trust a man. One suspicious move on my part, and he will be off like a rabbit.

"You geev me wahn ceegarette?"

"No. Chocolate. You're too young to smoke."

"For my papa. Wahn ceegarette for my papa."

In the twilight, his lifted face is ghostly in its paleness. His round, large eyes are pools of darkness. I dip into a musette bag and hand him a bar of bitter K-ration chocolate.

"No ceegarette?"

"No cigarette. Now scram."

"You no wanta nice girl. Foorteen."

"I thought you said sixteen."

"Foorteen. You no wanta?"

"Scram."

"Foorteen."

"I said scram."

He dashes a few yards, halts, turns, and spits in my direction. I walk away.

"Hey, Joe."

I pay no further attention to him. The cannon rusting on the beach; the blown bridge; and the rows of crosses. The lines of cots in a hospital tent. A boy in the dusk. Hey, Joe. The rear area from which the tides of war have receded.

She is not the girl of whom I dreamed. Oh, no. She is eighteen all right. But already shadows dance in the hollows of her cheek, and her eyes have the tiredness of age.

Her dress is black, but not velvet. It is a short, cotton affair that scarcely covers her knees. A broad belt, checkered with cracks, circles her waist. She wears no stockings; and the tiny shoes with the bright red bows turn out to be a pair of worn sandals.

Her hair is in braids, and the long strands glisten in the brassy light. Her hands are long and fluttery; her body, far too thin. There is a shyness in her attitude, which does not fit the bold toss of her chin. Perhaps, too many soldiers. So what? The corner of her eye is cocked my way, while she sits primly, modestly. That is good.

The mother studies me with frank anxiety. *"Giovane,"* she finally says.

"Diciannove," Drago explains, as unconcernedly as if he were discussing merchandise. To me he says, "She thinks you are very young. It is well."

There follows a sputtering conversation in Italian; then

Drago announces, "I tell them you bring presents. You give me your bag."

I am embarrassed. The can of stew, another of beans, a small tin of cheese, a pack of cigarettes make a ridiculously small heap on the table.

One by one Drago picks up the cans and solemnly identifies their contents. "*Fava. Stufa. Formaggio.*"

The mother beams and addresses me in Italian. Drago translates. "She says you are most generous. Many thanks. You are in."

I am in. Drago excuses himself. His stay in town is to be brief; and he has many people to see before being off to the wars once more. A soldier in the American army with big doings ahead. God knows when he will be here again. *Grazie ed addio.*

I have a half-mind to follow him. Seldom am I at ease among strangers. And here I am doubly uncomfortable. I do not understand the language of these people. I feel far more at home in the lines. I do not smoke; so there is not even the business of a cigarette to occupy hand and brain.

The father sits in silence, drumming gnarled fingers on the table. As head of the family, he has dignity to maintain. A kindly perplexity shows on his face. Doubtless he wonders what to do with this young whippersnapper of an American soldier.

A fat paragraph of Italian is thrown my way by the mother. I shake my head. She raises her voice and continues. Evidently she believes that volume will succeed where vocabulary has failed. Again I indicate lack of comprehension. She responds by elevating her tone to a shout.

The situation grows ludicrous. Suddenly I burst into laughter. And Maria joins in with a giggle. The parents are puzzled. Then they see the humor. The ice is broken.

I draw a small dictionary from my pocket and pass it to the father. He gravely peruses its contents, nodding approvingly.

73

A word catches his eye. *Calzolaio*. He points it out to me and taps himself on the chest. A shoemaker.

The dictionary is my undoing. The father eagerly races through the pages, finding new words.

"*La guerra male*."

"*Sì*, the war is bad."

"*Mussolini uomo traditore*."

"Yes, Mussolini is a treacherous man."

"*Per Italia dannoso*."

"For Italy he is evil indeed."

"Hitler."

He searches through the pages of the dictionary, but can find no suitable word. So he slashes his finger across his throat, clicking sharply with his tongue. I repeat the international gesture, indicating that I am in complete agreement. Hitler should have his throat cut.

"*Germano arrogante vizioso*."

"*Vero*. It is true. The Germans are arrogant and vicious."

"*Mio figlio soldato*."

"Your son is a soldier?"

"*Morto*."

"Dead?"

"*Morto*."

"I am sorry. It is the war. *Io tristo. La guerra*."

"*Nessun rancore. La guerra male*."

I have heard such talk from conquered people before, but this man seems in earnest. It is the war that is bad, says he. Hatred for one another we must not hold in our hearts.

The game is Maria's idea. We sit about the table throwing dice. There is a board on which is drawn an oval race track divided into segments. The points we make with the dice indicate the number of blocks over which we move four buttons. But suppose my "man" arrives in a square occupied by a rival? Too bad. The unfortunate button must return to the starting spot while mine takes over the position. The person who gets all his buttons "home" first is the winner.

Years ago in Texas, I played the identical game with my brothers and sisters. What now of time and distance? Briefly the memory returns: the checkered oil cloth, the warm kitchen stove, the wail of the wind about a shanty. I shake the thought from my mind and concentrate on the matter at hand.

I have never been hotter. I talk to the dice in the loving manner of a G.I. who has his month's pay at stake. They respond beautifully. The way those "tens" and "twelves" turn up is a miracle. As my buttons gallop around the board, Maria squeals with delight.

Under the table, my knee finds her leg. She gives no sign of even noticing. Perhaps she thinks it an accident.

Despite his ill-fortune with the dice, the father still has his sober dignity. With a wife and daughter looking on, he must not lose face.

The mother sighs, *"Ah, la fortuna."*

In quiet desperation, the father picks up the dice; rattles them slowly. Abruptly he pauses, his face flooded with alarm.

The wail of an air-raid siren falls over Naples. It is like no other sound on earth. The blood runs cold at its eerie warning.

The excited parents grab coats and blankets. No time for the dictionary now. They shout at me in Italian, accompanying their speech with wild gestures. I shake my head firmly. I have only one night in town, and I have no intention of spending it in the cold, damp depths of a bomb shelter.

"Come," says Maria. "Come." She tugs at my arm, but I will not be moved. Suddenly she gives up and sits down determinedly beside me. Her parents grow frantic. The siren's wail continues. Maria turns a surprising spit-fire. Arising, she wrathfully stamps her foot and hurls words with the rapidity of machine-gun fire.

The mother's voice assumes a pleading note. Maria grabs both the father and mother and starts dragging them toward the hallway. The lights go out; a door slams. The siren has ceased. For a moment I can hear nothing but the beating of my own heart. Then the soft squeak of sandals sounds in the darkness.

She sits opposite me at the table again. In the light spread by one tall candle, her white face seems to float. A marvelous change has come to her eyes. In their depths is a smile, a calm, strange smile that is like a veil hiding all that lies within.

In the distance, the ack-ack is opening up. The crack of the guns grows into a fierce, churning rhythm. I reach for the dictionary and search for a word.

"*Spaventato?*"

"No," she replies. "I am not afraid. And you?"

"You speak English?"

"A leetle. You not afraid."

"Sometimes, but not now. No, I'm not afraid now."

"Good."

She lights a cigarette and holds it awkwardly between her fingers. Puffing lightly, she blows the smoke from her mouth without inhaling. An amateur, obviously.

"Why didn't you speak English when your parents were here?"

"My father do no lak eet. The English keel my brawther een Africa."

The drumming of the ack-ack is louder. We can now hear the popping of machine guns also. The first wave of the planes must be on the outskirts of the city.

"Then your father must have hated me too. I was also an enemy."

"He do not hate. He love my brawther too much. He do not lak hees own seester remind him with speaking English. That ees all. To theenk too much ees—how you say—to go crazy."

"I am sorry."

"No sorry. Eet ees the war. You die too maybe. One cannot be sorry for all who die."

"Why not?"

"Eet ees too much."

"I know."

Five bombs explode. The house rocks. The candle flame leaps and is almost extinguished.

"Why you talk sad? Eet ees not good."

"I don't want sad talk."

"Good."

She gets up and blows out the candle.

"Geeve me your hand."

Fumbling in the pitch darkness, I find her outstretched fingers; they are as cool as the waters of a spring.

The gunfire is deafening. The bombs are falling much closer. But after the front lines, it is nothing to get excited about. We live until we die. When the house shudders in the blasts, Maria's clasp on my hand tightens.

"I am glad you stay," she says.

"Why?"

"Eet ees not lonesome. Eet can be so lonesome when the bombs fall."

"I know."

Rising to my feet, I put my arms around her. The body trembles. I kiss her full on the mouth. The trembling stops.

Quietness again. But the all-clear has not sounded. The raid will probably last until dawn. The planes are coming over in spaced waves, keeping all of Naples on the alert. In the periods of silence, I hear the breathing of the girl. It is silky, like a wind stirring through the willows.

Finally I ask, "Why did you act so shy when I first came here? It is not your true nature."

"Shy?"

"Yes, timid."

"Teemid?"

"Bashful, I mean. You did not seem pleased at all."

She catches on and tinkles with laughter. "Oh, that. I am—how you say—shy girl when my parents are here. Eet ees my brawther again. He says leetle seester ees to have nothing to do weeth soldiers. They are bad men. He knows. He ees a soldier heemself."

"And you believe it?"

"Maybee."

"Then I am a bad man?"

"Maybee. But we do not talk of eet."

Her finger tips move through my hair. A ragged pom-pom of the ack-ack begins again on the fringes of the city. For a moment I visualize the pips dancing on the scope of a radar instrument; the strained eyes of men, who are swiftly, deftly plotting the fire range; the tired, cursing gunners returning to their positions of action. Then I fall into a deep sleep that is not haunted by dreams.

It is Maria who awakens me. "You must go queekly," she says. "Eet ees all over. The day comes; and my father returns soon. Hurry."

A pearly light is already in the streets when I pause at the door.

"I'm sorry I slept," I say.

"Eet ees all right. You were tired. Not even the guns awaken you. How could I?"

"I am used to the guns."

"I know." The hollows are back in her face. Her eyes are red; and in the cold air she shivers.

"You have been crying," I say.

"No crying."

"Don't kid me. You've been crying."

"Eet ees not true. You must go queekly."

"I'll be back."

"You no come back."

"I'll write. I'll send you a letter tomorrow."

"No. A soldier never writes; never come back. Eet ees not the first time."

A civilian muffled to his ears in a tattered overcoat shuffles by. From a neighboring tower, a clock strikes.

"You must hurree. I am cold."

"Goodbye. I'll write. I swear that I will write."

"Goodbye. *Addio.* Go with God."

That was how it was. Blocks later, I remember that I forgot even to say, "Thank you."

Ahead of me staggers a G.I., singing in a high tenor voice. I race up the street, yelling, "Kerrigan!" He is hatless, coatless; and his jaw has a long shallow gash. He looks at me through bleary eyes, still continuing his song.

"What in the hell happened?"

"Happened?" he shouts indignantly. "That bitch. That gold-toothed slut. She—where's my coat?"

"You probably hocked it."

"Where's my hat? Where's my money? You want to know? That lower than a goddamned snail's belly of a gold-toothed slut. She stole it. Rolled me cleaner'n a whistle." Suddenly he cackles, "Horse-Face—that sonofabitch—thinks he knows women. Hell, man, I *invented* women."

With one arm around him and an eye cocked for military police, I move him toward the parking lot. A group of Japanese-American G.I.s round a corner and advance toward us at a brisk walk. Kerrigan halts, blinks his eyes incredulously, and crumples to his knees.

"My god," he groans. "All is lost. The Japs have captured Naples."

7

KERRIGAN does not have time to shake off his hangover before simulated combat again closes about us. For three days we storm a dummy beachhead. Naval artillery pounds the shore. The barrage lifts. We leap from landing craft and, falling, crawling, firing, advance upon assigned objectives.

Then abruptly the maneuvers cease. We are put on a strict alert, confined to the company area, and, except for a final inspection of equipment, given a day of rest. We know the signs. "Tomorrow" is on everybody's lips. Chaplains hold special services. There is much letter writing. We still have no idea of our destination. I am too sick to care.

I lie on my cot, sweating and shivering alternately. The malarial attack puts me in an embarrassing situation. If I go to the infirmary I think that it will seem I am deliberately trying to avoid the coming action. I lack the guts to take being thought a coward.

Kerrigan finally reports me. My commanding officer sends for me and orders me to report to the medics. Novak accompanies me to the infirmary. With an arm around my waist, he steadies my reeling body, while I curse Kerrigan furiously.

As we wait our turn at the infirmary, I get a fresh hold on my spinning mind. The sweat drips from my face. To Novak I say, "Don't leave me. I'll be back."

"Damned fool. Don't come back."

"Wait for me."

"I wait."

"Remember the beachhead in Sicily. At first it wasn't so bad. Then Jackson got it; and after him, Pope. We needed men."

"By gah, I forget that Jackson. He steal the goat in Africa and tie it to Snuffy's bunk."

"Yeah. That was Jackson. Remember the time you and I went awol from the boat in Casablanca and that second louie got so mad."

"By gah, he bust a gut. And you tell him. What you tell him?"

"He threatens to bust us. And I say to him, 'Sir, we're already buck privates in the rear rank. What are you going to do? Make us civilians?'"

"By gah, that's what you tell him."

"And just as he was ready to throw the book at us, the trucks come to move us up toward the front."

"Yeah. We wave back at him."

A medic approaches, flicks a thermometer, and thrusts it under my tongue. Withdrawing it, he scans the scale, whistles sharply, and leads me back to a captain.

The officer rolls back my eyelids and puts a hand on my forehead. "Get him to the hospital," he says.

"I don't want to go. My outfit's leaving."

"Get him to the hospital. Report him to his commanding officer. Malaria. Temperature 105. Absolutely unfit for duty."

"But, captain."

"That is all."

I go out to Novak. "I'll slip off. I swear I will."

"Damned fool. Go to bed. We have a dry run maybe."

"The hell you will. I know."

A wave of giddiness seizes my brain. I sink to a chair. "Okay, Novak, turn in my equipment."

"I do it."

"And when you get where you're going, dig a big hole and keep the coffee hot. I'll be up. So help me, I'll be up."

"By gah, I dig the hole."

I lie on a cot. Darkness strikes. I wake up in a hospital in Naples. A nurse, a pretty brunette with violet eyes, bends over me. "Do you feel better?" she asks.

"I feel like hell. What's wrong with my feet?"

"Nothing."

"There is too. They're all swollen."

"It's only a symptom. Nothing's wrong with your feet. Go back to sleep."

"Nurse. What happened to the Third Division?"

"I don't know."

"The hell you don't. What happened to it?"

"I tell you I don't know."

"Where is Novak?"

"Novak?"

"The little short guy that brought me here."

"You came in an ambulance."

"Then what happened to Novak?"

"I don't know. If you want to get well, go back to sleep."

"How long will it take?"

"A few days, if you don't act stubborn."

"I'm not being stubborn. I've got to join my company. It's leaving. Did you know that?"

"No. Go to sleep."

Again I drift into space. Hours later, Violet Eyes awakens me to give me medicine. I feel much better, but some dim regret bothers my conscience.

"I talked out of my head, didn't I?"

"You said nothing."

"I remember talking."

"It's all right. You did nothing wrong. Down with your medicine now. Bottoms up."

In less than a week, I am among a boatload of replacements headed for Anzio. Fifteen of us, just released from the hospital, are returning to our outfits. One man, who has had gonorrhea, bitterly claims he is not cured. He still has a "run."

"That's the only kind of discharge you get in this army," dryly remarks a doughfoot.

When we arrive, bright afternoon lies over the beachhead, which looks calm enough. Many boats stand offshore. Ducks and trucks drone over the sand with supplies.

But scarcely have our feet touched land before five German planes buzz over at high altitude. The new men scatter like frightened chickens. But an experienced eye can see that the krauts are after the boats. Black puffs of flak smoke blossom in the sky. The bombs fall into the sea, sending up spouts of water. The planes wheel up the coast. In five minutes they will be safely back over their own territory.

As we hike inland, jeeps drawing trailerloads of corpses pass us. The bodies, stacked like wood, are covered with shelter-halves. But arms and legs bobble grotesquely over the sides of the vehicles. Evidently graves registration lacks either time or mattress covers in which to sack the bodies. My step quickens. I have an urgent need to learn how my comrades have fared.

At divisional headquarters, we stop. A sergeant spots me. He is a regular army man who throws his weight about plenty. He boils at the irreverence for authority on the part of wartime soldiers. I try unsuccessfully to duck him.

"Hey, you."

"Speaking to me?"

"Who'd you think I'm talking to. Unload your pack. I've got a detail for you."

"Sorry, Mac, I'm going up to my outfit."

"The hell you are. This is an order."

"Oh, go bury your head in the sand."

"In the old army—"

"To hell with the old army."

"I'll report you," he screams. "You'll get the book."

"Report me. Then come up to the front and get me."

"What's your name?" he rages.

That is all I need to know. "George S. Eisenhower Bradley.

Rank: acting private. Serial number: one billion two and a half."

"Let me see your papers."

"Aw, go to hell." Slinging my carbine on my shoulder, I start up a road marked by an arrow and blue diamond, which is the code symbol of my regiment.

As I plod along, I study the terrain instinctively. As a farm youngster, the land meant either hunger or bread to me. Now its shape is the difference between life and death. Every roll, depression, rock, or tree is significant.

The earth over which I walk is flat, offering practically no cover against automatic fire. Drainage ditches criss-cross the land. These would give shelter to the stationary enemy. The advance must have been murderous. In the distance is a chain of wooded rises. I guess that is where the Germans have dug in. The enemy and his eternal hills that must be taken with blood, guts, and steel.

Night is falling when I reach the battered farmhouse in which our company headquarters is located. I push aside the black-out blanket in the door and see a sliver of light.

Alone in the orderly room, Anderson is typing out reports by a gasoline lantern.

"Hello, Anderson. You can stop writing your letters of condolence. I'm back."

He returns the greeting with a sardonic grin. "Welcome to Hell's Junction. We can sure use you."

"Been rough?"

"Jeezus!" His head shakes slowly, soberly. "Plain slaughter. The company's down to thirty-four men."

He resumes his typing; and my heart starts pounding.

"The third platoon?"

"Beat up pretty badly. Incidentally, congratulations."

"What for?"

"You've been promoted to staff sergeant."

"Where's Kerrigan?"

He lifts an impatient eyebrow. "In the rear. Shell splinter in his leg, I think. Nothing serious. He should be back up tonight."

Tap. Tap. Tap. More figures go on the paper.

"How's Little Mike?"

"Who?"

"Novak."

"He's dead."

"Dead? When?"

"The third day, I think."

"How'd he get it?"

"For chrisake. How would I know? I don't run the meat wagon."

Tap. Tap. Tap.

"How about Swope?"

"Wounded."

"Badly?"

"Man, I'm just the company clerk, not a medical report. Swope was knocked out. Wounded. That's all I know—except that I'm twelve hours late with these papers. You'd better check in with the old man. He's asleep in the next room."

"What are our orders?"

"The same as they've been for two days. Attack."

Tap. Tap. Tap.

I open the door and hear the sound of laborious breathing. "Sir."

He awakes with a snort.

"Murphy reporting for duty."

He lights a cigarette; and in the brief flare of the match I see that his face is etched with worry and weariness.

"How's the malaria?"

"I'm okay."

"Good. Feel like taking out a reconnaissance patrol?"

"Suits me."

He spreads out a map by the orderly room lantern. I glance at the details for a sketchy picture of the terrain. Fields; patches of trees; to the right, the Mussolini Canal; parallel to it numerous ditches called *fossi;* at right angles a road; beyond it a highway; a railroad; a town called Cisterna.

The captain points to the roadway. "The krauts," says he, "are in this area and thicker than flies. They're up to something. We suspect that they're bringing up armor. It'll be your job to get behind the lines and find out. I'd stick to the fields as much as possible. Your direction will be about north northeast. Any questions?"

"Who's going with me?"

"Martinez and Evans have volunteered. Are they all right?"

"They're okay."

"You'll report to Sergeant Beltsky. Lieutenant Ward is dead. Goddamned sniper got him the first day."

"Yessir." I turn on my heel to go.

"Murphy."

"Yessir."

"When you're challenged in the area of our lines, for godsake, sing out quickly. The boys are trigger-happy. They'll shoot at a shadow."

"Yessir."

Outside the night is crisp with winter. A chilling wind blows in from the sea, and in the western sky hangs one golden star. From the German lines floats a stream of white tracers, followed by the chatter of the gun. A spasm of loneliness seizes me. I am not one to question the way of things, but, almighty God, why did it have to be Little Mike?

I find Beltsky's dugout and slide in. He fastens a shelter-half over the entrance and strikes a match to a candle. Mud covers him from head to foot, and he looks as though he has not slept in a week.

It is a deep hole. The bottom is sticky with ooze; water seeps in from the sides. Poles, grass, and sod form the roof. Bandoleers of cartridges and a case of grenades lie in a corner.

"Nice place you've got here."

He smiles tiredly. "I always wanted a home in the country. Guess this is it. Cooper's in here with me. And every time a shell hits within a quarter of a mile, he grabs a shovel and starts digging us in deeper."

"He's a funny guy. I've seen him cool as a button during a fight."

"Yeah. He's got a kink in his mind. Thinks it's the big stuff that'll get him."

"Where's he now?"

"Out rounding up Martinez and Evans for a patrol. You like to get in on it?"

"I am. Just got all the dope from the old man."

"Good. Not too shaky?"

"I'm okay."

"You heard about that armor business? If the krauts can get enough tanks in the field, it's the end for us. I hear we've not got enough stuff on the whole beachhead to stand up to a real armor attack."

"I feel my malaria coming back."

He grins. "You'll be back in the hospital soon enough—if you live."

"Kerrigan won't be up in time for the patrol?"

"No. This is a rush order."

"I'd sure like to take that character along. Next to a shortage of booze, he hates patrols."

"I wish you could wait for him."

"You know how Swope and Little Mike got it?"

"No. Things were pretty awful. We got the holy hell kicked out of us. I did see Prouty get his. Burp gun caught him in the neck. I was about ten yards away, but pinned down. He must've bled to death. I saw him before he was carted away. Looked like a stuck hog."

"You knew his family."

"Yeah. Back in the states, I used to go home with him on passes. He had a nice old lady and a dreamboat of a sister. Named Laura."

"You going to write them?"

"Chris' no. What'd I say?"

"He was a good man."

"Yeah. He was okay."

When the other men enter, Beltsky is all business. "Don't take any unnecessary risks," he warns; "and under no circumstances will you fire unless caught in a real jam. The krauts expect you. Two patrols didn't get back last night."

"Jeezus!" says Martinez. "I volunteered for this job; now I think I'll un-volunteer. Why don't we just get the jerries on the phone? It'd save a lot of time and walking."

We toss our helmets to the ground. One clank of their steel would be like ringing a bell to the keyed-up ears of the enemy sentries. Then we scoop ooze from the side of the cave to smear on our hands and face.

"This stuff is supposed to make you pretty," says Evans. "Women use it all the time to smooth the wrinkles from the skin. Maybe I'll open a beauty parlor when I get out of this man's army."

"It don't work," Martinez declares. "I know an old girl who's had dirt on her face from the time she got out of diapers; and she's still as ugly as a horny toad. Lives in Fort Worth."

"Is that a town?"

"You never hear of Fort Worth, Texas?"

"Never even heard of Texas till I met a guy in my induction center. He claimed it was a state. I argued it was a brand of gasoline."

Martinez spits mud from his mouth. "Evans, you're the most

ignorant sonofabitch I ever knowed. In central Texas, we got cow pastures bigger'n Illinois, Chicago to boot. In east Texas, the cotton grows so high we have to train monkeys to pick it. In west Texas—"

"I know. All you need is water and a few good people. That's all hell needs."

We buckle on grenades; throw shells into our carbine chambers; check the safety locks.

Beltsky blows out the candle. "You'll run into Kraft at the outpost. He'll show you through the wire. Password is 'Melancholy Baby.' Get back before daylight and, for chrisake, be careful. We're short of men."

We pause outside to adjust our eyes to the darkness. The sky is strewn with pale stars. The black ruins of a house loom in the foreground. Lakes of shadow mark the open fields.

Martinez trips on a root. Evans and I flop down beside him and await breathlessly.

"Halt!" The voice is barely audible.

"Murphy. Reconnaissance. Melancholy."

"Baby. Come on up. What the hell you guys doing? Wrestling?"

"Martinez stumbled."

"He forgot his seeing-eye dog."

Kraft snickers. "You ever hear about the blind man who—"

"Yeah. Couldn't get in the army because his seeing-eye dog had flat feet."

"It's still funny."

"The hell it is."

Kraft waves his hand toward the German lines: "There it is; and you're welcome to it. Go to your right about a hundred yards. There's a flare set straight ahead."

We hit a plowed field and advance over it, crouching. The spongy soil absorbs the noise of our footsteps, enabling us to move with a degree of swiftness.

Suddenly the sky is quivering with light. We fall and freeze. It is an enemy mortar-flare. In the shimmering white light, I feel like a naked child. I think: If a man could only pull the earth over him like a blanket.

I raise my eyes slowly. Fields and scraggly trees dance about us. To our right is a ditch, on whose banks weeds begin stirring. My body snaps to tautness; relaxes. It is only a gust of wind.

The glowing core of the flare sinks to the ground. Starlight again. And silence, utter silence. We rest the carbines in the crooks of our arms and crawl forward on knees and elbows.

Perhaps thirty, perhaps sixty minutes go by. I have a watch, but on these patrols we are concerned with only one factor of time. Dawn.

We halt to check our compass. As I cup the luminous dial in my hand, Evans gasps. I screw my head in his direction. Not twenty yards away is the blurred silhouette of a half-kneeling man.

In this darkness we cannot depend upon rifle aim. I ease a grenade from its case, pull out its firing pin, and wait. Tickety-tickety-tickety. The beat of the wrist watch is loud in my ears. The kraut is finally satisfied with his observation. He utters something in German. Three other forms rise from the ground and steal off toward our lines.

We give them time to get out of hearing range, then gulp air into our lungs.

"Jeezus," whispers Martinez. "I could already see the old lady cashing my life insurance."

We return the pins to the grenades and again slip forward. Soon from the left come the thud of picks and rattle of spades. Now the same noises are on our right. We inch our way through the enemy lines and pause.

Our trained ears interpret each sound. There is no joking among the Germans. They are working earnestly and hard. That means they are going in deep for a defensive stand. The throttled-down churn of engines and a cautious clanking of steel tell us that tanks are being sneaked into the area. I listen carefully. There seem to be six. That is not too bad. The armor is probably only for infantry support. The humming of trucks and the plopping of boxes to the ground reveal that the krauts are stacking in a lot of supplies.

I remove the leather cover from my watch and check the time. It is nearly one o'clock. Our teeth chatter with the cold as we start back toward our own lines.

Now a flare pops near our company position. A machine gun blurts. The German patrol has evidently run into trouble. As we hug the earth on the fringes of the light, I think that we must be doubly careful now; otherwise we may be shot by our own men. For the remainder of the night, they will be jittery of anything that moves.

We approach our lines, crawling. A body lies before me. I slide up to it. It is a jerry all right. One foot is buckled under the torso.

"Kraft," I call.

"Halt!"

"Reconnaissance. Melancholy."

"Baby. Is it you, Murph?"

"Yes. For godsake hold that gun."

"Come on in."

"What happened?"

"A kraut patrol. We got 'em. One of 'em was moaning, but I wasn't going out to investigate. I'm froze. What time is it?"

"About three o'clock."

"What are the jerries doing?"

"Digging in."

"Chris', that means we do the attacking tomorrow."

"I guess so."

"What I wouldn't give for a cup of coffee and a cigarette."

"What I wouldn't give for a lot of things. Good night; and don't get shot."

In the orderly room, Captain Buckman is shaving a stubbly

beard from his chin. He has cut himself, and a streak of blood shows on his cheek.

"Where the army gets these blades I wouldn't know," says he. "I'd sooner use a trench knife. What did you find out?"

He dries his face with a handkerchief and hauls out the map.

"The krauts are digging in about four hundred yards this side of the road," I report. "They're moving up tanks—about six—and supplies. The ground between here and their lines is still dry enough to support armor, but I don't believe they've got it in strength. Looks like they're going into a defensive."

"Yeah. They'll let us do the attacking until they figure we're bled white, then they'll try to knock us off the beachhead. Was it bad going?"

"Nosir. We passed the patrol that Kraft knocked out. Otherwise it was routine business."

"Okay. You'd better turn in. Hell will likely be popping tomorrow."

"Yessir. Good night."

When I re-enter the dugout, Beltsky is still awake, but Cooper is snoring vigorously.

"I've been putting up with this every night. Artillery I don't mind. But this sawmill gets on my nerves. What happened?"

"The jerries are digging in and moving up tanks."

"Godamighty!"

"Yeah. The old man didn't seem to like our situation at all."

I pour a canteen of water into a helmet and try washing some of the mud from my face. Then I roll into a blanket and stretch on the ground. My brain whirls; and my body shakes. For a moment, I think the malaria has returned. But it is only the cold and exhaustion.

Toward morning shells begin falling in our area. I open my eyes. The cave shudders, and dirt falls from the roof. I try to go back to sleep, but the effort is useless. Only Cooper and men like Snuffy can sleep in such noise.

Beltsky comes in with a box of rations. He strikes a light and begins counting out cans of corned beef and beans. The very sight of the stuff makes my stomach go queasy.

"You'd better get some grub to your men," says Beltsky. "It's almost daylight." His eyes alight on the still slumbering Cooper; and his head shakes in wonder. "Look at that sonofabitch. If he knew what had been falling around us, he'd be shoveling us into China." He gooses Cooper with his foot. "Rise and shine, you ground hog, and greet the goddamned dawn."

I find my squad and distribute the tins. Snuffy and Kerrigan share a foxhole. They are both awake. Without asking, I know that the artillery aroused Kerrigan, and he punched Snuffy to consciousness.

They greet me with hearty curses, and I return the compliment.

"Since when did you and the reverend begin bunking together?" I ask.

"Tonight," Kerrigan answers. "The bird-brain owes me ten bucks; and I aim to keep an eye on him. It's blood money. On the boat coming up, I bet him a tenner I'd get hit before he did. Now he won't pay off."

"We said *hit*," Snuffy argues. "If you call that scratch a wound, I'm the man who took Sicily singlehanded. A blind man could've seen that splinter coming, but this sonofabitch steps right into it. He howled for his money, before he howled for the medics."

"You can trust the medics, but who can trust you? You'll fall in a hole some day and break your neck. Then where'll my dough be?"

"In the hole with me."

"Is that any way to treat a genuine, concubined member of the distinguished order of the Purple Heart?"

"Heart, did you say. You oughta spell it different."

Kerrigan turns to me. "Say, have you been sucking around the old man again? I hear you got pushed up to staff?"

"You heard right. I'm going to look for more respect from you characters."

"Go to hell," they chorus.

A cannon cracks; a shell whizzes overhead. The banter goes from Kerrigan's voice. He thoughtfully fumbles with his shoe laces.

"You heard about Swope and Little Mike?"

"Yeah. Anderson told me."

"I always said that coffee would be the death of him."

"How'd it happen?"

"They went into a shack to heat up some java and got a direct hit from an 88. At the aid station I talked to the medic who tended Swope. He lost his right leg at the hip and part of a hand. He was conscious, but the medic said he never made a sound and never had any expression at all on his face."

"He had guts."

"Yeah. You can say that again. Mike was blown all to hell. Hardly enough of him left for identification. Stove was still burning. Medic told me where I could find it. But not me. I don't want to see it again. Wish they could bury it with Mike."

"Remember the time he got it caught in the bushes and the sniper started firing at him."

"Jeezus! That was funny. There was Little Mike, jerking his pack, wrestling with that bush, and hollering 'sonsabeeches.'"

"He was a good soldier."

"Yeah, you'd have thought he was fighting a holy war."

"Maybe he was."

"Are you nuts? All he ever got out of life was work. What had he to save? A brain-baking job in a goddamned steel mill. A room in a slumgullion boarding house. A lousy dame who took his dough and then didn't have the decency even to answer his letters. Man, he had plenty to fight for. When I think of some of those 4-F, draft-dodging bastards I know back home,

I want to spit nails. Whose the hell war is this? Was it Novak's? Is it mine? Is it yours? Is it Snuffy's?"

"If it's mine," says Snuffy, "I'd like to turn it in on what I owe you."

Light trembles in the east. To our left an artillery duel is growing fiercer. We hear the crack and thunder of our own guns; the whine and crash of incoming German shells. Kerrigan stands in his chest-deep foxhole and leans with his elbows on the bank. He studies the eastern horizon and shakes his head in mock ecstasy. "Gee!" says he, "another beautiful day."

8

THAT AFTERNOON we attack. It is a major assault designed to expand the beachhead. The build-up of our strength is steady but slow. And days may pass before we are ready to attempt a smash through the encircling German strongholds.

Meanwhile, there is an urgent necessity of extending the terrain we have conquered. Every square foot of the beachhead is still in range of the enemy guns. Night and day they batter the men and materiel reaching the area. There is no question about it. The guns have to be shoved back. Otherwise they will continue crippling our forces and draining our power, thus delaying our offensive indefinitely.

In the operation, my company is assigned to clear a section of a highway along which the Germans are entrenched. We have been shown the maps, explained the details, and given our orders. Now we move forward.

Stripped down to the essential equipment for combat, we advance by squads along the flanks of a dirt road that stretches toward the enemy lines. The weather is sunny; and though it is January, beads of sweat roll from our skin. Fear is moving up with us.

It always does. In the heat of battle it may go away. Sometimes it vanishes in a blind, red rage that comes when you see a friend fall. Then again you get so tired that you become indifferent. But when you are moving into combat, why try fooling yourself. Fear is right there beside you.

Experience helps. You soon learn that a situation is seldom as black as the imagination paints it. Some always get through. Yes, but somebody usually gets it. You do not discuss the matter. It is quite personal. But the question keeps pounding through the brain:

This time will I be the one that gets it?

I am well acquainted with fear. It strikes first in the stomach, coming like the disemboweling hand that is thrust into the carcass of a chicken. I feel now as though icy fingers have reached into my mid-parts and twisted the intestines into knots.

Each of us has his own way of fighting off panic. I recall Novak and try working myself into a rage against the uniformed beings who killed him. But that proves futile. At this distance the enemy is as impersonal as the gun that blew Little Mike's pathetic dreams into eternity.

I turn my mind to faraway things: the meadows at home with the wind in the grass; a forgotten moment of laughter; a girl's face. But this also accomplishes nothing. The frosty fingers tighten their grip. Sweat drips from my forehead.

The German lines are nearly a mile away, but our scouts prowl cautiously ahead with eyes alert for surprises. Over a long section of the front our artillery pounds to prepare the way for our small arms.

Behind us the communication crew trails us with strings of telephone wire. In the gang I recognize Dillon, who wears the shamrocks in his shoes. A green kerchief is knotted about his neck. He would not go into battle without it. That is another of his charms against bad luck.

Horse-Face waves to him. "Ever play poker with that guy?" he asks.

"No," I reply.

"Don't. He's won nine thousand bucks since we left North Africa. Bought himself a farm in Arkansas."

"That's one way of making the war pay off."

"Yep. It'd took him nine years to collect that much gal-bait in Arkansas. That place is worse than Texas."

Thompson, a young replacement, walks just ahead of us. This is his first action. Horse-Face gives me a wink, strides forward, and taps him on the shoulder.

"Pardon me, son," says he. "But did you volunteer for service in this outfit?"

"What if I did?" replies Thompson, mildly belligerent.

"Well, sir," continues Horse-Face with mock concern, "I hope you knowed what you was gettin' into."

"I can take care of myself."

"Good. But let it be my painful duty to inform you that you've got yourself hooked up with the roughest, toughest, rootin', tootin' division in the ETO and parts of the South Pacific."

"Oh yeah?"

"Oh, for chrisake," says Kerrigan, "here goes Johnson again."

"Yessir," remarks Horse-Face, "when we leave a field, the blood is runnin' knee-deep; and bones stick up like sprouts in an Alabama new ground. Another whole division has to be sent up to fight off the buzzards while the burial squads snatch up the bodies."

"Aw, go to hell."

"It's the dyin' truth, son. Seen buzzards knock out three tanks once. North Africa. Boys called 'em Arab turkeys. They come in so thick the sky wouldn't hold 'em. Thousands had to walk.

See 'em movin' over the desert sands like a flopping ocean of tar.

"Colonel orders the tanks to start blastin'. Like tryin' to stop the Mississippi with a sandbag. Them birds didn't hesitate; swarmed right over the tanks, a-pukin' and a-squawkin', and smothered every man inside.

"Our whole battalion fixed bayonets and charged, but it was like fightin' a swarm of locusts with a slingshot. Buzzards parried with their beaks and stirred up such a wind with their wings that they blowed our helmets off. Fell back and called for the heavy artillery. Took two days, two nights, and fourteen hours on Sunday—"

"Will you shut up?" snaps Kerrigan in a rare mood of depression. "Let the kid alone."

"It's for his own good. Saw them buzzards with my own eyes."

"Oh, blow it. We've got trouble ahead. Those krauts are staying too quiet to suit me."

"They don't aim to suit you," says Snuffy.

"Step to hell."

Thompson walks stiffly. His chin is thrust forward defiantly.

I catch his ear and say, "When we contact the jerries, stick with one of the old men. Brandon or Kerrigan. Watch them."

"That sonofabitch thinks I'm scared."

"He's only kidding. He tells that wild yarn to every new man."

"It ain't funny."

"Okay. It's not funny. But do as I say. Keep an eye on Kerrigan or Brandon. And if you get through this fracas, you'll know as much as the rest of us about this combat business."

"And when you fill your drawers," adds Mason, "don't stop to take 'em off. It'll give the medics something else to cuss about."

He is a drawling Georgia boy, who has just returned from the hospital.

"How do you feel?" I ask.

"Scared to death. It's always harder to go back up after a long rest."

"Yeah. You can say that again."

"Lying there in the hospital, a man has too much time to think. And that's bad. He gets in the mood to live again."

"I know what you mean."

"A man in my ward had lost a leg; and he was as happy as a catbird in a cherry tree. Shipping out for home next week. Wisconsin. Figures he'll be out of the army by the time the fishing season opens."

"How's your shoulder?"

"It's a little stiff, but I'm okay. Muscle was cut up pretty badly; the doc said if the splinter had been just an inch higher, it would have clipped the bone."

"Yeah?"

"Yessir. One way ticket to Georgia."

Speech ceases. Our artillery fire is dying off. We see the fresh sod thrown up by the shells and know that we are near the enemy lines. Nervously the men give a final check to their gear and weapons. We pause while the crouching scouts move ahead.

This is the worst moment. Just ahead the enemy waits silently. It will be far better when the guns open up. The nerves will relax; the heart, stop its thumping. The brain will turn to animal cunning. The job lies directly before us: Destroy and survive.

The scouts wave us forward, motioning us to keep close to the ground.

It happens with the suddenness of lightning. From hidden positions two *flakwagon* guns churn. One of the scouts is caught squarely in the chest; and the upper part of his body is turned into a shower of seared, torn flesh.

"Oh, the dirty bastards," mutters Kerrigan as he plows into the earth beside me. "They're using 20-millimeter stuff."

These are deadly small shells that explode upon contact. According to the international rules of warfare, they are supposed to be employed against planes and armor, never directly against men. But somebody is always forgetting the rule book.

As if the fire were a prearranged signal for action, all hell erupts. From a dozen points come bursts of automatic fire. Branches and leaves clipped from the trees rain amid the whizzing steel.

Two men caught in the open squirm frantically for the doubtful cover of a slight ridge. Bullets kick all about them. They twist in every direction, but the spurting lead follows. The gunner finally gets his range. The bodies writhe like stricken worms. The gun fires again. The bodies relax and are still.

"Where are our goddam tanks?" fumes Kerrigan. "They're never up when we need them."

Other men have the same idea. From all along our lines comes the call. "Tanks. Get the goddam tanks."

A scream rises from a wounded man, but the noise is lost in the whistle of an incoming shell. The German artillery has begun a barrage. The shells fall to our rear, forming a wall between us and reinforcements; between us and the possibility of retreat.

Now a second barrage is hurled directly upon us. Flames spurt; and the earth seems to roll weirdly.

From right and left comes the cry: "Medics! Medics! Over here. For chrisake, come up! Over here. This way."

We open up with everything we have, shooting blindly. The mass fire is supposed to still the enemy guns until we are close enough to pry out their positions. But the Germans are dug in too well. The fiery blanket woven by their guns never lifts. We may as well be hurtling naked bodies against a wall of spears.

I drag myself under a fence, pause, and intuitively run my

fingers over the grenades I carry beneath me. My blood chills. The pin is missing from one of the grenades; and I lie directly above the prospects of being blown to bits.

A precaution, born of experience, is all that has saved me. When preparing my equipment, I stuck thin strips of adhesive tape around the levers controlling the grenade fuses. I mutter a brief thanks to Little Mike, who got the idea and passed it on to me.

I grasp the grenade in my fist; and on one elbow inch backward, find the pin, and replace it. Then I lie, blowing dirt with my breath. Once seized I could have tossed the grenade away, but that would have endangered the men about me. Besides, I have no grenades to waste.

Mason is ahead. He is stretched in a gutter so shallow that it barely covers his body. I wiggle forward and stop a few yards from him. We exchange grins, but there is sickness in them.

"What happened to the kid?" he asks.

"Thompson?"

"Yeah."

"He's with Kerrigan on the other side of the road."

"Where the hell are our tanks?"

"Better ask the War Department."

"Does anybody know what we're supposed to do now?"

"Knock off a few million krauts and get the war over by sundown."

"Well, we can't hang around here. This spot's hotter than the hinges of hell."

Pi-toon! A sniper sends in his calling card.

"That sonofabitch," says Mason. "Think I'll walk over and twist his goddamned ears off."

I move down the ditch, seeking a position from which I can shoot. A patch of seared weeds offers fair cover. I thrust my rifle barrel through the vegetation and wait.

Pi-toon! The German seems to be behind a fallen tree. I

turn to signal to Mason. But he is already rising to his knees, with pointed rifle.

The shriek of a huge incoming shell sounds. I drop to the bottom of the gutter and drive my head into the bank. The explosion is tremendous. It seems to lift me bodily into the air. For a second I lose consciousness. Then I find myself frantically crawling up the ditch. My brain whirls; my ears ring with the noise of a hundred bells. Greasy black smoke drifts over the earth; and the stench of burnt powder fills my nostrils.

"Mason!"

He does not answer.

"Mason!"

I squirm up to him. A glance tells me he is dead. His head is twisted unnaturally; thin trickles of blood come from the mouth and nose. His brown eyes stare glazedly. I place my ear to his chest. The heart is still. No piece of metal touched him. The concussion alone was sufficient.

I remove the helmet and straighten his head. His eyes are as empty as an unused grave. Briefly a picture trembles in my mind. It is that of a white-haired woman who stands before a cottage on a shady street in Savannah.

"I am his mother," she says. "What were his last words?"

"Said, 'Think I'll walk over and twist his goddamned ears off.'"

"Whose ears?"

"Those of a German who was trying to kill us."

"My boy went to his God with a curse on his lips?"

"His God will understand."

I tap my forehead with my fist. Am I going batty? I shake the picture from my mind. For a moment, I consider covering the body with the raincoat I carry in my belt. But Mason will not need it, and I may. I attach a strip of white bandage to his bayonet, which I drive into the bank above. The marker will help the burial squad to find the corpse at night.

I crawl over the body and advance up the ditch, which

grows more shallow by the yard. I can go no farther without exposing myself; so I twist myself around and retrace my path.

The German sniper is strangely silent. Through parted weeds, I study the log behind which I suspected him of hiding. But I see no indication of him. Perhaps, he thought the big shell got both of us and moved on in search of other game.

Or did Mason fire? I cannot remember. He could have. The crack of his rifle would have been lost in the shriek of the huge projectile. But surely he did not stand there like a fool and deliberately give his life to take that of the sniper's. Yet he might have.

Near the roadway up which we marched, I find Kerrigan and Thompson. They are sprawled behind a small mound, which is covered with scraggly, bullet-chewed shrubs.

"Where have you been?" asks the Irishman.

"Out for a walk. I got restless."

"What's wrong with your nose? It's bleeding."

"Concussion, I guess. A big shell landed near me. It killed Mason."

"Good god!"

Two of our tanks have moved up beside a farmhouse. They lower their cannon barrels and commence firing. The vicious explosion of their shells is like a sweet melody. Now the krauts are getting a dose of their own medicine.

In a few minutes, a German clambers out of a ditch and starts running at a half-stoop up the road. I draw a bead on him, but Thompson's rifle pops first. The German falls, tries to get up; and Thompson shoots again. The body sinks quiveringly to the dirt.

"Well, I'll be goddamned!" exclaims Kerrigan admiringly. "The boy has talent."

Thompson gazes at his handiwork in silence. When he turns to us, his eyes are bright with awe. He purses his lips and looks incredulously at his rifle. "I got him," he finally announces in a half whisper. "Do you think he's dead?"

"He's dead," replies Kerrigan. "You are now a full-fledged member of the Brotherhood of International Killers. Let me be the first to congratulate you."

The tanks have evidently terrorized a pocket of Germans. In their fright, they forget caution. One starts up the road; and I pick him off. Then Kerrigan gets another; and Thompson, two more. It is like knocking off ducks in a shooting gallery. Before we are done, nine gray-clad bodies are sprawled in the road.

"There's a lesson for you, Thompson," says the Irishman. "That's what happens when you lose your head under fire. A hog should have known better than to take off up that road; but not men, when they blow their toppers."

But our shots have revealed our hiding place. A machine gun is trained upon the knoll. Bullets buzz about us like mad hornets. It is time to check out. The krauts will likely start lobbing over mortar shells any moment.

Flattened to the earth and keeping the mound between us and the enemy, we crawl to a gutter in our rear. But we have scarcely settled down before we are ordered to advance with the aid of the tanks. Again we try the tactic of mass fire. The rattle of gunfire grows into a continuous ribbon of noise. We move forward for a hundred yards and are stopped cold. The Germans remain firm and throw back as much as we give them. In fact, more.

Their artillery fire is pulled up from the rear. And once more the earth is a seething hell of flame and whining metal; of screaming cursing men. The ground erupts in thunderous explosions; and in the ghastly rain of debris are the limbs and flesh of men.

In the furor, I catch sight of Brandon. He lies at the edge of a burning haystack, firing methodically, coolly with a Garand.

Behind the stack, Snuffy sits with his helmet off, frantically jerking the bolt of his rifle.

The gun evidently has a jammed cartridge; and he refuses to consider the problem of extricating it logically. Finally he hands the weapon to Brandon, whose skillful fingers quickly remove the shell. Snuffy moves to the opposite side of the stack; fires two fast clips; then he begins jerking the rifle bolt again.

The enemy locates our tanks and fires at them pointblank. For a few minutes they stand their ground with cannons churning. A German shell hits the house. A section of the roof lifts; collapses. The tanks clank to the rear of the building. They are through.

Before dusk we give up. My platoon is left to cover the withdrawal of the remainder of the company. We scatter and continue firing furiously to confuse and distract the enemy. Then we pull out ourselves.

Artillery shells follow us down the road, but once out of range of the small arms, we breathe more easily. Twelve men are missing from the platoon.

On the roadside a body lies near a snarled spool of wire. About the neck is the green kerchief. At some moment during the artillery barrage, Dillon's luck ran out.

There is little sleep that night. The artillery thunders for hours; our foxholes are wet and cold. Cheerless rumors have spread. Our men have been beaten back over the entire front. The day has but served to deplete our forces. We are to attack again tomorrow.

Tired and irritated beyond measure, we awake in a savage mood. The madness of battle grows within us. So does our indifference to life and death. We clean our weapons and wait for the dreaded order. By noon it comes. Attack.

Like robots driven by coiled springs, we again move forward. This time the German artillery meets us. We spread out in the open fields and plunge directly into the fire. Our ears are delicately tuned to the sound of the oncoming projectiles. Instinctively we calculate their probable points of landing.

The holes that they blast offer cover. We dive into them, sometimes before the smoke has cleared, get our breath and bearings, flounder out and move on.

Thompson is near me. He has changed vastly since yesterday. In a single afternoon he has acquired the cautious eye, the up-cocked ear, the wary assurance of an experienced combat man.

The whistle of an 88 shell has a threatening note.

"Get down!" I yell to Thompson. I brace myself on the earth; close my eyes; open my mouth. Wham! Rocks rattle against my helmet.

I raise my head. The shell struck about twenty yards away. When the smoke clears, I see the upper part of a body with a rifle still clutched in the hand. Somebody got a direct hit.

Who? Names dance fearfully through my brain. Brandon? Kerrigan? Johnson? Ward? That is who it was. Ward. He returned to the company last night after three months of schooling in mountain warfare.

I turn to Thompson. His face is white with horror.

"I saw it happen," he quavers.

"Saw what happen?"

"He was lying there flat."

I struggle for a grip on my own nerves.

"Forget it. Come on."

"He was just lying there flat."

"Come on."

"I can't."

"Goddammit, you've got to. You can't stay here."

"Who was it?"

"Fellow named Ward. Come on."

"He was just lying there."

"I know, I know. Let's move now. We've got to get to some cover."

"Is he dead?"

"Half of his body is missing. Can't you see?"

"I don't want to look. I got a headache. I got a bad headache."

I crawl over to examine him. He suffers only from an acute case of panic. His teeth chatter; and his lips twitch in rising hysteria. I seize him by the shirt front and slap his face hard.

"Now come on. If we stay here, we'll both get hit."

He picks up his rifle and moves toward the battle line. In a little while he becomes calm.

"You've got to learn to forget what you see," I say. "You remember those Germans yesterday. They lost their heads; so they lost their lives. Remember?"

"I'll be all right. Don't tell the other guys."

"I'll say nothing. It was just the shock. Nothing to be ashamed of."

"But I can't forget it."

The Germans have evidently been reinforced overnight. The lash of their small arms has grown more terrible. Our artillery bores into their lines. Our tanks slam steel into every obvious strongpoint. We kill men by the score. But always when we come into range, a cyclone of automatic fire sweeps through our ranks.

Repeatedly we get the signal to advance. We snake forward. A quick call on a German telephone sends their shells directly on top of us. The big guns have us zeroed in. Living now becomes a matter of destiny, or pure luck.

The medics are bloody as butchers. Unarmed and with plainly marked helmets, they are supposed to be spared by the Germans. But the projectiles have no eyes. And I see one medic fall dead on a man whose wounds he was dressing. A scrap of metal severed his backbone.

Horse-Face duels with a sniper. The German is behind a chimney on a roof top; and Johnson deliberately moves into the open to draw his fire. I set my sights on one side of the chimney. A gun barrel appears. I begin the squeeze on my trigger. But the German changes his mind and disappears behind the masonry. His gun cracks; and the bullet hits within a yard of Horse-Face, who now raises his Garand.

Tensely I aim again. But the jerry is partial to Horse-Face. Their two guns seem to fire simultaneously. The German tumbles to the roof, rolls, and stops just short of the eaves. Horse-Face crawls over to me grinning pleasantly.

"Seen a man knock a guy off a roof like that in a picture show once. Trick is to take it easy. Makes the other man nervous. Figured I'd get that guy's goat when I crawled out into the open. Did. Seen a man bluff a bull one time. Out in Indiana. Bull charged. Man picked up a rock and hit him smack in the eye. Bullseye. Son, that was a bull's eye, wasn't it?"

The indestructible Horse-Face Johnson. His humor is as imperishable as his body. Under a hail of fire, he talks constantly of things as remote as the moon.

All afternoon we throw ourselves against the enemy. If the suffering of men could do the job, the German lines would be split wide open. But not one real dent do we make.

Again we are forced to withdraw.

We straggle to the rear, exhausted. It is an orderly retreat, not a rout. We still have spirit, but the company strength has dwindled drastically. Replacements cannot begin to keep pace with the slaughter.

On the third morning, a chaplain visits our company. In a tired voice, he prays for the strength of our arms and for the souls of the men who are to die. We do not consider his denomination. Helmets come off. Catholics, Jews, and Protestants bow their heads and finger their weapons. It is front-line religion: God and the Garand.

Staggering with weariness and snarling like wolves, we meet

the Germans again. Doubtless they know our condition. Today
they are more arrogant than ever. We slip to within two hundred yards of their lines before they turn the full force of their
weapons upon us. Obviously they intend our complete annihilation.

Under the furious punishment, a man a few yards from me
cracks up. He begin with a weeping jag; then yelling insanely
he rises to his feet and charges straight toward the German
lines. A sniper drills him through the head; and a burp gun
slashes his body as he falls.

By night we fall back to our original lines with orders to
hold at all cost. Some of the companies have been reduced to
twenty men. Not a yard of ground has been gained by the murderous three days of assault.

9

NOW time becomes a dreary succession of light and darkness.
Neither the day of the week nor the date of the month is re-
membered. We snatch food and sleep whenever we can as the
endless cycle of hours ticks its way into eternity.

A doomlike quality hangs over the beachhead. Just what it
is I cannot say, but it is everywhere. I feel it in the howling of
the wind; the falling of the rain; and the mud that sucks at our
feet. It is in the yellow rays of the sun and the blue rot of trench-
foot. And, above all, it is in the eyes of the men.

Beltsky is gone. A shell fragment sheared off part of a leg;
his combat days are over. I am in charge of the platoon.

There is no thrill in the promotion. Already we old men feel
like fugitives from the law of averages. Loosely we cluster together, bound by a common memory and loneliness. The need

for reinforcements is desperate. But we are suspicious and resentful of the new men that join us. As the days pass, if they prove their worth, they gradually grow into our clique and share the privilege of riding other replacements.

Jackoby does not yet understand this. He has just come into the lines; and he has a chip on his shoulder. He wears his rig like a rookie. There is no excuse for such sloppiness of dress on the part of one from the rear area. His speech is sullen; his eyes, bitter. His attitude must be straightened out immediately.

A detail is being sent out to bury three cows whose bloated carcasses have been causing a stench in our section of the front. Kerrigan and Brandon are in charge of the job. They curse me cordially and profusely for the assignment as they await their helpers' arrival. We stand in a blacked-out room of a partially demolished house which we have made into a forward command post.

To Jackoby I say, "Shed your gear, and go with these men."

"What for?"

"To bury some cows."

"I ain't no gravedigger for a bunch of cows. What've they got to do with winning the war?"

"Plenty. Get your shovel."

"I come up here to fight."

"You'll get plenty of fighting."

"I ain't eat."

"You'll eat later on. Cut out the argument."

"I'm tired. I been walking all evening."

"Get your shovel."

"I ain't gonna be ordered around."

Brandon growls. Kerrigan steps forward. "Murph," says he, "it's my turn. You got to beat hell out of the last one."

"Stand back. This is my job. For the last time, soldier, I'm telling you to get your shovel."

"Goddammit, I said—"

I drive my fist into his stomach. He buckles; and I follow

with a clip to the jaw that sends him sprawling. Then I jump astride his body, seize him by the throat, and batter his head against the floor.

Brandon peels me off the prostrate man; and Kerrigan pulls him to his feet.

He glares at me, but evidently he has decided he has had enough. "I'll report you," he snarls. "So help me, I'll turn you in tomorrow. A noncom hitting—"

"Oh, go to hell. Are you ready to get that shovel?"

"You'll report nobody," says Kerrigan in a voice trembling with rage. "Up here we don't run to headquarters with our problems."

"I know regulations. A noncom—"

"We left regulations in the rear. They were too goddamned heavy to carry."

The muttering replacement slips off his pack, removes his shovel, and follows the men into the night.

In a little while I join them. Enemy artillery fires intermittently, but it is not trained on our sector. I hear the murmur of the laboring men; smell the cows; and wonder how it would seem to have the odor of death out of my nostrils once more.

Jackoby is silent. He works willingly enough. Perhaps, he imagines he is digging the grave for me. I do not mind, because I understand how he feels, and it is one way of getting the soil heaved. I ignore him. To betray softness would be to undo the lesson in not questioning orders in the lines. When he pauses in his labor, his eyes turn toward the flash of the German guns.

We dig for several hours. It is a fine feeling to get out of the cramped and muddy foxholes for a change. Our bodies sweat; muscles stretch freely. Brandon hums. Kerrigan swears softly.

"If anybody hands me a shovel after the war," says he, "I'll brain him with it. An idiot's spoon, that's what it is. Dig. Dig. Get a good hole made, up you move. I've been fighting the whole war with this idiot's spoon."

"It's in the proper hands; an idiot's tool for an idiot."

"Go to hell."

"Reminds me of an old girl," remarks Horse-Face.

"Something always reminds you of an old girl," says Brandon. "Did this one have a face like a shovel?"

"Hell, no. She was a beaut. But she was an idiot if I ever saw one. Comes up to me in a USO club in Nashville, Tennessee. Says, 'Soldier, you're lonesome lookin' as a duck in a henhouse. What's wrong?' Figure she's the sentimental type. Try appealin' to her sympathies. Say, 'Lady, I got a lot on my mind. Just standin' here thinkin' about my dear old mother out in Idaho. Raises potatoes. Writes me the crop this year is a total ruin. Bugs got everything on top of the ground; moles got everything under.'

" 'Had a mama myself once,' says she. 'Loved horses. Always wanted to be a bareback rider in a circus.' 'You?' says I. 'No,' says she, 'mama. Run papa off with a double-barreled shotgun. Didn't like the way he had his hair cut. Too much off the back. Repented later. Went to a fortuneteller to see if he could help find papa. Liked the looks of the fortuneteller. Took off with him. Reminds me. Got my car outside. How'd you like to go for a spin?' Said, 'I'd love to.'

"Takes me riding in a yellow roadster."

The story is snapped by a jerry shell that lands nearby. We see the belch of flame, hear the whining flutter of metal.

"The midnight mail," observes Kerrigan casually. "Sonsabitches never forget. Now watch them start a waltzing barrage." His voice rises thinly to a melody, which is interrupted. "Huh uh. Here she comes."

The diggers drop to the bottom of their holes. Kerrigan and I dive behind one of the cows and ram our heads into the smelly hides. Wham! Whizz! The Irishman raises his head with fingers pinched to his nose. "Cozy, ain't it?"

"What was that?" asks Jackoby with rattling teeth.

"Small stuff. An 88."

"Let's get out of here."

"What for? When your number's up, you go. When the old man with the sickle gives you the nod, it's one detail you can't goof-off on."

"As I was sayin', takes me ridin' in a yellow roadster."

"No use staying here and getting killed," says Thompson. "These goddamned cows can wait."

"Hell, man. That was nothing but the krauts saying, 'Good night.' Wait'll old Annie opens up."

"That's the big gun?" says Jackoby.

"Well," Kerrigan replies, "you wouldn't call it an air rifle. Rumor says its barrel's not over a quarter of a mile long. Krauts use old railroad cars for shells and a pile driver for a ramrod. Ever hear it?"

"No."

"You will."

"Takes me ridin' in a yellow roadster. Turns a hair-pin curve at—"

"No use us being damned fools," insists Thompson.

"How come you've got so gun shy? You were the guy that was going to clean up the beachhead singlehanded when you first come up. Couldn't wait to get into action."

"I'm just saying—"

"You want to live forever?"

"Oh, go to hell."

"Takes me ridin' in a yellow roadster. Turns a hair-pin curve at sixty-five. Try to get her to slow down. Says she, 'That's my speed, bub. Drove to California once by way of the Panama Canal. Three days; three nights. Never slept a wink.'

"Figure now I've got a nut on my hands. Vow never to go into a USO again. Errrrrra . . . Errrrrrra. Cop gets after us. Says she, 'Don't open your mouth while I lay the charm on this character. Used to be in the movies. Played opposite Valentino. Called him Rudy. He called me Cuddles. Folks said we were a born match.'

"'Tells the cop she's Martha Washington, and I'm the general himself. Says she, 'We're on our way to Valley Forge with a message from Abraham Lincoln. Curfew shall not ring tonight.' Cop thinks we're gettin' fresh; threatens to put the slug on us.

"Pull out my military courtesy. Say, 'Sir, I didn't claim to be Washington.' Says, 'Where'd you get hooked up with this dame?' Says I, 'At the USO, sir. Just standin' there thinkin' about my dear old mother out in Idaho. Raises potatoes.'

"'This woman's a snowball,' says the cop. 'She's fulla dope.' 'Hod damn,' says I, 'who'da thought it? Tells me she used to be leadin' lady to Valentino. Mama married a fortuneteller.' 'Valentino,' says he. 'She's a hop head from way back.' At this the lady lets out a scream and pastes the cop in the eye. Never seen such a wild cat. Still believed she could've whipped that guy if his pal hadn't pitched in. They finally get the cuffs on her. She starts yellin' that she'll foreclose a mortgage on the courthouse and threatens to get Roosevelt on the phone.

"Cop says to me, 'Drive her car into town; and don't try any funny stuff. Got you covered from the rear. May have to hold you as a witness.' 'Hell, nosir,' says I. 'Can't hang around. My outfit's leavin' tomorrow.' 'Where to?' says he. 'For parts unknown,' says I, 'to fight for the likes of you.'

"Biggest mistake I ever made. Mighta still been in Nashville sittin' in a nice warm cell instead of on this godforsaken beachhead playing undertaker to a mess of cows."

"Horse-Face," says Kerrigan, "where in the hell do you get such lies?"

"It's the dying truth. Every word. Trouble with you slummy characters is that you never get around high society. Reminds me of another old girl I met in New York. See her walkin' down Broadway leadin' a poodle on a leash. Says—"

"Oh, for chrisake."

"You want me to tell about that Naples trip?" He anticipates Kerrigan's swinging shovel and ducks.

When we quit work, the sky is paling. "You'll find rations at the C.P.," I say to Jackoby. "If you want to eat, ask the man on duty to give you something."

"I want to throw up. After smelling them damned cows all night, I feel like puking."

"Go ahead. Maybe it'll cheer you up."

"Why don't you quit picking on me?"

"You're picking on yourself. I don't care whether you eat or whether you vomit. But you'd better get some sleep. We've got another date with those cows tomorrow night."

"Goddammit I—" He breaks off his speech and walks away mumbling. Two more sessions with the shovels are required before the cows are under the sod.

On the third night, Jackoby snickers quietly at one of Horse-Face's yarns.

Rain falls in slanting black streaks, turning our area into a sea of mud. It pulls at our feet like quicksand. We slant the bottoms of our foxholes. Water drains to the lower ends; and we dip it out with our helmets. But when the storms really strike, we give up. For hours we crouch in ankle-deep water.

The enemy never lets up. During the day, if one sticks his head above the surface of the ground, he risks sudden slaughter. Often we must use ration cans as chamber pots, hurling them from the holes like grenades after they have served their purpose. When shells hit close, the soft walls of the dugouts crumble. Like turtles we dig ourselves out of the mud and try repairing the damage before another shell arrives or the water rises in our foxholes.

The rain is not without its blessing. As long as it keeps the ground swampy, enemy armor bogs down and cannot move against us.

Once every twenty-four hours we slip into the ruins of the house and heat our tins of rations in the embers of a small fire. This can be done only at night. We are in plain sight of enemy observers. By day, smoke would show and bring the artillery down on us.

Stomachs go lumpy and sour. The bitter odor of vomit is everywhere. And it seems that the intestines themselves will be squirted out in diarrheal discharges.

Kerrigan gingerly swallows spoonfuls of beans, chewing them uncertainly. "It is not any longer a question of losing your guts," says he. "It's only a matter of from which end."

Snuffy cocks open an eye. "Wanta make a bet?" he asks.

"On what?"

"Which end."

"Shut up."

"I's jist askin'."

"Shut up."

In the house we have discovered a barrel of wine. It is of dirty reddish color and smells like bad vinegar. The men sip it wryly. Only Snuffy can down enough of it to get drunk.

It happens one night when he is manning a machine gun. A German patrol trips one of our flares. When the light pops, there is no response from Snuffy. I hastily crawl to his emplacement to investigate. He is stretched on the ground, sleeping as peacefully as a cradled child. His mouth is open; and his breath reeks of wine. I straddle his body, seat myself on his hips, and fire the gun at skipping shadows until the flare dies. The noise does not awaken Snuffy. Nor do I. Brandon takes over the watch; and the incident is not reported.

Through our hearts and minds, resignation and futility crawl like worms. We cannot advance. And we cannot retreat another yard without adding further peril to the slim security of our beachhead.

Rumors slide from hole to hole. The British are pulling out, while the pulling is good, leaving us holding a gigantic and ferocious wildcat with a very small grip by a very short tail. The Germans are only waiting until our build-up is worthy of a major attack. They will then thrust through the middle of our defenses, split our forces, and drive us into the sea. We believe nothing; doubt nothing.

Our function we know. It is to hold the lines until enough men and materiel arrive to try again cracking the iron wall that lies before us. We listen to the moan of the wind, curse existence, and snarl at one another. There is no escape with honor except on the litter of the medics or in the sack of the burial squads.

Smathers leaves in a mattress cover. He should have been more careful. It was a foolish way to die; and he wanted so much to live. A Toledo girl, to whom he was engaged, occasionally sent him copies of *Better Homes and Gardens*. The magazines arrived frayed and dated. But Smathers perused them gravely, grinning at the sardonic comments of the other men.

We all liked him, but kidded him plenty. He had joined us somewhere near Salerno, a lean, tanned, handsome fellow with humor and calm courage. I will never understand how he forgot that at night men on the outposts are as jittery as drunks with hangovers.

Hearing our machine gun, I rush to the spot, but he is already dead when I arrive.

Cates bends over the body, frantically loosening the clothes and muttering, "Oh, Jesus Christ! Jesus Christ!"

"What's the matter?"

"Oh, Jesus Christ! It's Smathers. I've shot him. Get the medics."

I lean my ear against the sprawled man's chest. There is no sound. "He's gone."

"No, he's not. He was talking a minute ago."

"What did he say?"

"He said—he was saying—he just said, 'Oh god.' Get the medics."

"He's dead."

"No, he's not. Get the medics. Go get the medics. He was talking just a minute ago."

"I'm telling you: he's gone."

"He was up helping string barbed wire. I hear somebody running my way and challenge him. He keeps on coming without singing out. And I've got to let him have it. I thought he was a jerry. I was sure he was a goddamned jerry."

"You can't be blamed. You better go back and tell the old man. Stop at the C.P. and tell Kerrigan to send me a couple of men."

"What'll I say to the old man? I thought he was a jerry."

"Just tell him what happened. He may chew you up for being trigger-happy, but that's all he'll do."

"I challenged him; and he didn't sing out."

"I know. I know."

"And, Jesus Christ, he was a pal of mine. We used to spend passes together. But I couldn't see who it was. You know I couldn't see who it was."

"Nobody's blaming you."

"Let's try the medics. It won't do any harm to try the medics."

"I tell you he's dead. You know he's dead. Get hold of yourself."

"But he was talking just a minute ago. He said—"

"I know. Now you better go back and see the old man."

"Oh, Jesus Christ." His voice breaks into a sob.

"Do you want to stay here while I go back."

"No. No. I can't stay here. He was a friend of mine. And, Jesus Christ, I couldn't see him. I challenged him, and—"

"Get going, Cates. Get going. We've got to have another man on this gun."

"I'm going. But I'd like to try the medics."

"Get going."

He stumbles off through the night, still muttering crazily.

Kohl comes up and takes over for him. Caskill helps me carry the body back to the command post. We drop it in the mud outside the door and enter.

"What's wrong with Cates?" asks Kerrigan. "He's acting like he'd gone nuts."

"He killed Smathers. Thought he was a German."

"Good god!"

"Said he challenged him, but Smathers didn't answer."

"Where is he?"

"Outside. You want to see him?"

"Good god, no."

I ring company headquarters on the field telephone.

"What!" shouts Anderson after I have passed him the news.

"Don't get excited. We're still holding the lines. Nothing serious has happened. Cates mistook Smathers for a German and shot him. Tell the old man it was an accident. Smathers didn't sing out when Cates challenged him."

"That's going to make the old man mighty unhappy."

"I can't help that. Notify G.R.O. They'll want to pick up the body before morning."

"The old man liked Smathers."

"So what? We all did. Tell the buzzard detail not to drive past your station. We're expecting the kraut artillery any time."

"Sure. Sure. Anything to oblige."

"Thanks."

I hang up the receiver and grow sick at my stomach.

Kerrigan is pensive. "What a shame," he says. "Remember that girl in Toledo?"

"Remember the time we rode him so about his flowers?"

"Yeah."

Remember the time:

We sit in a tent in our camp near Naples. The mail has just arrived. Smathers reads his batch of letters and turns to the magazine with the pictures of houses and gardens.

Caskill, noticing, winks at Kerrigan. "I have a problem, dear. Will it be petunias or gladiolas this year?"

The Irishman takes the cue. "Pit-tunis! Pit-tunis!" he replies, mimicking the pop and spit of bullets passing near the ear.

"But, dear," minces Caskill, "how about poppies. They do look so sweet on a grave."

"Oh, you mean man, what a horrible, horrible thought!"

Smathers lifts a good-natured eyebrow. "Rave on, you bastards. But I've already got the lot."

"In a military cemetery, I presume. That's grave."

Smathers tosses the magazine aside. "Don't worry. I'll get home," he says. "You guys will be pushing up the poppies while I'm pushing the baby carriage. But I won't forget you. Oh, no. There I'll be sitting in a nice, little breakfast nook. Bacon and scrambled eggs beside me; and the best coffee in the state of Ohio. Boy, can she make coffee!

"The little woman will be right there opposite me, with that adoring look on her face. And, brother, can she adore! 'Honey,' she'll say, 'tell me about Caskill and Kerrigan again.' 'Those sonsabitches,' I'll answer. 'Not at the breakfast table.' 'Oh, but do,' she insists, 'it sounds so funny the way you say it.' 'Okay. The last time I saw them their faces were as green as Kerrigan's brain; and the flies were blowing them.'"

"Reminds me of an old girl," says Horse-Face.

"For chrisake, what now? The blow flies?"

"Breakfast nook. Train engineer's wife in Alabama. Met her at a comin' out party."

"Coming out of what?"

"Her clothes. Says—"

"Will somebody please throttle that bastard. I'm too tired to move."

Two men bearing a litter come into the ruined house.

"Where's the body?" asks one.

"Outside. I'll show you."

"Tore up?"

"Not bad. A machine gun."

"Good. I never seen so many messy ones as we've picked up on this beachhead. That damned artillery."

They pull a mattress cover over the body and roll it on the stretcher.

"Boy, am I tired," says one of the men. "We been packing meat all night. This guy got his dog tags?"

"He's got everything. If you find a package of magazine pages in his pocket, put them among his personal effects."

"Magazine pages?"

"Yeah. Magazine pages. That's what I said."

"Jeezus! Now I've heard everything. This business gits daffier and daffier."

The men stumble off through the darkness. I return to the ruined house, roll up in a blanket, and go to sleep.

10

MEANWHILE the boats wallow in from the open sea. Planes bomb them, and fluttering shells from enormous railroad guns crash among them. But the creaking of winches and lowering of ramps continue as precious cargoes of men and materiel are dumped upon the beach.

At night armor rumbles into places of hiding. Camouflage nets are spread over the cannons. Replacements, many of them miserable and frightened men, unload their gear and dig in. Command works desperately on new tactics.

Time. We must have time.

The threat of a German counterattack becomes more imminent. The enemy cannot help realize that daily we grow stronger. But the rain which we so heartily curse has turned the earth into swampland in which the ponderous armor flounders impotently.

When the sun shines and the wind blows, we study the forward area anxiously. The crusting of the ground has become all important.

We are using the remaining portion of an upstairs room in our ruined house as an observation post. One morning I am scanning the terrain through a pair of binoculars when I spy a German tank. My hands start trembling. As I sweep the enemy lines with the glasses, more tanks appear. I count twenty of them. That is all I care to see. Grabbing a map, I roughly estimate the position co-ordinates of the enemy armor, seize the phone, and yell for the artillery.

Our cannons blast, but the shells fall short of the tanks. Gradually I correct the fire until one tank is hit. Its crew climbs out and starts running. I pick off one with a Garand. Two of his comrades drag him toward shelter. But I dare not shoot again, lest the Germans locate me and turn their guns on us. Exchanging this excellent observation point for a couple more wounded krauts would be a poor trade indeed.

The remaining tanks wallow back. Again I correct the artillery. The shells follow the armor in a hectic chase, but I soon lose sight of the krauts and notify our gunners. Wasting further ammunition would be senseless.

I sit down weakly. Sweat stands on my forehead; my knees shake; and the pit of my stomach seems to have fallen out.

The tanks are there.

Even the wrecked one worries me. I guess that when night falls, it will be picked up by a retriever, repaired, and sent against us again. True, it is only one tank among many, but to the foot soldier that is how the war goes. Infinite small threats make up the whole. Eliminate the little problems, and the big ones will take care of themselves.

I check the terrain with a compass; get my directions. Then I call company headquarters for permission to take out a patrol after dusk. Brandon, Kerrigan, and Snuffy volunteer to accompany me. Horse-Face is also willing. But I am afraid that he will take a notion to spin one of those wild yarns of his in the shadow of the enemy himself. I put him on a machine-gun watch and take Jackoby instead.

Yes, Jackoby is changing his tune. He has seen that at the front there is little bucking for rank and that nobody is the fair-haired boy. Each has his share in the work and common misery. So the chip falls from Jackoby's shoulder.

Loaded with rifles and antitank grenades, we slip through the night. Over the muddy ground, progress is slow; and frequently we must halt for breath. Snuffy deliberates over a Molotov cocktail, which is simply a bottle of gasoline with an ignition fuse attached. It is supposed to set the tank afire, but Snuffy does not trust it.

"If it works," says he, "I'm a blue-tailed monkey's uncle. And if it don't work, we're in a hell of a fix. I'll lay anybody three-to-one that them krauts have got that tank guarded. Any takers?"

"Keep your voice down," urges Kerrigan. "Did anybody ever see such a fool? Must have learned to whisper in a sawmill."

"And when this mulatto cockytail conks that tank, what happens? Clank. Them krauts are goin' to start blazin' away. Four-to-one. Any takers?"

"Maybe he's right," observes Jackoby.

"He's never right. Let's move up and get this damned job over."

"Gittin' nervous?"

"Hell, no. I'm getting cold. Come on, you hillbilly. Let's go to war."

When the Germans evacuated the tank, they left a light burning inside. It sends a glow through the open manhole, marking our target perfectly.

Leaving the men to cover me, I crawl to within range, rise on one knee, and hurl a Molotov cocktail. The bottle crashes against the steel. In the stillness, the noise is like a bell. But nothing else happens. I try again with no better luck. The fuses are obviously faulty.

I hear the voice of a German and know that I must work in split seconds. Swiftly sliding up a ditch, I lob a grenade through the open manhole. The explosion does not even extinguish the light. I crawl back a short distance and begin blasting off the treads with rifle grenades.

The operation stirs up a hornet's nest. Two enemy machine guns bark. Tracer bullets streak about me. I follow the ditch as far as possible. Then I kick caution out of the way and take off like a jack rabbit.

My comrades, hearing me coming, get a fifty yard start on me. But I catch up before we pause to rest our aching lungs a quarter of a mile away.

"Jist lack I said. Them mulatto cockytails should be give back to the Russians. They damned nigh got us slewn," pants Snuffy.

"Where in the hell did that guy learn to speak English?" asks Kerrigan.

"Rat where I'd like to be now. In them Tennessee hills so fur away."

"Will the Germans follow us?" Jackoby inquires anxiously.

"Keerist, no," Kerrigan snorts. "You couldn't pry them out of their holes with a crowbar. They wouldn't know where we'd be laying for them."

"Yessir. We'd done better with far-crackers."

"Far-crackers? What in the hell you talking about now?"

"Far-crackers, you dumb ass. Ain't you ever thowed no far-crackers on the Fourth of July?"

"*Fire*crackers, for chrisake!"

"That's what I said; far-crackers."

The next morning the ruined tank is still visible. Evidently it is no longer worth repairing. The Germans never retrieve it.

Now the rain starts again; the water drips; and the wind moans. We slog through the mud on routine duty; wait for night; wait for day. Even the sound of the guns fits into the pattern of tedium. And the utter boredom of static warfare drives men to strange deeds.

Kerrigan discovers he is a poet. He composes some verse to which Snuffy adds a monotonous folk tune. In a quavering, rusty voice, he sings:

> *Oh, gather 'round me, comrades; and listen while*
> *   I speak*
> *Of a war, a war, a war, where hell is six feet deep.*
> *Along the shore, the cannons roar. Oh, how can a*
> *   soldier sleep?*
> *The going's slow on Anzio. And hell is six feet*
> *   deep.*
>
> *Praise be to God for this captured sod that rich*
> *   with blood does seep;*
> *With yours and mine, like butchered swine's; and*
> *   hell is six feet deep.*
> *That death awaits there's no debate; no triumph*
> *   will we reap.*
> *The crosses grow on Anzio, where hell is six feet*
> *   deep.*

It is a major achievement. Kerrigan is flattered and has to be severely discouraged from indulging in further literary efforts.

Movement gives the illusion of progress; and that illusion is our greatest need. Monotony often achieves more than either pleading or patriotism. To spike the rot of existence; to get out of our holes and relieve irritation by a slash at the enemy, we volunteer for dangerous patrols.

One misty night three of us are in the command post, playing poker by candlelight. The telephone jingles. Kerrigan reaches for the receiver.

"Hello. No, this is not the boneyard. It's Lil's place. Yeah. Anderson. The hell you say. Now ain't that just ducky? Yeah. Yeah. I'll tell him."

"What is it now?" asks Berner, a corporal who has had a losing streak all evening.

"Anderson. The old man says intelligence has got to have some prisoners. Asking for volunteers to go out and round them up. Count me out. It's too damp outside."

Berner throws down his cards. "Just as my luck was changing," he grumbles.

"Don't worry about that. You'll need all your luck now. Every time I come into this hole to get warm, I land up on one of these murder details."

"Go break the news to Kohl. We'll need his German lingo," I say. "And tell Caskill to get his rear-end here and look after the phone."

"What's wrong with my German, *arschlock?*"

"Too vulgar. For this we need that delicate touch."

"Kohl's going to love this."

"It'll give him some exercise."

The first hint of the Germans' presence is the smell of strong tobacco smoke. We tread softly with weapons ready. A murmur of voices sounds in the night. But in the mist we can see nothing. We sling our rifles on our shoulders and grasp grenades.

A hut looms suddenly in the fog. Again the odor of tobacco hits our nostrils. Inside the house, a man laughs.

Like cats we creep to a window and flatten ourselves against a wall.

"Tell them to come out," I whisper to Kohl.

"Hey, *Wir sind Amerikaner. Alles kaput. Hände hoch! Komm 'raus."*

Only silence greets his words.

"Tell them to come out; or we'll blast them out with grenades."

"*Komm 'raus. Oder wir pfeffern eine Granate 'rein!*"

There is a scramble inside, but still the door remains shut.

"Tell them this is the last warning."

"*Wir warnen euch zum letzen mal.*"

"No response comes from the house.

"Okay. Let them have it."

We hurl four grenades through the window and dart to a safe distance. The hut rocks; and in the fumes of powder is mingled the smell of powdered masonry. Berner and Kohl cover us with rifles. Kerrigan and I dash forward, kick open the splintered door, and jump to the sides.

"Ask them if they've had enough," I say.

"I don't think the bastards are alive. *Na habt Ihr die Nase voll?*"

The low groan of an agonized man comes through the door. We enter with fixed weapons. Guided by the moans, I reach a hand to the floor, find a body; and my fingers become sticky with blood. I grab the uniform and drag the man from a hole in the floor.

He gasps and becomes still. I bend my ear to his heart. It has stopped beating.

I fish into the hole again and pull out another body. The legs kick spasmodically; and the breathing seems horribly loud. It sounds as though the man had a throatful of phlegm. I run my hands over the chest and find a gaping hole from which the blood spurts like a fountain. There is nothing we can do about it.

Frantically I try once more. The third man, protected by the flesh of his comrades, has escaped the blast. I jerk him to his feet and frisk him for weapons. He trembles like a frightened bird but is otherwise unharmed.

Kohl addresses him in German. "*Warum könnt Ihr nicht 'raus?*"

The prisoner replies with muttered words.

"What does he say?"

"I don't know. I asked him why he didn't come out when we called. But he's either too scared to talk or he's speaking a dialect I don't understand. Sounds like he's tongue-tied."

"Well, get him to the rear quickly."

"The same way we came?"

"Any damned way. Just get going."

From outside comes the thud of running feet.

"Keerist!" Kerrigan exclaims. "Here's old man trouble. His pals, no doubt."

Kohl and Berner grab the prisoner by the shoulders and hustle him off through the mist. Kerrigan and I edge to a corner of the house. A jerry calls, "Hans! Hans!" We answer with two clips of cartridges.

Then cautiously we steal away in a direction at angles to that taken by Berner and Kohl. The running continues on the right. Shouting comes from our rear. We now hear the pounding of footsteps on our left. Dropping to our knees, we shoot in both directions. Six rifles return the fire. The Germans have evidently guessed the nature of our mission and are attempting to head us off. It is the prisoner that concerns them most. Captured men often give out information that has disastrous results.

Wheeling to our right for about fifty yards, we shoot again. The Germans make no response. Maybe they are waiting for us to plunge into their trap. If so, our ruse has worked.

We retrace our steps. And I check my compass for the straightest direction to our lines. Stealthily we walk for a couple of hundred yards; then we run like deer. With relief I remember that we have encountered few antipersonnel mines in this area.

The Germans, now aware of the trick, blast wildly. Bullets sing overhead. I increase my speed; trip on a snag; and pitch on my head. For a moment, I think my ankle is sprained. Kerrigan pulls me to my feet. I test the joint gingerly. The sound of our pursuers grows louder.

I hear the click of the safety lock on Kerrigan's rifle.

"Don't shoot, for godsake," I say. "They still don't know where we are."

"Damn 'em. They'll never get me."

"Go ahead."

"Can you walk?"

"If I can't, I can crawl like hell. Go ahead."

"Don't talk like that to me, you hop-headed goon. I can just see myself leaving you here."

"I can walk."

"Then let's move."

Resting one hand on Kerrigan's shoulder, I manage to limp at a rather fast pace. But hours seem to pass before we reach the security of our lines.

Kohl and Berner are waiting in the command post. They have already delivered their prisoner to company headquarters. Now they stand with foolish grins on their faces.

"No wonder I couldn't understand that German," says Kohl. "The guy was a Polack. The old man had Paderwicz talk to him. He'd been in this area only three days and was about as full of information as an empty barrel."

"Besides," adds Berner, "he was half drunk."

"He was sure of only two things. He wanted to go home; and he had lost his bottle."

Kerrigan sinks to the floor. Placing his forehead in the palms of his hands, he rocks his head back and forth.

"Holy keerist!" he sighs. "I thought his breath smelled familiar."

During our absence the mail has been brought up. I thumb through the packet of frayed envelopes. There is nothing for me. I toss a letter to Kerrigan. A flourishing feminine hand has addressed it in violet ink.

Then I finger a small paper. It is directed to Private Michael

Novak and must have escaped the eye of the company clerk. Seeing the name of a dead man on such an intimate thing as mail gives one a queer feeling. I slip the paper from its encircling sheath; turn the pages.

It is a company publication. Under a headline (OUR BOYS AND GIRLS IN SERVICE) is a picture of Novak. Yes, Little Mike as a civilian. He must have been quite like the man we knew as a soldier. He has the same crooked nose, with a smile to match; the stubborn chin; the need of a shave; the tousled, black hair; the broken depths of thought and sadness in his eyes. And his necktie is knotted at the throat like a noose.

Beneath the photograph:

> *Private Michael Novak. "Little Mike," as he was familiarly known among his co-workers at Eureka, is now with the Seventh Army in Italy. That is bad news for the Germans. During the four years he was with us, Mike, though on the quiet side, endeared himself to all with his industry and unfailing good humor. We are expecting great things of him in the war. According to his sister, Mrs. Zigmund Sowa, he has already seen considerable combat. Keep up the good work, Mike. We are proud of you.*

I glance again at the picture, then turn the page. Another headline: EUREKA QUINTET LICKS EAGLE CAGERS 52-36.

> *In an unbroken string of victories, the Eureka basketball team added another scalp to its belt when it tangled last week with Eagle Consolidated. It was a bitterly contested game until the last whistle. Outstanding performances were contributed by John "Red" Cathy, as right forward, and—*

Folding the paper, I return it to its holder, and above the typed address, mark "Deceased."

Kerrigan scowls over his letter. "Have I gone nuts?" he asks. "Or is this dame crazy? Listen to what the bitch writes.

Dear honeybunch. It is little me again. How are you? I'll bet you have already forgot your "blue eyes". I haven't heard from you in weeks and weeks. Well, I wish you could see my sailor. He is the "cat's whiskers". Ha-ha. I am just kidding. You know I am strictly an "army girl". Honey, I do miss you. I was over at Sally's last night. She has a new "love". You know Sally. He is an oil man. Runs a filling station. Ha-ha. He wanted to bring a friend along for me. But I said, no siree. I don't sit under the cherry tree with anybody else but my Irishman. We went out to Joe's "joint" and drunk some beer. I never seen the like of soldiers. And I want you to know that your little "blue eyes" has not lost her "sex appeal". Three soldiers tried to move in on our party, but believe me I gave them "the old elbow". I get lonesome, but after all you are "the tops" in this girl's life. I tell every man I go out with about you. Oh, honey, I do miss you. This awful war "gets me down". But if it hadn't been for the war, I maybe wouldn't have met you at all. And that would have been "tragic". When I think of all the "good times" we had together, I want to cry. Well, don't take any wooden nickels. With oodles of love. Cora.

"Brilliant. Simply brilliant," remarks Kohl. "That's the very kind of girl I always wanted to meet. The home-loving type. Who the hell is she?"

"Some broad I used to shack with in Boston. No, I guess it was New Haven. She's living in Boston now."

"Was she a pro?"

"Hell, no. I still had a good amateur standing until I came overseas. 'Blue-eyes.' I must've been drunker than usual if I called her that."

"Who was Sally?"

"I don't know. But this I must say for Cora. If I remember correctly, she was first-class in the hay."

Regularly combat patrols are sent out to harass the Germans. We must continue to remind them that we still have a striking force. Our present defensive stand is not to be mistaken for weakness. Usually these missions include fierce, bloody skirmishes; and often not even the tedium of the foxholes impels enough men to volunteer for them.

One day reconnaissance informs us that the krauts have moved up their forward outposts in our sector. It could be the prelude to an attack. A patrol is organized to knock out the positions. In our platoon Kerrigan, Berner, and Thompson get tapped for service.

The Irishman groans; Berner swears softly; Thompson alone is silent as they buckle on their gear.

During the course of action, Thompson vanishes. Nobody can explain what happened to him. He simply disappears.

"Going up the road, I kept an eye on him," says Kerrigan. "He was in a hell of a mood. His eyes kept darting about like a rat in a cheese factory. I asked him what was wrong. He said, 'I got the bellyache. Somethin' I eat I guess.' I told him we wouldn't be gone long; then when we got back, if he was still alive, he could get some baking soda. If he was dead, he wouldn't need it. Maybe I shouldn't have said that. He looked at me in a funny way."

"When we stopped for a rest," adds Berner, "he lay on his back with his eyes closed. I told him to cheer up. He may get shot in the leg and get a big rest. He told me to go to hell. I said, 'Thanks. I'm on my way.' I don't remember seeing him after that."

"The jerries threw a lot of stuff at us," continues Kerrigan. "Mostly mortar and machine-gun fire. A couple guys got killed; several more were wounded. And I was too busy watching out for my own hide to study about the kid until we started back. Then I missed him. I asked the other fellows if they'd seen him, but they hadn't."

"There was a lot of confusion," remarks Berner. "Maybe he moved in too close and got himself captured."

"Or hit."

I check with the aid station, but Thompson is not among the wounded. Routinely I report him missing in action.

Three days later he is found cowering in an abandoned hut in the rear area. A deserter. He is placed under arrest and confined in the prison stockade. I guess what has happened. His nerves gave way; and he could not force himself to face the enemy guns again.

Thompson was not a coward, but from the army point of view his offense is a serious matter indeed. It could set a disastrous precedent among worn-out, frightened men who know that they must continue hurling their flesh against the enemy until death or a wound honorably relieves them of duty.

I am called to the rear to testify in the court-martial proceedings against Thompson. As I walk over the terrain, my mind is awhirl. Which of us knows when his own nerves may collapse and he will do something equally as foolish as Thompson? Is it fair to judge a man legally for some act committed in the unnatural situations of war? But is not desertion a crime against us, his fellows, who must stay at our posts and keep plugging the breaches in the dike as the flood rages? I can find no answer.

Before the court, my testimony is brief and factual. On Wednesday of last week, Private Thompson was assigned to a combat mission. I myself delivered the order to him. He left with the patrol; he failed to return with it. I reported him missing.

A chair creaks as the army twists its rump about. Previous to the incident, had Thompson been a good soldier? Yessir. As far as I am concerned, his conduct had been entirely satisfactory.

Then to what do I attribute his act? To nerves. To fright.

"Hmmmm," muses the army. To fright? Do I think that Thompson has a corner on fright? Nosir. I have my own share of fear. But you do not desert? Nosir. Do I believe that Thompson deliberately sought to avoid hazardous duty with his act? Yessir. I think that it obvious, but under the influence of fear. Hmmmm! It is natural to be afraid. We all are. But no soldier can let his fear govern his conduct to such a degree. Is that understood? Yessir.

A droning officer tells the details of finding the soldier in the shack. Then Thompson himself takes the stand. He has little to say.

The court ponders the case briefly, and hands out a verdict of guilty. Thompson is sentenced to twenty years in prison.

The jeep that returns him to the stockade has to go toward the lines for a distance. So I crawl in for the ride. Thompson is silent as we bounce up the road.

"I had to report you," I say finally.

"I'm not blaming you."

"You could have easily been killed or captured."

"I said I wasn't blaming you."

When I get out of the jeep, I shake hands with him.

"Good luck."

"The same to you."

Suddenly we both laugh.

"I don't guess it's funny," I say. "I'm really sorry for you."

"Sorry for me? I'm sorry for you. I got only twenty years. If I serve the whole sentence, I'll be just thirty-nine when I get out. But what happens to you? Why, you poor sonofabitch, you go back into the lines. You attack. If you live, you attack again. And you keep on attacking until you're dead. What's twenty years compared to a corpse?"

Before I get to the front, night has come, and the rain is falling again.

11

IN the constant cold and wetness, feet turn blue, and flesh rots. I send the worst cases to the rear for treatment. The men are given cans of foot powder and promptly returned to the lines, still shivering and hobbling.

When Caskill comes back, he is still barely able to stand. For several days I have been staggering under a malarial attack. With feverish brain I direct the routine operations of the platoon. I am like a baited animal, enraged at myself and everything I see. Now the anger flames at the picture of Caskill.

I seize the field telephone and ring the aid station.

"Give me a doctor."

"A what?" asks the switchboard operator.

"A medical officer."

"Who?"

"Anybody with bars on his shoulders."

"Oh. How're things up there?"

"Rougher than hell."

"Wait a minute. I'll get you Captain Hoff."

"The fat guy with the glasses?"

"Yes."

"Put him on."

"Ye-es. Captain Hoff. What do you want?"

"Sergeant Murphy, captain. I've been sending men with trench foot back to your aid station."

"Ye-es. I know. I know."

"You do! Well, goddammit," I shout, "don't shove them back up here with a couple of aspirins and a pack of foot powder."

"Who do you think you're talking to, sergeant?" he screams over the wire.

"I don't care. I'm telling you: Don't send my men back up here before they can walk."

"Are you drunk?"

"I'm sick."

"Of what?"

"The whole mess."

"We're busy back here. I can't waste time."

"You're busy! Now isn't that too bad. We're slightly occupied ourselves."

"I'm running this station," he yells in a choking voice; "and, by god, remember that you may be through here yourself."

"God spare me."

The receiver clicks in my ear.

"You shouldn't have done that," says Caskill worriedly. "It's no use. You'll only get yourself in trouble."

"Trouble! How can a man get into more trouble?"

"It's no use."

"Okay. Okay. It's no use."

Caskill, doubtless seeking to change the subject, says, "While waiting at the aid station, I read some old Chicago papers."

"What's new?" asks Brandon.

"Charlie Chaplin wants a second front."

Snuffy looks up from a steaming can of beans. "Come again."

"Charlie Chaplin wants a second front."

"A second front! Jeezus! Give him this one."

"A man was killed in southside Chicago. Body, riddled with bullets, was found lying in the streets. Slayer escaped, but left a yellow handkerchief as a clue."

"Is that supposed to be news?" asks Brandon.

"I suppose so. Papers gave it headlines. Call it 'The Yellow Handkerchief Murder.'"

"Jeezus!"

"The cigarette shortage continues; and people are demanding an explanation for the scarcity of tobacco."

"My piles bleed for them."

"The public is warned that meat rationing will be more severe in coming months."

"Meat?"

"Yeah. The kind that doesn't come in cans. Remember?"

"Lord, yes. Steak."

"Night clubs may be forced to close at midnight to conserve fuel and the energies of factory workers who like to guzzle too late."

"I can't stand it."

"The miners are talking about a strike."

"A strike?"

"Yeah. You know: People demand higher wages, shorter hours, better living conditions. If they don't get them, they quit work."

"Americans?"

"Why, hell, yes. Who do you think they are? The Chinese?"

"Are you kidding?"

"It's the truth. It was right there in the papers."

"Jeezus!"

I start from the room to check our machine guns for the night. Not far from the ruins, my knees give way; I collapse in the mud; and darkness blots out the mind.

Later I learn that Kohl and Berner carry me to the rear on an old door. I am but dimly aware of the aid station. A face floats over me. I argue with it that my feet are bursting out of my shoes. Then I faint again. When I regain consciousness, I am among a row of cots in a hospital tent.

The next day I meet Helen. She is one of the nurses, and a remarkable human being. As she glides up the aisle, I notice the brightness of her blond hair. The heads of the sick and wounded twist to greet her. She pauses briefly at each of the cots, calling the men by name, asking silly little questions, and deftly parrying their feeble attempts at banter and impudence.

When she reaches my cot, I have my mental defenses up. She ignores my sullen glare and speaks in an eager whisper, as if fearful of disturbing the patients next to me.

"Well, you look better this morning."

"I feel better."

"Lord, you were mud from head to foot when brought in last night. Remember?"

"No, I was blacked out. Regulations, you know."

"You were a regular mud man. I helped clean you up; and I wasn't even on duty. Say, 'Thank you, nurse.' "

"Thank you, nurse. The plumbing broke down up in the lines."

She leans over to straighten my pillow. "Now. Now. At least, you could have taken a whore's bath."

Undisturbed by the surprise that leaps to my face, she continues, "Yes. A whore's bath. We call them that, too."

"Just cold water and a helmet?"

"And, of course, a little soap."

"It was no use. You try at first; and then you give up and let the mud take over."

"I know." She touches my wrist and glances at me with anxious eyes. They are as blue as a summer sky.

"Your pulse is pounding. What's wrong?"

"I don't know, goddammit. You're the nurse."

"Oh." A smile dances in her eyes. "It's nothing. I sometimes forget that I'm a woman."

"I don't."

"None of you do, except with your language."

"I'm sorry about the cussing."

"Don't apologize. You should hear me when I get riled. It's the crying I can't stand."

"Do they cry?"

"Some of them. Their nerves fold up; and they can't help it."

"What do they cry about?"

"Most of them don't know. They just get on weeping jags like some drunks do."

"They'll never make me cry."

"Who?"

"Anybody. I'm not the crying kind."

"I'll bet you aren't. We were discussing your age last night. How old are you?"

"Nineteen."

"You look younger."

"I can't help that. I'm nineteen."

"What are you doing in the army?"

"I asked for it. Wanted to play soldier."

"And now you've had enough."

"I've got a bellyful."

"But you wouldn't quit if you had the chance."

"No. I wouldn't quit."

"Why not?"

"I never thought about it. Maybe I feel—What are you asking all these questions for? They've got nothing to do with malaria."

"They've got everything to do with malaria. Maybe you feel what?"

"Oh, hell. As long as there's a man in the lines, maybe I feel that my place is up there beside him."

"Is that all?"

"That's all I can think of."

She hands me a glass of bitter medicine. I hold my nose and swallow it. "Now will you let me alone?"

"You're too tense. Why don't you get off that Irish high horse for a bit?" she asks.

"I'm all right."

"Perhaps you need a back-rub to loosen those muscles. Tell you what I'll do. If you take down those dukes and be a nice boy, I'll give you a rub when I get off duty."

"Don't knock yourself out."

When she passes to the next cot, I close my eyes; but the

vision of her face still waltzes through my mind. The nose is bent slightly; the mouth is large and sensual, but droops, as if from sadness, about the corners. Her skin is as fair as apple blossoms.

As the hours sift by, I sleep fretfully and wonder if she will return. If I had known how, I would have been more pleasant.

At dusk I hear her brisk voice as she moves up through the lines of cots. My blood quickens, but I hastily assume a mask of surly indifference. It is all the defense I have.

"Hello, Irish. Did I take a ribbing? The girls found out."

"Found out what?"

"That I'd decided to give you a rub."

"What's wrong with that?"

"Nothing, except we save it for our specials."

"Your special whats?"

"Our special interests."

"Don't knock yourself out."

"You said that before."

"I didn't ask you to do it."

"Of course, you didn't. Now will you try to relax? I'm tired and don't feel like fighting with you."

"Then why the hell don't you go to bed?"

"It would do me no good. I get so tired that I could collapse. But I can't sleep any more."

"Yeah. I know what you mean."

Her skillful fingers pry into the muscles of my back, causing shivers to prowl up and down my spine.

"What did the kids call you in school? Red or freckles?" she asks.

"They called me short-breeches."

The fingers hesitate.

"Short-breeches. Oh, that's funny."

"Is it? Then laugh."

"Oh." The fingers resume their movements. "I didn't mean to say anything wrong."

"It's all right. If you're so damned curious, maybe you'd like to know how I got the nickname."

"I would."

"When I was in the fifth grade, I had just one pair of over-alls. My mother washed them every night and dried them by the kitchen stove. They shrunk halfway to my knees. So the guys started calling me short-breeches; and I'd slug them. I fought every day."

"That was bad."

"I didn't say it was good."

"But what does all this fighting get you? You're fighting me now."

"It gets me the opportunity of being let alone until somebody else crosses my path."

"Meaning I'm not welcome."

"I didn't say that."

"You couldn't make it more obvious if you hit me in the head with a bed pan."

"I'm sorry. I guess I was trying to prove that I was as good as any of them. I lived on the wrong side of the tracks."

"Oh."

"Does it shock you, nurse? I wouldn't want to shock you with a few little details about a hungry kid dreaming about a ban-quet."

"Get that chip off the shoulder, Irish. You don't have to prove anything to me."

"I don't give a damn about proving anything to anybody, except maybe to myself. It doesn't matter. Nothing matters. You do your job the best you can and forget the rest."

"I know. Oh, how I know."

"I'm not mad at anybody. I'm glad that things happened as they did. We had a lot of kids in the family and needed food. So I hunted a lot and learned to shoot straight. I couldn't afford to miss. That comes in handy now.

"Sometimes I had just one shell. Sometimes in the field, I

dream of walking in the darkness with that one shell. The Germans are all around me; and I know that I don't have the ammo to stand up against them. I wake up with the shakes. Do you know what being hungry is?"

"No," she says softly, "not really hungry."

"I do. I've seen the time when I put pepper on molasses to make it seem something different from what I'd had the day before. The pepper burnt my stomach and made it feel full. I still like hot food."

"I'll swipe you a can of pepper from our mess, and you can take it back up with you."

"Don't strain yourself. Now is there anything else you'd like to know. I'm just rearing to spill my guts."

"I understand your Irish now. You're still fighting the battle of little short-breeches."

"No. I honestly don't care. I laugh when I remember the people whom I once thought were the great ones of the earth. I've learned who the great ones really are. They're men like Brandon, Kerrigan, even Snuffy."

"Who are they?"

"Some guys I know up in the lines. They bitch; they cuss; they foul up. But when the chips are down, they do their jobs like men."

For a while she works in silence. The faint thump of the cannons drifts through the night. From somewhere a soft moan rises.

"You want to hear some more?"

"I want to hear it all."

"For godsake, why?"

"I don't know. I used to be a hell of a cynic. Among my crowd in Omaha, it was supposed to be a fashionable attitude. And good old Helen was always fashionable. But for the past few months, I've had the curious feeling that I'm developing an enlarged heart."

"Yeah? That's bad."

"I know. When the breaks come, they're bigger, too."

"I don't know what you're talking about."

"Skip it. Do you write home regularly?"

"I've got no home."

"But your mother?"

"She died when I was sixteen."

"No."

"She had the most beautiful hair I've ever seen. It reached almost to the floor. She rarely talked; and always she seemed to be searching for something. What it was I don't know. We didn't discuss our feelings."

"No?"

"No. There was nothing to say. But when she passed away, she took something of me with her. It seems I've been searching for it ever since."

"You'll find it."

"I don't think so."

"What happened then?"

"I hooked up with the army, learned to eat my oatmeal, and kill my quota of men; so I got promoted to staff. That's my story. Now are you satisfied, nurse?"

She does not answer. Her thumbs swiftly circle my shoulder blades. I watch the shadows cast by a gasoline lantern skipping over the tent walls.

"Can you guess what the kids called me?" she asks.

"I wouldn't have the slightest idea."

"Droopy-drawers."

A direct shell-hit could not have been more effective in shattering my defenses. I crane my head around to meet her smiling eyes.

"Droopy-drawers?"

"Yes," she snickers. "You wouldn't think it now. But I was a thin little child. And the elastic on my panties was never tight enough."

"Old droopy-drawers."

"Wouldn't it have been wonderful if we'd been in school together. Can't you see it? Chalked on the fences; carved in the trees: 'Short-breeches loves droopy-drawers.'"

I flip over to my back. "Is the elastic still loose?"

"No. No. It's very tight. Has to be in this man's army."

"Why'd you join up?"

"Oh, I don't know. Maybe to escape the monotony of civilian life. Being a bachelor girl is not all peaches and cream."

"Good lord! You came into the army to get away from monotony?"

"I get what you mean. But the monotony of one muddy, broken body after the other is not the same as the monotony of a dozen shabby romances or a thousand cocktail parties."

"I guess not."

"Five years ago, I finished college with a science degree; and about all I did with my knowledge was to experiment in mixing new kinds of drinks. Good old Helen. Always comes up with something different. I build a hell of a martini. Do you like martinis?"

"Never drank one."

"No. Of course, you wouldn't have. Anyhow when the war struck, it was a cinch with my science background to get into the nurses corps. So here I am. Good old Helen, right on the job."

"And have you had enough?"

"Yes and no. Like you, I couldn't leave until the last stretcher case was brought in. You can't get away from it now. I had a friend, an infantry lieutenant, who tried it. He got the medal of honor and was sent home, a hero. God, how he hated that word. He was given the full treatment. Bands, flags, dinners, speeches. Then the army handed him a desk job, but it lasted only a few weeks. When he saw how casually people back there were taking the war, it broke his heart. He asked to be returned to his unit overseas.

"I met him in Naples. You couldn't imagine the change in him. He seemed to be in a daze; and snapping him out of it was harder than getting you off your Irish. I finally took him to a hotel."

"I knew I should have held out. Pulling that droopy-drawers business wasn't fair. I was a sucker for it."

"No. No." A grin flashes over her face. "This was an emergency; and Nurse Hansel was right there on duty. In the darkness, I could feel his temples throbbing. Then he began to spill. It all came out. Little things made him blow his topper: people simpering over a cut of steak; new fashions in the show windows; men yawning over battle headlines. He couldn't take it. So he began to hit the bottle. That only made it worse. He wanted to cram what he'd seen over here down people's throats. But he couldn't. So he came back.

"We had a couple of days together before he moved up to the front. When he left me, his eyes were shining again. A few weeks later he was killed. I didn't grieve much, because that's the way he wanted it. Now I hope that family of his doesn't snatch his body back after the war. I know he would want to lie among the men with whom he fought; men who understood him."

"So would I. And the women too."

Her nose wrinkles impishly. "Well, I'd better be ducking now, or these other fellows will get jealous. It's amazing how closely they check up on us nurses. The man in the far right corner has been here only a week, but he already knows the date of my menstrual period. How he found it out I wouldn't know. I usually forget it myself. But I checked the calendar; and he was right."

"Good night, droopy-drawers."

"Good night." She hesitates. "Be sure you address me properly when the head nurse is around. She's a bear for rank; and I'm always in hot water with her."

"You would be."

As she moves down the aisle, she is followed by a sleepy chorus of "Good night, nurse."

Before the week is up, I am fit to return to the lines. Helen accompanies me to the outside of the tent. In the sunlight I notice that tiny wrinkles have gathered about her eyes.

"Well, so long, short-breeches," she says. "I'll be thinking of you up there in that nice cool hole while I'm down here slaving over hot bed pans."

"Goodbye, droopy-drawers." I start away; then turn. "Thanks."

She makes a face at me; and that is the last I see of her. Word that the hospital area has been under bombardment and several nurses killed filters up to the front. I try, but never find out whether Helen was among those who got it.

12

SPRING comes to the beachhead, and on the ruined land new green glistens in the sunlight. When the guns are quiet, we can hear the song of birds; mate calls to mate, their voices swelling uncertainly.

Near the command post a cherry tree bursts into bloom. The leaf buds swell; the petals sift to the ground; and one day the hard, green fruit hangs upon the branches.

Kerrigan is touched by the sight and composes a new song to express his feelings.

> *We've got cherries on Anzio;*
> *Cherries, yes; but women, no.*
> *Don't ask me how, but it sure is so.*
> *That's the hell with Anzio.*

Brandon frowns upon the song. He studies the tree with a thoughtful eye and talks of April in Kentucky. His daughter, who has just turned ten, wants to cut off her pigtails. It is a problem that concerns us deeply. Through the months of ruin and despair, the little girl with her braids and freckles has served to remind us that somewhere on the earth utter innocence still exists. But if those pigtails go, what then? We group around Brandon while he reads her letter aloud.

"Deer dady, the boy who sits behind me in school pulls my hair and it is a mess for granny to brade everyday so i think i will have it cut off like all the other girls are doing. Mary who is my new friend who moved from chicago says her mama says she can get a perment wave so i think i'll have my hair cut off. Granny won't let me unless you say ok so i hope you say ok. from your loving daughter Marion. P.s. it look turable stringy anyhow."

"Oh, no," groans Horse-Face. "Don't let her. Keep her a kid as long as you can."

Kerrigan glances at him queerly. "You getting sentimental?"

"Me?" says Horse-Face, his lips curling. "I'm the most unsentimentalist guy you'll ever hope to meet." Inspiration shows suddenly in his eyes. "Pigtails just reminded me of an old girl I knowed out in the state of Arizona. Apache Indian. Wore braids that reached to her knees."

"Oh, my god," moans Kerrigan. "I should've kept quiet."

"Cut off your gab, and you'd bust a gut," says Snuffy, without opening his eyes.

"See her standing in front of a shack. About to perish from thirst."

"The girl?"

"No, me. Walking telephone lines across the plains. Summer. June. July. Maybe August. Give out of water, and damn near give up the ghost when I see the girl. Go up to her and say, 'How?' Says she, 'What the hell you mean how?' Says I, 'You speak English?' Says, 'English, German, French, and some Chinee. Name's Minnie-choo-choo. Daughter of Chief Iron Horse. Grandma got scared by a railroad train in the old man's prenatal days. Come in, Lonesome Stranger. You like some beer?' 'You got some beer?' says I. 'No,' she says. 'You like some coffee?' 'Sure, sure,' says I. 'You got some cream?' 'Cream?' says she. 'We ain't even got some coffee. Drink sheep's blood.' Say, 'Make it sheep's blood then.' Hands me a gourdful. Drink it, and must've got a sunstroke. Start a-baaing and a-butting Chief Iron Horse. Daughter conks me with a tomahawk. Makes me mad. Butt the old man clean out the door. Girl gives a big whoop and jumps astraddle of my back. Take out across the plains a-baaing and a-bucking, with the girl flamming me with a cactus plant. Line gang finds me under a mesquite bush. Girl's gone. Take me to a hospital. Lay there baaing like a sheep for fourteen days and thirteen nights. Doctors said it was the damndest thing they'd ever seen. When it comes to drinking sheep's blood, been a teetotaller ever since."

Flack, an earnest, young replacement, is fascinated. "What happened to the girl?"

"Well, sir," replies Horse-Face, "story had a strange, queer ending. When I get out of the hospital, I meet an old timer and ask him about them Indians. Says, 'Knowed both Iron Horse and Minnie-choo-choo well. Killed in 1902. Tornado.'"

"You're kidding."

"It's the dying truth, son."

"They were ghosts?"

Horse-Face shrugs. "Call them that if you want to. But that tomahawk was mighty real. Look." He parts his hair and reveals a long jagged scar upon the crown of his head.

It is a sunny day, and a warm wind blows. The front is deceivingly still. We sprawl upon the ground on the seaward side of the command post. Hope has returned with the season.

No longer do we feel like orphaned underdogs. Our forces are driving up from the south, and the beachhead bristles with accumulated power. An all-out attack is imminent. We are eager for it to begin. Our every thought and action is concentrated on getting the war over before another winter comes.

Replacements have strengthened our platoon. Flack came into the lines with eagerness. A pale boy who looks as though he scarcely had strength to lift a rifle, he has volunteered regularly for patrols. He works with a quiet thoroughness. Since joining us he has already made corporal, and I have recommended him for a sergeancy.

The old men regard him with tolerant amusement. It is strange to see a man bucking for promotion at the front, where an advance in rank only puts him closer to death.

Through casual conversations, I have learned that his mother is the mainspring of his drive. In a small-town Iowa school, Flack was evidently a leader; so it was a great disappointment to his mother when he had to enter the army as a private. But she is sure that he will eventually be commissioned.

If Valero, a tough Italian from the slums of Chicago, ever heard of a school he gives no indication of it. He does not discuss his past, but he is a born soldier. In many skirmishes, he has proved himself as nerveless as he is merciless. He asks no quarter, gives no quarter; and his face lights up with savage joy when his gun is spitting. But with the men he is as friendly as a shaggy dog, calling everybody "Pal."

But his favorite is Constantino, a meek little Italian who is also from Chicago. The friendship often proves trying. Valero is constantly volunteering for dangerous missions. "And, of course," says he, "muh old pal, Constantino, wants to go along. I got to look after him." Constantino, who apparently would prefer looking after himself in the security of a dugout, blanches and picks up his gun.

Bergman is a redheaded, blue-eyed Swede from Minnesota. On occasion he forgets completely that there is an "h" in the English alphabet. When we are caught in the inevitable foul-ups of the military machine, he says, "I trow up bote hands. I quit." But he never does. Muscular and loose-jointed as a young ox, he has a keen sense of irony that serves as a damper for his quick temper. I later discover that his ability to take punishment is exceeded only by his capacity for cognac.

In late May, we realize that the vast operation is beginning. Night after night practically every cannon on the beachhead blasts the enemy positions. The Germans, at first, answer with furious barrages. But that is according to plan. The krauts are being tricked into expending their precious ammunition while we are still under cover.

During the terrible months immediately preceding, our command has studied every detail of the terrain over which we must pass. The enemy strongpoints are known; the mine fields, mapped; the gun positions, plotted.

But time has also favored the Germans. It has enabled them to bring in reinforcements and to strengthen their defenses immeasurably. Obvious facts inform them that the assault is impending. Now with the tables turned and their backs to the wall, they are prepared to fight like insane men. They must. If we shatter their lines and merge with the main body of our army pushing up from the south, Rome is doomed and their men in the area face annihilation.

Our final artillery barrage is so intense that it seems nothing could be left of the German lines. The grinning soldiers, listening to the thunderous explosions, say, "Hitler, count your children." Under the spinning shells we turn from the holes in which we have cowered for nearly four months and march toward the enemy. Directly overhead our 50-caliber machine guns lay a cover of bullets that crack in their passing like millions of bullwhips.

The Germans stagger; but fanatical and desperate, they recover. From the ruins of buildings, from field and forest, their deadly guns stutter.

The first major task of my company is to cut the railroad running south of Cisterna. The Germans have dug in along its sides; and the track bed is protected by a lashing stream of automatic fire. We pause behind a high stone wall to reconnoiter and co-ordinate the movements of our three platoons.

The track in this section passes through a deep cut. To cross we must slide down the bank, sprint over the bed, and clamber up the opposite slope. To our right, near a concrete culvert, the Germans have two machine guns trained directly toward the cut through which we must run.

Valero attempts to knock out the weapons with a Browning automatic. He bores into the emplacements with spurts of lead, but the guns are too strongly shielded to be silenced by small arms.

Meanwhile, important moments slip by. The first platoon begins the crossing; and the enemy guns are strangely quiet. The second platoon goes over. I crawl to the edge of the cut, turn, and wave my men forward one at a time.

Johnson.

When Horse-Face reaches the roadbed, he leaps the tracks and scrambles up the embankment with bullets singing about him. At the top, he twists his head toward me, thumbs his nose, and wriggles off on his belly.

A crackle of mass fire begins on the opposite bank. I have the sudden, sickening feeling that we are being lured into a trap, but I cannot hesitate.

Brandon. Jones. Valero. Flack.

For some unaccountable reason, the young corporal pauses in the cut. It is only for an instant. But down the tracks the Germans press their triggers. Flack drops to his knees, then crumples across an iron railing.

Berner. Kohl. Bergman. Kerrigan.

I am the last. Scanning the banks, I pick my path, draw a deep breath, and start sliding. The handle of a trench shovel fastened to my back wedges between two protruding rocks; and I hang like a pigeon upon the bank with lead spattering all about me. Rock dust from the bullets fills my nostrils. My throbbing temples seem ready to burst.

Glancing up, I see the look of horror on Kerrigan's face. He gets up, measures the distance to me with his eye, and tenses his muscles for the jump.

Yelling for him to keep down, I free myself with a desperate heave and bolt across the tracks.

Sweat stands on Kerrigan's brow. "You ignorant bastard," he spits, "are you hurt?"

"No. Just a slight heart attack and a nervous breakdown."

"Why the hell didn't you look to see where you were going?"

"I was interested in the scenery. Come on."

A low rock wall parallels this side of the track also. Along it the panting men lie with their heads in the crooks of their arms. A German machine gun rips the air. Bergman raises his head to investigate. A sniper's bullet clangs against his helmet, spinning it around without knocking it off his head.

Cautiously he feels for blood. Another bullet shatters the stock of his rifle.

"Jesus Christ!" he exclaims. "They got no respect for my equipment." The first bullet has lodged between his helmet and its liner. But by freakish luck, he has not been scratched.

We roll over the wall and find ourselves in the range of two enemy strongpoints. But for the moment, the krauts are ignoring us. They are absorbed in trying to split the two groups of men that preceded us.

A sergeant in the first platoon senses the predicament. If his men are isolated, they will likely be destroyed. He makes his decision quickly. Motioning his men to follow, he rises and with a submachine gun charges head-on toward one of the enemy positions two hundred yards away.

On the flat, coverless terrain, his body is a perfect target. A blast of automatic fire knocks him down. He springs to his feet with a bleeding shoulder and continues his charge. The guns rattle. Again he goes down.

Fascinated, we watch as he gets up for the third time and dashes straight into the enemy fire. The Germans throw everything they have at him. He falls to the earth; and when he again pulls himself to his feet, we see that his right arm is shattered. But wedging his gun in his left armpit, he continues firing and staggers forward. Ten horrified Germans throw down their guns and yell, *"Kamerad."*

That is all I see. But later I learn that the sergeant, ignoring the pleas of his men to get under cover and wait for medical attention, charged the second enemy strongpoint. By sheer guts, he advanced sixty yeards before being stopped by a final concentration of enemy fire. He reeled, then tottered forward another few yards before falling.

Inspired by his valor and half-insane with rage, his men took over, stormed the kraut emplacement, and captured it. When they returned to their leader, he was dead.

This was how Lutsky, the sergeant, helped buy the freedom that we cherish and abuse.

With the immediate opposition removed, we advance toward a row of houses from which comes bitter enemy fire. I am scuttling for the cover of a field of tall wheat when I hear Snuffy howl.

"Eeeeyowl" he hollers. "Git the medics. I'm hit."

With skipping heart, I hurry to his side.

"I knowed they'd git me," he groans. "Git the medics. I'm bleedin' like a stuck hawg."

Quickly examining him, I pause between anger and amusement. The bullet has punctured a can of beans in his pack; and he has mistaken the trickle of sun-warmed juice for blood.

"You damn clown," I mutter. "Get moving."

"I'm a dyin' man. The bastards shot my back clean off. Go git the medics."

I thrust my hand in his pack and draw forth the punctured can.

"There's your back; and there's your blood."

He blinks incredulously and pulls out his plug of tobacco.

"Well, I'll be a dirty name," he says reflectively. "Who'd ever thought I could've been so mistook."

One of our tanks has halted behind the stone wall on the opposite side of the railroad. It lowers its gun and begins pumping shells into the enemy-held houses. The Germans run from the buildings and scatter like frightened quail. As unemotionally as if we were shooting skeets, we pick them off with our guns. Then we close in.

I enter the first house with my finger on the trigger of a submachine gun. We take no chances; trust nothing. I start at the sight of a rifle barrel sticking through a door. A footstep sounds. Firing a short burst through the door, I kick it open.

In the room I find Snuffy. The natural sallowness of his face has paled to a corpse-white. I have missed killing him only by accident.

"Why didn't you holler?" I ask. "I thought you were a damned kraut."

"Was that you 'at far-ed?"

"It was."

He hurls his helmet wrathfully to the floor.

"Which side are you on?" he asks.

"What did you expect me to do? Knock or ring a bell?"

"I quit. When your own pal tries to slaughter you, it's time to quit. You got anything to eat?"

"How'd you like some beans?"

"Whyn't you fergit that?" he asks with a sheepish grin. "I knocked over a kraut after you left me. And I hope it was 'at bastard 'at shot up my beans."

"Find him sleeping?"

"What you mean, sleepin'?"

"For you to hit him, he'd either have to be dead or sleeping."

"Nosir. This'n was runnin' like a scared turkey. I ups with my heater and lets him have it right in the fanny. Sure cure for the constipation. What you got to eat?"

I find a fruit bar and some dog biscuits in my knapsack.

Snuffy glares at the rations resignedly. "Hot damn army grub. Biscuits break your teeth off. Fruit bar makes 'em ache. Pass 'em over."

With the hard crust of his defenses broken, the enemy begins a withdrawal. Though reeling like a punch-drunk fighter, he pounds us with cannon and harasses us with small arms. We are deathly tired, but we must keep hitting the Germans while they are still off-balance.

In a forest we stop to reorganize our forces. The area has been recently occupied by the krauts. Their foxholes pit the earth; and the ground is littered with debris and abandoned equipment. Our rapid advance has taken us temporarily beyond the reach of our supply lines. Our stomachs growl with hunger. We search through the trash, hoping to find some food.

We have not long to look before a heavy artillery barrage is turned on us. The shells hit the trees, explode; the woodland shrieks with steel fragments.

I dive into a foxhole. This is a job for our big guns. We can do nothing until the fire lifts.

I am sitting with my helmeted head between my knees when a body tumbles into the pit. It is Horse-Face. His face is ash gray; his smile is feeble.

"So they've got you scared at last?" I say.

"Got a drink of water?"

I hand him my canteen, but it slips through his fingers.

"What the hell is the matter with you?" I ask.

"Think I strained my back."

He slumps forward. I rip off his shirt. It is a small, ugly wound just under his left shoulder blade; and it does not bleed much.

"Nothing but a scratch," Horse-Face insists. "A goddamned silly scratch."

"Scratch, hell. Take it easy while I go get a medic."

"No. Keep down," he urges. "You wouldn't get two yards. Shells are thicker'n whores at an Elks convention."

His eyes grow cloudy.

"Oh, God," I think. "Not Horse-Face."

When he speaks again, blood bubbles from the corner of his mouth. "If I get any mail from South Carolina, burn it, Murph," he says. "Might be forwarded to the wife. Damned army efficiency at the wrong time."

He forces a grin; and for the moment the shadows go from his eyes. "Expecting a letter from an old girl who lives in Charleston. Comes up to me at a company dance and says, 'Hello, general, how're things lookin'.' Say, 'Looks like war.' Says—says . . . Don't remember what she says. Brunette. Got some water?"

I scramble from the hole and run through the thundering forest, shouting for a medic.

"Over here."

I find him crouching in a dugout.

"A man's hurt bad. Hurry!"

"Have you gone nuts? We can't get through."

"The man's dying."

"Then what can I do?"

"Come on," I say slowly. "Or so help me, I'll kill you with my bare hands."

The distance is short. But when we reach the spot, Private Abraham Homer Johnson, otherwise known as Horse-Face, is dead.

The medic studies the wound and shakes his head. "The fragment probably nicked his heart. I couldn't have helped at all. Nobody could."

I close my eyes. A roar surges through my brain, muffling the scream of the shells.

Knowed an old boy in the army once. Named Horse-Face.

"He was a pal?"

"We'd been together since North Africa."

156

*Biggest liar in the whole division. Says, "Met an old girl who
owned a pet seal up in the state of Michigan."*

"Jesus," says the medic, "that's too bad. I lost a buddy on
Anzio. Was he married?"

"Yeah. He was married."

*"Named Dolly Christine." The girl? "No, the seal. Goes onk,
onk every time I make a pass at her." Pass at the seal? "No,
the girl."*

"Any kids?"

"No kids."

*"Throwed her fish to keep her quiet." The girl? "No. Dolly
Christine. Spent fourteen dollars and sixteen cents on sliced
mackerel. Biggest mistake I ever made."*

"Must've been a good joe."

"Yeah. He was all right."

*"Seal falls in love with me. Woman gives me the go-by. Blows
with a first lieutenant. Air corps. And I take off for parts unknown to fight for the likes of her."*

"Well, that's war for you."

"Yeah."

In a little while the shelling lifts. We climb out of our holes,
regroup, and plod toward a flaming town.

Early that evening we are again hit by artillery fire and are
ordered to take cover until dawn. Brandon and I bed down in
a deep foxhole which lies beneath the limbs of a solitary tree.

"Old Horse-Face won't have to get up in the morning," says
Brandon.

"No. He can sleep from now on. And I just hope a burial
squad don't find us here. I'm so dead, they might shovel us
under by mistake."

"I wouldn't mind much."

"No. I wouldn't either."

I wrap up in a blanket and shut my eyes, but my mind will
not let the body sleep. The earth quivers gently with bursting

shells, and the sky is light with the glare of burning buildings. I smell the raw earth in which we lie and think of tomorrow.

"Are you asleep, Murph?"

"No, I can't relax."

"I've been lying here studying how much longer we've got."

"It doesn't matter. Tomorrow . . . the next day . . . next month . . . next year. What's the difference?"

"I'd sort of like to get home once more. Lot of things I'd like to straighten up before I check out. But I guess things can take care of themselves."

"Yeah. Everything'll work out all right."

"Until today, I thought maybe there was a chance of getting through alive. But when Horse-Face got it, I gave up. That guy wasn't born to die like that. He was one fellow the war didn't break."

"No. He wasn't the breaking kind. He's probably got the devil cornered with a yarn right now."

"Yeah," snickers Brandon. *"Met an old girl once just inside the gates of hell. Prostitute who forgot to reform."*

I take the cue. *"Says, 'What's the big sweat about, general?'"*

"Say, 'Still got on my long-johns, lady. Come from a cold climate.'"

"Says, 'We got a c-o-a-l climate here, general. Just waiting for John L. to arrive and pull off a strike that'll top the devil himself.'"

"Say, 'Haw! Haw! Sounds like a hell of a strike.'"

We both laugh heartily and feel better for it. But at this moment the grave seems merely an open door that divides us from our comrades.

A runner stops at the edge of our hole.

"Murphy."

"Yeah."

"You're wanted at the C.P."

"For godsake, what for?"

"How should I know. I'm just the Western Union boy with the singing greetings. You'd better get going."

"Probably want to give you a furlough," says Brandon.

"More likely a short arm. Any message you want to send to the colonel?"

"Tell him I've come around to Roosevelt's viewpoint. I hate wah."

"We all hate wah."

"But we got wah."

To reach the command post, I have to pass through an area that is under heavy bombardment. As I hurry, cursing and crouching, over the exploding earth, I wonder why I am so urgently needed at headquarters.

I find the command post in a shattered barn. And I detect the odor of whisky mingled with the fumes of manure. The lieutenant on duty greets me with a thick, uncertain voice.

"Sergeant," he mumbles.

"Yessir."

"Take out a patrol."

"A patrol?"

"Yes, goddammit. You know what a patrol is?"

"Yessir."

"Well, get going."

"Where am I to take the patrol?"

"What?" he asks irritably. "Where do you usually take patrols? Get you some men and find the krauts."

"But I don't know this terrain. Wouldn't it be foolish to risk the men?"

"What!"

I make no reply.

"Sergeant, did you hear me?"

"Yessir."

"Then get moving; and keep on moving until you hit the krauts."

"Then what?"

"Then what?" he repeats sarcastically. "Now, by god, that's a fine question. Do you want to get busted?"

"I don't give a damn."

"What!"

Again I do not answer.

"Sergeant! You've got your orders. Now get going, and report back to me before daylight."

"Yessir."

Realizing that he is blind drunk, I return to my hole and ignore the order. If he remembers tomorrow, I may well find myself in trouble for refusing to obey him. But tomorrow can take care of itself.

Before turning in, I decide to make a final check of the platoon's posts. The sound of heavy snoring comes from the earth as exhausted men snatch a few hours of sleep.

I find a tank track and walk in it across the field. The weight of the heavy vehicle would have exploded mines had they been buried along its trail. In the dim light, I pause before a depression. It is a partially filled foxhole with a curious object thrust upward through the dirt. The shape is extremely familiar. But my tired brain refuses to identify it. Carefully I grasp the thing. Then realization dawns. It is a boot; and inside it is the foot of a man. The flesh is still warm.

Yelling for help, I start clawing up the dirt with my hands. Two men are unearthed. One is already dead. The other, struggling horribly for breath, is unconscious when the medics carry him away.

What happened is obvious. Not even the noise of the tank awoke the men as it passed overhead, caved in the sides of the hole, and rolled on.

By dawn the artillery barrage has shifted to our area. We dare not stir. During the night some rations have been distributed. Brandon and I have a single can of beans between us. As we sit dipping our spoons by turns into the tin, a shell hits nearby. Dirt showers over us. We are unharmed, but the bean can which Brandon still holds carefully in his hand is filled to the brim. We remove the dirt and resume our breakfast.

Daylight reveals that the tree above us is filled with ripe cherries. We are thinking of risking our lives for the fruit when Brandon gets a bright idea. He lies on his back and with bursts from his tommy gun clips off branches of the tree. They fall into our hole; and we eat.

Between strongpoints the German retreat develops into practically a rout. We march up a highway in columns with small patrols scouting ahead on either side to protect our flanks against surprise.

We are rounding a curve when five planes dive at us. They strafe and bomb our ranks fiercely. We spurt for cover, leaping the soft shoulders of the road to avoid possible mines. When the planes pull out of their dives we see on their wings the white stars that mark them as our own. The error of the flyers has cost us over a hundred casualties. The highway is strewn with the dead and wounded.

Exasperated beyond speech, the unharmed men stare blankly at the destruction. Occasionally one gets control of his tongue and sputters a volley of oaths against the air corps.

While waiting for the reorganization of our ranks, I stumble upon a German ration dump. I open a can of rice and thick, yellow chicken gravy. Then I call to my men; and we eat until our stomachs complain.

As we approach Rome, the enemy rear guard stiffens its defense. Our route is punctuated by merciless fire fights. Once the Germans force a captured lieutenant and sergeant to sit on the front of a tank that rumbles toward us. Evidently they do not believe that we will fire at our own men, but that is their mistake. Our commanding officer faces the facts without sentiment and quickly makes his decision. The order is given. The guns blast away. The sergeant leaps from the tank; the lieutenant topples off dead. But the shell that kills him stops the tank. Our advance continues.

13

ROME is but another objective on an endless road called war. During the bitter months on Anzio, we dreamed of a triumphal entry into the great city. There were plans, promises, and threats of wholesale drinking and fornication. Now that our dream is an actuality, a vast indifference seizes us. Pitching our tents in a public park, we sleep until our brains grow soggy and life oozes back into our spirits.

Snuffy is the first to recover. He sneaks out of camp and returns laden with bottles of wine, which he buries in a hole beneath his blanket. He is so fearful of growing sober that he even awakes at odd hours of the night to pull at the bottles.

When he has become thoroughly drunk, he is hit by religious fervor. In a tearful and wailing voice, he confesses his unworthiness to live, and rants of the mercy of God. In dead earnestness, he turns upon Kerrigan, begging him to repent and give up his sinful ways. Kerrigan tolerates the advice for a while before planting a very solid boot in the seat of Snuffy's pants.

"When you're drunk, let religion alone," says the Irishman quietly.

"The wrath of the Lord will be visited upon you," shouts

Snuffy. "He has taken you from the Valley of Death and delivered you from evil."

"Ah shut up."

"Why don't you let him alone? A little religion wouldn't harm any of us," says Marsh, a newcomer who joined us somewhere along the road from Anzio.

"Keep out of this unless you want to get hurt," Kerrigan advises. "Come on, Snuffy, let's hit the sack."

"I will not," cries Snuffy. "I will not sleep until you are saved. Repent before it's too late and you find yourself in the far and brimstone of hell, gnashin' your teeth and cryin' for water. Repent."

"I repent that I've waited so long to do this," says Kerrigan grimly as he taps him on the jaw with his fist. Snuffy folds up. We drag him to his tent, remove his clothes, and cover him with a blanket. It is two days before he can bear the sight of wine again.

We prowl through Rome like ghosts, finding no satisfaction in anything we see or do. I feel like a man briefly reprieved from death; and there is no joy within me. We can have no hope until the war is ended. Thinking of the men on the fighting fronts, I grow lonely on the streets of Rome.

As the battle lines crawl northward, the rear echelons pour into town; our attitude toward them is irrational. With the smell of mud and death still in our nostrils, we resent the pressed uniforms and gaiety of men who have spent the war in relatively safe areas.

One afternoon we are sitting in a café when a group of air corps men enter. Kerrigan, who has been drinking wine since morning, is in a foul mood. Brandon chain-smokes, drums his fingers upon the table, and hums abstractedly. Snuffy, as usual, is asleep. He has no memory of Kerrigan's slugging him and cannot explain the soreness of his jaw.

Two members of the air corps group are boisterously drunk.

Seeing our combat infantry insignia, they come to our table and offer to buy a round of wine.

"Keep your money," says Kerrigan, "and buy yourself some medals."

His sarcasm does not register. "Good old infantry," says one of the weaving airmen. "I got a buddy in the infantry. Souse Pacific. I got respect for the infantry."

"Is that so?" snaps Kerrigan.

"You're goddamned right. Air corps is all right. But give me the infantry any day."

"You can have it," says Snuffy, awakened by the conversation.

"Say," continues the airman, "you ever kill a man?"

"Thousands of them," replies Kerrigan. "All in the air corps."

"How's it feel to kill a man?" He crooks his arms as if he were sweeping the room with a tommy gun. "Rat-tat-tat-tat. I'd like to kill just one German."

"Go back to your pals," says Kerrigan. "Get the hell away from us before you fall and hurt yourself."

"Are you telling me, or asking me?"

"Either way you want."

"No goddamned dogface is telling me what to do."

"Okay, junior," says Kerrigan, rising. "I said get the hell back with your own crowd."

"Come on," says the belligerent one's companion. "To hell with 'em."

After they have rejoined their group, Kerrigan fills two large water glasses with red wine and hands one to Snuffy.

"Reverend," says the Irishman, "I feel like singing. Drink up to the Junior Birdmen."

Holding his nose to avoid the odor, Snuffy downs the wine without taking the glass from his lips. For a few minutes he sits with his mouth agape to see if the wine is going to stick. Satisfied that his stomach is once more in working order, he wipes his mouth with the back of his hand and begins.

Into the air, Junior Birdmen;
Into the air, Boy Scouts, too;
Into the air, Junior Birdmen,
And keep your nose up in the blue.

Kerrigan chimes in:

Up in the blue.

And when they make a presentation,
And hand out those wings of tin,
You too can be a Junior Birdman—
If you'll send those box tops in.
Oh, turn over, Gertrude.

A bottle sails over our heads and splinters against the wall. That is all Kerrigan has been waiting for. We meet the air corps, slugging. A chair crashes on Snuffy's head; and he sinks slowly to his knees, grinning like an idiot. I catch a blow on my left arm and connect with a right uppercut to somebody's chin. Kerrigan heaves a table at a staff sergeant and is sent spinning across the room by a sneak blow behind the ear.

Two men have tackled Brandon. Grabbing one by the shirt and belt, he lifts him bodily and throws him at the other. They both hit the floor simultaneously.

I feint with a left at a fat corporal. He ducks; and I follow with a haymaker just as a chair knocks me dizzy. When I shake the cobwebs from my brain, I see that Snuffy, back on his feet, has a headlock on a man. But he does not seem to know how to turn him loose or put him out of action. Kerrigan has a black eye, but otherwise his face glows with contentment. He picks up a table and flattens two men with it.

The fat Italian who runs the café screams for the police; and an air corps man throws a chair at him. He ducks and runs through the doorway. When he returns, he has two M.P.s in tow. One is a lieutenant. The fight stops suddenly.

"What in the hell goes on?" asks the lieutenant.

"We're just playing," says Kerrigan earnestly.

"Sure," adds the staff sergeant, wiping a bloody nose. "Just having a little fun when the eytie gets upset."

"For chrisake," says the M.P., "don't you guys get enough fighting in the field?"

"We were just playing," Kerrigan insists, helplessly.

"Well, you're going to play in the guardhouse. Don't you know you'll get the whole town off limits with this kind of roughhousing?"

"We didn't mean no harm," says Snuffy. "Somebody throwed a bottle."

"Who threw the bottle?"

The question is met by a series of blank looks.

"Who threw the damned bottle?"

There is dead silence as the scowling M.P.s scan the face of each man.

"I know who threw the bottle." All eyes turn upon the speaker. It is Kerrigan. "Yes, I saw him; and the guy was nobody but the damned eytie there who runs this joint. He didn't like our singing."

"Didn't like your singing, uh? Then why the hell did you start mixing it up with the air corps?"

"Fighting the air corps?" says Kerrigan with innocent surprise. "Why, sir, those guys are our pals. We been sitting here drinking together."

"Sure," cuts in an airman. "We were just sitting here talking. And when the Italian threw the bottle, we were so anxious to keep out of trouble that all of us rushed for the door at once and sort of got tangled up."

Sinking into a chair, the lieutenant holds his head between his hands. "I'll be a sonofabitch," he says finally. "Sometimes I wish I was back driving a truck in Nebraska. Okay. Let's get this joint straightened up; and somebody's got to fork over money for damages, or this joe will take his troubles to the army."

We restore the café as nearly as possible to its original shape, while the Italian rolls his hands in a wine-stained apron and jabbers excitedly. But when we line up by the bar and start planking our money down, his attitude changes. Kerrigan contributes his whole wad. "I haven't had so much fun," says he, "since a hog ate my little brother."

"Don't any of you ever come back here again," the lieutenant sternly warns as we leave. "If I catch you here, I'm going to run you in, or my name's not O'Reilly."

"Lootenant," says Snuffy, "I ain't even gettin' out of camp till the next invasion. You couldn't give me Rome on a platter with a order of potatoes thowed in on the side."

Walking up the street, Kerrigan gingerly pats his swollen forehead. "You know," he says, "that little scrap is just what we all needed. I'm beginning to feel plumb at home again."

Rome, for whose liberation we fought so hard, becomes less meaningful by the day. Each night more men linger about the camp. They bring in bottles of wine; and as the gray dusk falls, they gather in clusters to drink quietly and talk.

Elleridge, a schoolteacher before the war, has joined our company as a replacement. He has not yet seen combat; and being in Rome is a major thrill for him. He attempts to lecture us on the glories of our surroundings.

"Here we are," he says, "in the Eternal City. Along these streets buried Caesars have walked. When I visited the Colosseum, I closed my eyes and saw the mighty gladiators striding out to do battle with wild beasts. I heard the roar of the bloodthirsty multitudes; saw the savage lions leap into the arena. I held my breath as man and beast closed in brutal conflict."

Snuffy elbows me. "Fer chrisake, is the guy nuts?" he asks.

"It's all in the imagination," I explain.

"Then I wonder kin he imagine me a six-months furlough?"

"On the banks of the yellow Tiber," continues Elleridge, "I closed my eyes again. This time I saw the ancient Horatio, heavy with armor, plunge into the foaming current after destroying the bridge and saving Rome from the invaders."

"If 'at guy can see all 'at stuff with his eyes shut, what in hell couldn't he see wid 'em open?" asks Valero.

"You ought to be able to catch him," says Kerrigan. "This is your country and your town, Valero."

"The hell it is. Give me little old Chi any day of the week, and Cicero on Sundays."

"Did I hear somebody mention Cicero?" asks Elleridge.

"Me, bub. What's wrong wid Cicero?"

"Nothing. He was truly one of the great Romans—statesman, orator, man of letters."

"Tell about the beer. Cicero's got the best damned beer dis side of Milwaukee."

"Cicero and beer. I don't get you."

"It's the only place in Illinois where you can get the genuine true six per cent stuff. Take the head off a dray horse."

"We're not talking about the same things. I speak of Cicero, the Roman."

"Well, just keep on roamin', pal."

"The Tiber river which flows through the city of Rome is the father of all rivers. Along its banks civilizations have risen and fallen."

"To hell with the Tiber!" shouts somebody. Let's sing about the Swanee. Where's Marsh?"

Marsh has a fine tenor voice. He stands in the twilight with a bottle of wine in one hand and his head thrown back in song. The men join in. Other groups hear and take up the melody until the park rings with music.

> *Way down upon the Swanee River, far, far away,*
> *There's where my heart is turning ever,*
> *There's where the old folks stay.*

Sitting at night in a foreign land, we are strangely moved by these songs that are so much a part of our background. They call up long-buried memories and a tenderness of spirit that has no place in war. But we sing each night until the order comes to buckle on our gear and move.

Although we are sent to a training area, we do not know what we are being prepared for. Within a few weeks, however, we learn on the beaches of southern France.

14

TECHNICALLY it was called a perfect landing. The vast operation designed to crack the enemy coastal defenses in southern France had been calculated and prepared to the smallest detail; and it moved with the smooth precision of a machine.

Resistance, compared to that met in other invasions, was light. Several weeks previously our forces had broken out of the Normandy beachhead. They now slashed across northern France like an angry river through a levee breach. The eastern front was crumbling under the mighty impact of the Russians. German cities were being ground to dust by our air force.

The German situation was compared to a man who had occupied a stolen house. Now justice was hammering on both his front and back doors. As he dashed alternately between the doors, frantically trying to keep them closed, a trap door opened in the floor; and a third party started climbing up from the cellar. We were that party.

But we do not know, we do not see the gigantic pattern of the offensive as we peer over the edge of the landing boats that are nearing the coast of France. We study the minute detail of the front that lies immediately before us.

My regiment's first objective is a sandy stretch of shoreline bearing the code name of "Yellow Beach." The terrain looks harmless enough. It is early morning in mid-August. Beyond the beach, thin patches of mist hover over the flat farmlands; and above the mist, the inland hills rise calm and green.

About us in the bay lying between St. Tropez and Cavalaire is the now-familiar design of an amphibious invasion. The battleships have given the beach a thorough pounding. Now their guns are quiet, but the huge gray ships steam slowly in the background.

The rocket boat guns take over. As weapons, they are more intimate than the naval cannon. Fired in batches, their missiles sail hissing through the air like schools of weird fish. They hit the earth, detonating mines, blasting barbed-wire entanglements, and unnerving the waiting enemy.

Under the rocket barrage, scores of landing boats churn toward the shore. I stand in one; and the old fear that always precedes action grapples with my guts. Seeking to distract my mind, I glance at the men huddled in the boat. They look as miserable as wet cats. Though the water has been smooth enough, several are seasick; and others have the lost, abstract expression of men who are relieving their bowels.

Suddenly I see the comedy of little men, myself included, who are pitted against a riddle that is as vast and indifferent as the blue sky above us. My sense of humor has always been considered perverse because I laugh at big things and fret over small ones. Now I laugh.

Kerrigan cocks an eye at me. "What's the big joke?" he asks.

"Just take a look around you."

"I have. It's as funny as a graveyard."

"Yeah," says Valero. "It's de grav-y train if I ever see one."

"Maybe Elleridge would like to give us a lecture on what the well-dressed tourist will wear in France this summer."

"Mattress covers," says Snuffy.

170

"Sure," says Constantino. "Make with the fancy talk, perfessor."

"I feel like vomiting," says Elleridge.

"Better not," warns Kerrigan. "Save your food. We're short of rations."

I strike a pose with my carbine. "Let's sing," I say. "How about 'The Beer Barrel Polka'?" I start to sing in a lusty manner.

Nobody joins me, except Kerrigan, whose voice trails off into silence after the first few lines of the song.

"Nuts!" says Valero. "We ain't no mockin' boids."

"Come on," I urge. "This is how they make a landing in books. Sing like they do in the movies."

"Aw, close the flap-trap," says Kerrigan, peering anxiously at the shoreline. "We're almost there."

"Welcome to de land of polly-voo," says Valero. "Has anybody got any good telephone numbers?"

"Remember what we talked about," says Constantino.

"Don't worry, pal," says Valero. "I can see right now dis invasion's comin' off as smooth as a pup's belly."

We jump from the landing craft and wade ashore through the swirling water. From the hills the German guns begin to crack. An occasional shell lands in our midst. The medics roll up their sleeves and get busy.

An explosion sounds on my left; and when the smoke lifts I see the torn body of a man who stepped on a mine. A medic bends over him, rises, and signals four litter bearers that their services will not be needed.

Directly ahead of us is a strip of scrub and matted grass. We move quickly toward it for cover, stepping as gingerly as. if walking on eggs. We have discovered that the beach is loaded from end to end with mines which a few pounds of pressure will detonate.

We stop at the edge of a green meadow. Beyond are trim vineyards and scattered farmhouses; and each of the buildings is a potential enemy stronghold. I jump into a drainage ditch and wade up it with the mud sucking at my feet. Behind me is Valero.

From the windows of the house nearest us comes a volley of rifle fire. A hundred guns answer from the brush. Six Germans run from the building with their hands up.

From our ditch, we see another kraut racing for a barn. Valero gives him a burst with his Browning automatic. The German stops and for a moment stands tottering. Valero shoots again. The man falls and starts crawling slowly for cover.

Valero climbs out of the ditch and stands erect to get the advantage of elevation. His third burst does the trick. The German flops over on his back and is still.

"Mebbe I need glasses," says the Italian coolly as he inserts another clip of ammo into his weapon. "I shoulda got him wid de first burst."

The Germans turn mortar fire upon the beach. Our men leave the brush and race across the meadows to the vineyards. A shell hits a barn; and from it emerges a Frenchman leading a frightened cow by a rope. A second shell lands in the area. The bellowing cow jumps and starts running, dragging the Frenchman behind her.

"Put a saddle on her," shouts a soldier.

"Give her a flying tackle," another advises.

"Milk her on the run," yells a third.

The thin shell of resistance along the beach is soon shattered. We move rapidly inland. Three wooded hills lie to our right. From the center one protrudes a pillbox with the barrels of its cannon pointing beachward. Our secret information lists this hill as an enemy strongpoint. To my company is given the job of neutralizing it.

Under a glaring sun we move toward it in sweat-soaked clothes. My platoon is in advance; and I am bringing up its rear when searing automatic fire bursts from the wooded slopes.

I round the corner of a farmhouse that stands on the edge of a vineyard stretching to the trees. The whole platoon is pinned down. A few feet from me is Valero, who is bending over Constantino.

Constantino speaks with a bubbly voice; and I know there is blood in his throat.

"You won't forget," he mutters.

"You'll be all right, pal," says Valero. "De medics are comin'. You're outa this mess now. You're goin' home."

"Don't try to kid me. I know the score. I'm through."

"Sure. Sure. Thass what I been tellin' you, pal. You're all troo wit de war."

A breeze slips through the vineyard, softly rustling the leaves.

"Valero."

"Yeah, pal."

"Don't leave me yet."

"I ain't leavin' you, kid."

"You're sure you got my mother's address?"

"Sure. Sure. Right in my pocket. Wanta see it?"

"You won't forget to visit her?"

"No, pal. I'll be seein' you and her too. We're goin' to have some big times when we get home."

"Tell her that—" He dies before he finishes the sentence.

Into Valero's hard, seamed face has come a peculiar softness. I would never have guessed there was a thread of gentleness in his nature.

When Valero rises, he seemingly does not see me. His features are again set in hard, cold lines. He studies the wooded slope with glinting eyes. Then with BAR held for firing from the hip, he stalks forward. A rifle cracks. His helmet spins on his head. When I reach Valero, he is dead.

I am alone now, and the Germans have discovered me. They lay a blistering crossfire directly over my head. I roll into a ditch that runs parallel to a thick canebrake leading up the hill.

As I round a slight bend in the gully, I run head-on into two Germans. For an instant they recoil in surprise; and that is their mistake. My combat experience has taught me the value of split seconds. Before the Germans can regain their balance, I kill them both with a carbine.

Near the edge of the forest, I locate a group of krauts in a a series of foxholes. We duel until my ammunition is exhausted. Then I retreat down the ditch. To compete with the enemy's automatic weapons I need more fire power.

Below the farmhouse, I find a light machine-gun squad. The Germans have its members pinned to the earth; and no amount of arguing or cursing on my part can get them to stir from the spot. So I seize their gun and drag it up the ditch alone. It is perhaps best this way. I reason that if one man can do the job, why risk more?

I try setting the gun up in the ditch, but from this position the bullets fly harmlessly over the heads of the Germans. Despite the lack of cover I drag the gun out in the open field, directly in front of the enemy strongpoint. Now the advantage is mine. I am firing uphill and may lie flat upon the earth. But the Germans to shoot down the slope at me must expose head and shoulders over the embankments fronting their foxholes.

By the time my gun is ready for action, bullets are popping within a foot of my body. I judge the range, press the trigger, and turn the stream of lead on anything that remotely resembles a kraut.

Screams of agony come from the foxholes. I rip the position again and wait in readiness. But nothing stirs. I pick up my gun and stalk up the hill to investigate.

A young German, who appears no older than twenty, sits on the ground; his eyes are filled with unspeakable terror. I am on the point of giving him a burst when I notice that his left jaw has been shot off. He tries to say something to me with his half-mouth; and as his chin moves, blood spurts in jets from a severed artery.

I brace myself against sentiment. I can do nothing for the boy except put him out of his misery. I raise my gun, but cannot pull the trigger. His staring eyes, already filling with the shadows of death, still plead for life. I step around him and examine the other foxholes. Each contains a body or two. One stirs; and I give it a burst as a precaution.

Now an enemy machine gun opens up on me. I hit the dirt, but cannot locate the gunner. The fire, however, is coming from my left. I set up my gun and rake the area with lead until my last cartridge is spent.

Then I race for the cover of the ditch again and scuttle down it to reconnoiter. Recovering my carbine, I hold it ready for action while I wonder what to do next.

At the sound of a moving body, I wheel about. It is Brandon.

He grins broadly. "What are you trying to do?" he asks. "Win yourself a wooden cross?"

"Where are the other guys?"

"Pinned down, so they say. I found out you were up here all by yourself. And I says to myself, 'That Murph is trying to hog all the glory.' Couldn't let you get by with that."

"You shouldn't have come up."

"Why not? This is not a private war, is it?"

"I wouldn't know."

"Neither would I. Come on. They can kill us, but they can't eat us. It's against the law."

As we start up the ditch, the canes at our side suddenly part; and two Germans fire at us point blank. A bullet clips off part of Brandon's right ear, but he does not flinch. Whirling, he kills both men with just two shots from his carbine.

I examine his wound. The blood trickling from it runs down the side of his face and drips off his chin.

"Better go back and get it dressed," I say.

"And leave you? Oh, no. You don't pull that one on me."

"Don't be a fool."

He pitches me a clip of ammo and says, "I was born a fool and haven't improved since. Where do we go from here?"

The ditch has become decidedly unhealthy. A machine gun is feeling out our position; and from the opposite side of the canebrake, hand grenades are being lobbed at us. Sliding up the gully, we locate the machine gun. It is just up the hill from a foxhole sunk beneath a cork tree.

Putting a blast of fire on the gun crew, we dash for the hole. At the bottom of the chest-deep pit, two Germans sit with their heads between their knees. They never know what hit them. Quickly lowering our carbines, we shoot them carefully in the head and dive in on top of the bodies just as the machine gun opens up.

Smiling, Brandon wipes the blood and sweat off his face with his sleeve.

"Have you got any idea of how to get out of this spot?" he asks.

"No, I'm open to suggestion."

"We should have looked it up in the field manual."

Cautiously raising our helmets above the surface of the ground, we draw fire from the machine gun. The bullets pop at least two feet above us. At ground level, we decide that our heads will be relatively safe.

Heaving two hand grenades, we rise suddenly and empty our carbines into the gun emplacement. Our action is followed by utter silence. Then the Germans yell, "*Kamerad!*"

Brandon peers over the edge of the hole. "They're waving a handkerchief," he says. "I'll go get 'em."

"Keep down," I urge. "You can't trust them."

"Murph," says he, "you're getting to be a plumb cynic. They've had enough."

He climbs from the hole nonchalantly and stands upright. That is all the enemy is waiting for. I hear the slash of machine-gun fire. As Brandon topples back into the pit, he softly mutters,

176

"Murph." Stunned, I lie for a moment with the two dead Germans beneath me and my comrade on top.

Carefully I ease myself from under Brandon. An abrupt movement may cause his wounds to hemorrhage. I grab his wrist, but there is no beat to his pulse. I start yelling like an insane man for the medics, but I might as well be shouting at the moon. I am all alone; and the hill is rattling with fire.

For the first time in the war, I refuse to accept facts. While Brandon grows cold beneath my hand, I keep telling myself, "He is not dead. He can't be dead, because if he is dead, the war is all wrong; and Brandon has died in vain."

Then I get the curious notion that he needs fresh air. I lift the body from the hole and stretch it beneath the cork tree. Why I am not shot during the process I shall never understand. Instinctively I spin about to find a machine gun being trained upon me from a position a few yards to my right. I leap back into the hole, jerk the pin from a grenade, and throw it.

At its blast, I scramble from the pit with my carbine. But the grenade has done its work well. One of the two Germans manning the gun has his chest torn open; the other has been killed by a fragment that pierced an eye.

I pick up their gun and methodically check it for damage. It is in perfect condition. Holding it like a BAR for firing from the hip, I start up the hill.

I remember the experience as I do a nightmare. A demon seems to have entered my body. My brain is coldly alert and logical. I do not think of the danger to myself. My whole being is concentrated on killing. Later the men pinned down in the vineyard tell me that I shout pleas and curses at them, because they do not come up and join me.

When I find the gun crew that betrayed Brandon, the men are concentrating on targets downhill. They do not see me, and I have time to take careful aim before pulling the trigger. As the lacerated bodies flop and squirm, I rake them again; and I do not stop firing while there is a quiver left in them.

In a little while, all resistance on the hill has been wiped out. The company moves up, and we halt on the crest to reorganize.

The voices of the men seem to come to me through a thick wall. My hands begin to tremble; and I feel suddenly weak. Sinking to the ground, I wait until the company moves off through the trees. Then I go back down the hill and find Brandon.

I check his pockets to see that all of his personal effects are secure. I open his purse and take a last look at the little girl with the pigtails. I remove his pack and make a pillow for his head. Then I sit by his side and bawl like a baby.

An insect begins chirping halfheartedly. The leaves on the cork tree rustle. After a little while I get up, wipe the tears from my eyes, and walk over the hill to rejoin the company.

The pillbox in the area has proved to be a dummy. In this tiny section of France the war is over. Above us white clouds float beneath a roof of pure blue. It is just another summer day; and the farmers are already out inspecting their vineyards for damage.

When the company takes a break for a brief rest, I find Kerrigan.

"What's wrong?" he asks. "You look like an undertaker at a health resort."

"You haven't heard about Brandon?"

"Brandon?"

"He's dead. Machine gun got him."

Kerrigan reacts as if he had been slapped in the face. "Oh, this goddamned stupid goddamned war," he mumbles. "What'll happen to his kid?"

"She'll live. He wouldn't listen to me. Trusted everybody. I tried to keep him down."

"Yeah. He was like that, but," he continues, his tone shifting to savage irony, "we won the fight. The hill's cleared."

"It's not cleared of Brandon."

"It never will be."

Elleridge has been listening to our talk with gaping mouth. "Did a buddy get killed?" he asks awesomely.

We glare at him without answering.

"I didn't mean to say anything wrong. I don't suppose it's any of my business," says the ex-teacher in an embarrassed manner.

"It's all right," Kerrigan replies wearily. "Forget it."

The order comes: "Okay. Up on your feet. Let's go."

As the afternoon passes, the rage leaves me. Again I look at the Germans as an enemy to be hated only impersonally. Again I see the war as it is: an endless series of problems involving the blood and guts of men. And I accept the mysterious workings of destiny as I did yesterday.

But I do not want to think beyond this. I need to march, to shoot, to destroy, to do anything that creates the feeling of progress and accomplishment. So I volunteer to cut across country and contact the elements of our battalion driving inland a few miles away.

Only Berner and Kohl accompany me. We tread through fields and forests Indian fashion. It is a lazy afternoon. The quietness is broken only by the intermittent roar of cannon and occasional outbreaks of small-arms fire. But the area through which we walk is peaceful. We hear the chirping of insects, and sometimes the song of a bird.

From the hilltops we can see the beach. Boats still chug through the blue waters of the bay. There has been no let-up in the piling of men and materiel ashore. Files of replacements move up the hot roadways. Tanks crawl cumbersomely toward the cover of trees. The ships' cranes dump the contents of their cargo nets into waiting ducks. The heart jumps, the blood stirs strangely at the massive pattern of our offensive.

Near a farmhouse we are greeted by a native. He is an old

man whose white hair curls beneath a broad-brimmed hat. Berner decides to try out his high-school French.

"*Les boches sont partis?*" he asks.

"*Oui,*" replies the old gentleman, smiling.

"Good. He says the Germans have all skeedaddled."

Kohl is suspicious. "Wait a minute," says he. "*Les boches sont ici?*"

"*Ah, oui,*" answers the Frenchman pleasantly.

"You're nuts," says Kohl to Berner. "He says the Germans are here."

"*Sont partis les boches?*" Berner asks again.

"*Ah, oui.*"

"*Sont ici les boches?*"

"*Oui.*"

"There you are," says Kohl. "The Germans are here and gone at the same time. Well, that's the supermen for you." An idea strikes him.

"*Il pleut maintenant?*" he asks the Frenchman.

"*Oui, m'sieu. Certainement.*"

"He says it's also raining cats and dogs," explains Kohl.

"Ask him if he knows any loose women," says Berner.

"*Vous connaissez des femmes—des femmes chaudes?*"

"*Oui, m'sieu. Fait chaud.*"

"He says the weather is very warm."

"That's fine. Unless he has other interesting news, we'd better get moving."

"*Bien, m'sieu. Pour toute l'information, merci.*"

"*Plaisir, m'sieu.*"

"He said it was a pleasure to give us the information. I told you I could parlez-vous this lingo."

"You don't think he's playing dumb?"

"Not with that face. He looks about as dangerous as Santa Claus on Christmas Eve. *Au revoir, m'sieu. Merci encore.*"

"*Au revoir. Vivent les Américains.*"

"He says long live the Americans."

"How long?"

"That's what I'd like to know."

In a short while the French will become accustomed to our butchering their language. And our ears will learn to pick out a few familiar words from what seems volleys of gibberish.

On a hillside, the felled trees give away the German position. We sight the dead brush and crawl to the edge of the clearing. Wherever the krauts are, they are well camouflaged. For a while we can see no sign of life.

"They must have ducked," says Kohl finally.

"Oh, no. Look up there." Sunlight glints briefly on glass. The German officer lowers his binoculars.

"I can get him from here," says Berner, adjusting the sights of his rifle.

"Don't be a fool. He's not by himself. I can see the barbed wire now."

"Must be an observation post."

"Sure. That's what it is."

"We can pull out now, or—"

"The hell with that. Let's hit them."

After discussing the matter, we decide that Kohl will move to a position on the right; Berner, to another on the left; and I will remain in the center. We will try to give the impression that the place is surrounded.

"When you hear me fire, open up with everything you've got," I say, "and start yelling. If too many swarm out, take off like a bat out of hell. I'll meet you at the farm where we saw the old man."

"Just don't get in my way," says Kohl. "Or I'll run right over top of you."

I move out to a clump of brush and wait until I think a proper amount of time has passed. The German officer has gone, but I have located the head and shoulders of a sentinel. My rifle cracks. The bullet kicks up dust; the sentinel vanishes before I can draw another bead on him.

But immediately Kohl and Berner start firing rapidly. I yell like an Indian on the warpath, while my two comrades shout curses and threats at the krauts in German.

A white flag soon flutters from the emplacement. The German officer reappears. As he stands behind barbed-wire entanglements, I lower my sights on his heart and remain in concealment.

"Where is your officer?" he shouts in English.

"You'll see," I reply. "Up with your hands; and don't make another move. Tell your men if there's any monkey business, I'll blast out your liver."

"There won't be any tricks. Come on up."

I rise from a clump of brush and walk forward.

Five men stand behind the officer. He eyes me contemptuously and asks, "Where is your officer? I surrender only to an officer."

"Throw your gun to me."

He lowers a hand to his holster, pulls out a Luger, and deliberately tosses it aside. His men start. They have not decided to what extent I am bluffing. I have no alternative to playing my cards to the hilt now.

"I will give you exactly three seconds to do as I say. Pick up that gun and throw it to me."

The officer hesitates. My finger begins squeezing the trigger of my carbine. I think perhaps with a quick rake I can put most of the Germans out of action, but at this moment, I would give my chances at Paradise to have a tommy gun in my hands.

Then the German snorts, picks up his pistol, and tosses it over to me.

Kohl and Berner join me.

"Is anyone else inside?" I ask.

"There is nobody else," says the German.

"In that case, we'll disinfect the place with a grenade."

The German turns toward the dugout and barks a command. *"Komm 'raus!"*

Two sly-looking soldiers emerge with their hands up.

"Now march directly toward me. If there are mines in the path, you'll soon meet your maker."

Satisfied that the ground is safe, Kohl searches the place for more stragglers. But he finds none.

As we march the prisoners away, the officer asks, "Where are your other men?"

"I wouldn't know. You must be a fine officer to let a little noise and firing confuse you."

Before dusk, we have contacted our men. That night we bed down in a forest; and the next day the drive begins in earnest.

15

SMARTING under the wrongs and indignities endured during the years of German occupation, members of the French underground now emerge from their hiding and strike. Sometimes we find whole towns liberated by the F.F.I. and waiting our entrance. Maquis join our forces as guides and give us information on enemy strongpoints.

The German dead are often dumped in abandoned foxholes and covered unceremoniously with the soil they held in captivity. When it rains, their boots stick gruesomely from the mud.

Meanwhile, the Third Army continues its slashing drive across middle France. When we contact it, all the Germans in a vast section of the country will be caught in a trap. For three days we move forward in trucks, encountering only road blocks and pockets of resistance. After the slow battering months in Italy, our advance seems incredibly swift.

We experience great exhilaration, for there is nothing so good for the morale of the foot soldier as progress. Long ago we came to believe that our only way home lay through the Siegfried Line; and each mile that we move up the Rhone Valley of France is another mile nearer America.

The Germans react strangely to the situation. In one instance, twenty thousand of them surrender to a single American platoon. Yet often we encounter handfuls of men who fight like wildcats to slow our offensive.

One day we come upon a house in which a lone colonel has holed up. Before the building several men lie in a fanwise formation casually pumping rifle bullets through the wooden door. The colonel returns the fire with a pistol. He shouts in English that he will never be taken alive.

It is an interesting show, and we pause to watch. I study the situation as one would a mathematical problem. The walls of the building are made of stone, which gives the German ample protection from our small-arms fire. He must be shooting at a slant from a corner of the room. A couple of hand grenades should be sufficient to flush him, but we have used all of our grenades on a previous objective.

I finally get an idea. Borrowing a tommy gun, I creep down one side of the house and kick the door partially open. A volley of pistol bullets splinters the wood. Still using the wall as cover for my body, I thrust the gun around the corner of the door. Held sideways, the rattling gun rides around in an arc sweeping the room. At the thump of a falling body, I leap through the door.

The German is badly wounded in the back, but he tries to lift his arm and shoot me with his Luger. Jumping forward, I stamp his pistol hand with a heavy boot. But even after that, the gun has to be twisted from his grip. I put the weapon in my pocket and remove my foot from his arm. His lips are flecked with foam and blood. He slobbers like a mad dog. As the medics enter and examine his wounds, he curses them heartily in English.

Swift encircling movements by divisional units trap a large number of the enemy in the town of Montélimar. The city is an important communications center, but the Germans would willingly let it go if they could escape to the north. As the ring closes about them, they counterattack fiercely. An entire regiment of infantrymen hits my battalion. They are stopped by a heavy concentration of artillery and mortar fire.

We are ordered to drive straight into the resistance, by-pass the town, and enter it from the north. My company moves into the battle area just before daylight. As we advance over the flat, open fields, we nervously study the eastern sky which will signal the lifting of our cover of darkness.

Dawn breaks slowly; and in the dim light, we find ourselves faced by two 88-millimeter cannon and a strong detachment of men. Silently we drop to the earth. The Germans crawl out of their holes, stretch themselves, and start preparing breakfast. They are not aware of our presence until we open fire.

Though taken by surprise, they decide to fight. Quickly yanking the camouflage nets from the cannon, they commence firing. The projectiles whistle overhead. The barrels cannot be lowered sufficiently to fire directly into our midst. Fortunately we are too close to the guns.

But the krauts quickly wise-up and change their fire to air bursts. Slivers of steel shower our position. We crawl forward. In the open fields retreat would be suicidal.

Two of the tanks assigned to support our attack lumber up, but they hastily take cover behind a farmhouse. One glance at the situation was enough for the crews. Against tanks on such terrain, the 88 is a deadly weapon. The armor is not strong enough to deflect the shell. With one direct hit, the tank would likely be put out of action and most, if not all, of its crew members killed.

We understand this, but our present situation is not conducive to rationality. We shout curses and taunts at the tankmen, who remain notably undisturbed by our opinions of them.

Now from a score of foxholes flanking the big guns, the enemy unleashes his small-arms fire. The air is filled with whistling lead and foul language which we divide impartially between the krauts and our tank crews.

A man with a stubble of beard on his face is hit in the shoulder by a shell fragment. With a bewildered look on his face he rises to his feet, directly in the line of fire. The krauts cut him down, but before he falls, he turns slowly about as if for a last view of the familiar sky and fields. His body flinches as more lead is poured into it. When he hits the ground, he flexes his knees and rests his head in the crook of his arm as if going to sleep. I try to recall his name, but cannot.

Within a moment I am involved in a duel with a German who climbs upon a cannon to get the advantage of elevation. I see him as he lowers his rifle upon me and whip up my carbine. He fires. The bullet kicks dust in my face as my carbine goes off.

Frantically I try to blink the dirt from my eyes, knowing the German will likely not miss again. It is only a few seconds, perhaps, but it seems much longer before I can see. The kraut is sprawled in front of the gun. Later I discover that my lucky shot got him in the heart.

Piles of ammunition are stacked behind the gun. Suddenly I see the solution of our problem. Securing a bazooka, I move forward fifty yards and throw three shells into the ammunition dump. When the shells begin to explode, the Germans leap from their holes and start running for a ditch in the rear. As they race crouching over the ground, their buttocks stand out prominently; and we bore into them with small-arms fire.

With the big guns out of action, our lieutenant goes back to get the tanks into the field. My platoon is in the lead position. We rise to our feet, form a skirmish line, and stroll forward, shooting.

The Germans have not yet had enough. From the ditch, they bitterly return our fire. Bergman, who walks beside me, is hit in the upper leg. He casts a startled glance at the wound and says, "Well, what do you know? Looks like I've been hit."

I cannot stop now. "Wait here for the doc," I say.

"With a fight like this going on," the Swede snorts. "I hear you talking, but I don't get what you say."

Calmly inserting a fresh clip of ammo in his tommy gun, he limps forward while the blood soaks his trouser leg.

The tanks are backing us now; and the Germans see that the game is up. Around thirty throw down their weapons and hoist their hands.

One tries to escape on a motorcycle. As he dashes down the road, Kerrigan lisps, "You naughty, naughty boy. Trying to get out of taking your medicine." His rifle cracks. The motorcycle turns a flip, tossing the rider yards into the field.

While the prisoners are being frisked, we take a brief break and munch on breakfast rations.

On the outskirts of Montélimar, a huge enemy convoy has been caught by our artillery fire. In their haste to escape, the doomed vehicles had been moving two and three abreast. Our artillery zeroed them in. The destruction surpasses belief.

As far as we can see, the road is cluttered with shattered, twisted cars, trucks and wagons. Many are still burning. Often the bodies of men lie in the flames; and the smell of singed hair and burnt flesh is strong and horrible.

Hundreds of horses, evidently stolen from the French farmers, have been caught in the barrage. They look at us with puzzled, unblaming eyes, whinnying softly as their torn flesh waits for life to drain from it. We are used to the sight of dead and wounded men, but these shuddering animals affect us strangely. Perhaps we have been in the field too long to remember that innocence is also caught in the carnage of war.

A horse, trailing entrails from a split stomach, staggers down the side of the road. Mahler, a gentle Texan who lived on a ranch in civilian life, stops; and I hand him the Luger which I took from the German colonel.

He goes over to the horse and pats him on the neck. "What did they do to you, boy? What did they do?" he croons. Then he raises the pistol and shoots the horse behind the ear.

He hands the pistol back to me without speaking.

"Keep the gun for a while," I say. "You'll need it further on."

As we move up the road, he begins to talk. "I've known horses all my life," he says; "and there's not one dirty, mean thing about them. They're too decent to blast each other's guts out like we are doing. Makes you ashamed to belong to the human race."

"Yeah. I know horses too. For a time they were the only real friends I had."

"You couldn't have had better. If I ever get out of this war, I want to live so far back in the hills that I'll never see another human being."

During our advance, he steps stoically over the corpses of Germans to put horses out of their agony with the Luger.

I am with Kerrigan when we enter Montélimar. The krauts still hold part of the city. A freight train burns in the railroad yards; and though this section is clear of the enemy, one of our planes is busily strafing it. We keep under cover until the flyer has thrown all the lead he wants, and buzzes off into the blue.

Cautiously moving from house to house, we search for snipers. Leaping from the sunlight into the dim rooms, we must wait for our eyes to become adjusted to the change. As we stand in one house, the door of a room creaks open. Suddenly I find myself faced by a terrible looking creature with a tommy gun. His face is black; his eyes are red and glaring. I give him a burst and see the flash of his own gun, which is followed by the sound of shattering glass.

The horrible being that I shot at was the reflection of my

own smoke-blackened self in a mirror. Kerrigan doubles with laughter. "That's the first time I ever saw a Texan beat himself to the draw," says he.

In the late afternoon our job is done. My company is ordered to hole-up and wait for further orders. In a section of the city, a brisk fire fight continues. From another part of the town, an enemy artillery piece lobs occasional shells. But we are not disturbed. The chances of our receiving a direct hit are not worth considering.

I take over part of a house to serve as quarters and command post for the night. A machine gun is set up outside the door; a field telephone connecting us with headquarters is moved in; and we relax.

Bergman has refused evacuation. His wound has proved to be only superficial. He lies on a pallet, smoking and swearing cheerfully.

Kerrigan stands at the door with his eyes turned toward the sky. Over the rattle of distant fire comes the sound of a striking clock. A shell explodes; the house trembles.

"Afternoons like this make me homesick," says Kerrigan, turning from the door.

"Homesick fer what?" asks Snuffy. "You never had it better."

"Didn't I? Well, I used to know a girl, a real, decent girl. We—"

"Hawl" exclaims Snuffy. "You're suffer'n from shell shock."

"We used to spend this kind of afternoons on a river."

"On who?" says Bergman.

"What's the use?" says Kerrigan wearily. "After associating with you rumdum bastards, I couldn't make the grade in a two-bit whorehouse."

"Ain't it the truth," says Snuffy.

Footsteps sound, and our mouths gape as a girl enters the room.

"Where'd that come from?" asks Kerrigan.

"That ain't the point," says Snuffy, "where's it goin'?"

She holds a bowl of grapes in her hands, and her glance roams uncertainly from one of our faces to another. Apparently in her early twenties, she is not bad looking at all. Her face is of a smooth olive color; and glistening black hair tumbles to her shoulders. At first I mistake a slight scar near the corner of her mouth for a dimple.

Kerrigan recovers from the shock of seeing her and bows from the waist.

"Mademoiselle," says he, "what can we do for you?"

"The question is what can she do for us," says Snuffy.

"Quiet, fool. This is a situation calling for tact and finesse."

"Then you'd better send for the chaplain."

"You speak French?" Kerrigan asks the girl.

"Get that," says Snuffy. "What'd you think she spoke? Chinee?"

Kerrigan eases toward the girl like a cat stalking a bird.

"You speak French?" he repeats.

"*Oui, m'sieu.*"

"Honey, we miss you too," exclaims the Irishman, embracing her wildly.

"*Mais non,*" sputters the girl, shoving him aside. "The seek soldier. *Blessé, n'est-ce pas?*" Her eyes turn upon Bergman.

"Him?" snorts Kerrigan. "He's about the most unblessed man you'll ever hope to meet. We call him the Milwaukee misfit. At the age of eight he was put in the pokey for horse stealing. At ten, he turned alcoholic. By the time he was twenty he'd served seven raps for murder. I wouldn't trust him with my aunt Lizzie even if he was in a straight jacket. Stay away from him."

The girl obviously does not understand. The Swede, grabbing the cue, closes his eyes and groans piteously.

"*Ah, pauvre, pauvre,*" exclaims the girl, rushing to Bergman's side.

"Well, I'll be a suck-aig mule," says Snuffy. "Better haul out that tack and start fur-nessing."

Bergman feigns delirium. Threshing around on the blanket,

he mutters curses at Kerrigan and proclaims that his own sexual prowess is unsurpassed.

The girl claps a hand to his forehead. *"Fièvre,"* she declares. *"Chaud. Chaud."*

"Sho, sho, baby," Kerrigan replies disgustedly. "He's sho going to cop a feel if you're not careful."

"She says he has fever. His forehead's hot," says Kohl.

"He's got brain fever."

"You Irish bastard," mumbles the Swede. "I can get more women with my eyes shut than you can with them open."

"Qu'est-ce qu'il dit?" asks the girl in alarm.

"He's speaking—how do you say—of his dear old mother," explains Kohl. *"Il parle de sa mère. C'est la fièvre."*

"Ah. Sa mère. Pauvre. Quelle triste."

"She says it's a sad situation."

"He's a sad sack; and that's no mistake," says Kerrigan. "Think I'll go out and step into a bullet."

"Make it an 88," mutters Bergman.

"Qu'est-ce qu'on fait?" asks the girl.

"She wants to know what we should do with this dying soldier."

"Give him a drink," gasps Bergman.

"Cognac, mademoiselle. Vite."

"Oui. Mama, cognac. Vite."

The kitchen door flies open; and a middle-aged woman darts into the room with a bottle in her hand.

Grabbing the cognac, Kohl takes a healthy swig of it himself. The woman casts a puzzled look upon the proceedings.

"Pour le blessé," she insists.

"I was just testing it for vitamins," Kohl explains. *"Pour voir s'il bon."*

"Il est bon," says the woman.

Sighfully Kohl turns to Bergman. "This is going to hurt me far more than it'll hurt you," he says. "Go easy on the stuff, you sonofabitch."

"Quit stalling, and throw me a slug," mumbles Bergman.

"*Qu'est-ce qu'il dit?*" asks the girl.

"His mother again. *La mère encore. Toujours la mère.*"

"*Ah, pauvre.*"

During the war, I saw many strange things, but few were stranger than the sight of the Swede's lying flat on his back and downing a quarter of a bottle of cognac without coughing, sputtering, or strangling. Even Kerrigan admitted that it was a noteworthy achievement.

The next day Mahler is hit. He is on a routine patrol when he is struck in the back by a fragment from an air burst. His spine is injured; and I hear that his legs are paralyzed. Remembering his face as he patted and shot the horses, I wonder whether he will ever ride again.

16

SNUFFY's rear-end hangs over the edge of a medical jeep. A sniper caught him in the hip as we fought our way toward Besançon. Kerrigan and I arrive on the scene just as the jeep is pulling out. Seeing us, Snuffy hoists his buttocks in our direction and lovingly pats the large bloody bandage.

"So long, you miserable sonsabitches," he yells. "I just got that million-dollar wound."

The jeep bounces off down a road; and we never see Snuffy again.

"Wouldn't you know he'd get out the easy way," says Kerrigan.

"I'm glad he did."

"So am I. If that wound's bad enough, he'll never see any more action."

"He saw enough."

"Yeah." Kerrigan pulls a dirty fold of paper from his pocket. "Snuffy's poker debts," he explains. "Forty-five dollars, two thousand lira, seventeen hundred francs gone to hell." Grinning, he tears the paper to bits and casts the pieces to the wind.

We look at each other, but find no words to continue the conversation. Of our original gang only we two remain.

In a short while we are again in the thick of battle. Our forward units knife through the enemy lines, leaving pockets of resistance for mopping-up crews. The noises of combat come from all sides.

The swift advance has drained our energies and most of our supplies. Now hungry and sleepy, we rest on a roadside waiting for orders. Our artillery fires over us. We lie on our backs, listening to the crash of the shells.

A motor roars up the road.

"It's a tank," somebody yells. We leap to our feet, with our ears cocked in the direction of the ominous noise.

"It's a truck," declares Kerrigan.

"The hell it is. That's a tank, and a big one."

We scramble for cover. If it is a tank, we have no weapons powerful enough to cope with it. I grab a BAR and run for a clump of brush on the edge of the road.

A German truck lumbers around a curve. For a moment I do not move as the wonderful feeling of relief floods through my body. Then I set my sights on the windshield and pull the trigger. The truck lurches from the road and hits a tree. I keep down long enough to see if anything develops. Nothing does. The stalled motor coughs and dies. I pour another burst into the cab and move toward it cautiously.

The two krauts in charge of the truck lie slumped to the sides. I poke them with my BAR, but they do not react. The vehicle is loaded with supplies. I kick aside what appears to be a strong box, grab an armload of cognac and bread for the men, and take off. The steel box, I later discover, contained a small fortune in francs. But right now money is without meaning to the famished men who sit gulping cognac and bread.

Giddy on the liquor, Marsh begins to sing, "Bury Me Not on the Lone Prairie." The rest of the platoon takes up the tune, and our morale gets a hefty boost.

That night we crash into Besançon and fight until morning. Within a few days, the city is secured; and once more we take up the pursuit of the Germans.

My platoon is bringing up the rear when a road block halts the company. It is a very minor action; so I start walking to headquarters for instruction. My platoon may be needed for a flanking movement.

Mortar shells begin to pepper the earth; and I halt to talk to a group of men until the fire eases up. From their pallid faces, I can tell that several of them are replacements.

Their sergeant grins at me. "I've been telling 'em there's nothing to be afraid of," he says. "They ain't seen nothing yet. This is practically the rear echelons."

"They'll get used to it. What's the old man going to do about the road block?"

"If he asked my advice, I'd say call out the air force. A couple hundred bombers should be able to take care of that little old road block in a matter of a few hours." He winks at me, while his hand traces the motions of a diving plane. "Zoom. Bawoom! Zoom. Bawoom! Right, sergeant?"

"Right," I reply.

"Then why don't they send for the air force?" asks a youngster with blond hair and bright blue eyes.

The sergeant turns upon him scornfully. "Are you kidding?" says he. "The air force is taking the day off to run off a new batch of medals. Bunch of flyers knocked out a jerry latrine day before yesterday and go gliding home through the wild blue yonder to get their medals. And what do you know? There wasn't a medal left. Plumb broke the spirit of them flyers. No, we can't depend on the air corps. But maybe a tank—yeah, a tank ought to be able to do the job, except—"

"Except what?"

"Except a tank's never around when you need it. But don't be downhearted. We've still got the artillery. That's your friend."

"Then why the hell doesn't it get busy?"

The sergeant shakes his head mournfully. "The artillery means well," says he, "but it couldn't hit a bull in the back with a bass fiddle. So who's it? Who's always it? The infantree. Right, sergeant?"

"Right."

"Yeah," the sergeant continues reverently. "The Queen of Battles. Stick with it and you'll be getting slivers up and down your spine."

"That's just what I figured," says the recruit, grinning.

"Now you're getting the spirit. Just always remember, there is no other branch of the army that offers so many chances for the Purple Heart, the Distinguished Wooden Cross, the Royal Order of the Mattress Covers. You want to be decorated, don't you?"

"I'd like to be decorated with a discharge."

The mortar shell comes in almost soundlessly. It is practically under my feet before I am aware of it. I have just time enough to think, "This is it," before the blast knocks me unconscious.

When I come to, I am sitting beside a crater with a broken carbine in my hands. My head aches; my eyes burn; and I cannot hear. The acrid, greasy taste of burnt powder fills my mouth.

Methodically, I run my hands down over my legs. The limbs are still there. But the heel of my right shoe is missing; and my fingers are sticky with blood.

My groggy brain picks up a voice. "Are you all right, sergeant?" it asks.

"My foot."

"Just a gash. It doesn't look serious."

"Then I'm okay."

I wipe the tears from my smarting eyes and look about me. The sergeant and the young recruit are dead. Three other men are wounded. They were all further than I from the projectile.

When a mortar shell explodes on contact with the ground, it throws its fragments upwards and outwards in a cone-shaped pattern. I was standing next to the base-tip of the cone and consequently caught only the beginning of the shower. Had I been three feet farther away, I would most likely not be alive to tell about it.

After a few days in the hospital, I get myself a new pair of shoes and return to the lines. It is late September. Drizzly rains sweep over the hilly, wooded country through which we move; keeping warm during the night has already become a problem.

The leaves of the trees are turning color. The gold and red contrast sharply with the evergreens; and the camouflage men must start mixing new paints to conform with the changes in nature. It is the prelude to another long, grim winter.

We plod up the wet roads doggedly, wondering vaguely which of us will still be alive when the new leaves return to the trees. The Germans fall back stubbornly, but steadily. Each day, however, their resistance grows stronger, their retreats shorter. As they approach strongly prepared positions in the Vosges mountain area, they lash back at us with counterattacks. My regiment is on the verge of some of its hardest fighting of the entire war.

One morning as a chilled, misty dawn breaks over the earth we wait for the signal to tackle a hill known only by number. Our artillery is softening up the point with a barrage. We lie on our backs, shivering and silent, as the gray light grows about us.

Near me a sergeant checks a 50-caliber machine gun, which is set up in a large round hole edged by a wall of sandbags. The weapon, stationary for the time being, will be used to cover our advance and, if necessary, our retreat.

The sergeant, satisfied that his gun is ready for action, lolls back upon his elbows. Beads of water cling to his mop of wavy black hair. He is extraordinarily handsome. With his fine, sensitive features and broad shoulders, he looks like a Hollywood producer's dream of a soldier. In the army we would immediately classify him as a lady-killer.

He lights a cigarette and turns to me with a grin. "God pity you guys," he says; "that hill's going to be a humdinger. It's crawling with krauts."

"Yeah?"

"And they're plenty mad."

"Thanks for the encouragement. When I'm up there, I'll be thinking about you lying back in that nice warm hole. I hope the krauts don't start chunking artillery in this direction."

"Keep an eye peeled for their automatic stuff. They've got plenty of it up there."

"Any more cheerful information you'd like to pass out. Our morale is just boiling over."

"I'll give you a tip. Next time you join the army, don't let them shove you into public relations. I know a man who was. He broke all of his fingernails on a typewriter."

"Too bad."

"It was a downright calamity. Well, you guys can move up any time now. I'm getting hungry."

"Then why don't you eat?"

"For a very simple reason. I've got no rations."

"I've got no appetite."

"Don't worry. Those jerries use forced-feeding methods. You'll soon have your belly full."

"Now that's a hell of a way to draw your rations."

The barrage lifts. I say, "Good luck," to the sergeant and move over to my platoon. In our rear one of our cannon whams. We hear its projectile fluttering through the air hesitantly, as if reluctant to bury its nose in the cold, wet earth. The sound instantly reveals to an experienced ear that the shell is defective. Though our own, it may explode anywhere. Shouting to my men to get down, I hit the dirt just before the crash comes.

The blast seems to be directly over us. In the silence that follows, I mentally examine each part of my body for the burning sensation that reveals wounds. I find none and stand up. The new men are fearfully dabbling their fingers over their clothes in search of blood. I know their feeling. That a shell could hit so close without doing damage is a miracle to the uninitiated.

I glance toward the machine-gun nest. The sergeant still lolls, but a man is hastily twisting a tourniquet about his leg. His left foot has been sheared off cleanly just above the shoe top. There is no expression of pain or panic on the sergeant's face. He strikes a match to a cigarette and puffs calmly.

"Okay. Don't move your leg now," says his comrade. "You might start bleeding again."

Flipping away the butt of the cigarette, the sergeant picks up his foot, examines it curiously, and tosses it aside.

"Well," says he, as if talking to himself, "there goes my dancing days."

His comrade begins to shake nervously. "Don't go away," he says, "I'll be right back with the medics."

The sergeant smiles. "Now, Mac, just where the hell do you think I'd be going," asks he. Then I see his eyes close and his face freeze into a grimace as the pain strikes.

He was right about the hill, but at first it seems that the objective will be easy. As we sneak up the slopes, we hear only the creaking of our boots and the patter of water from the trees. The Germans remain silent. But we have seen them pull this trick before, and will not be fooled by it. We advance from point to point, using trees and huge rocks for cover and examining every possible foot of the ground that lies before us.

The quietness disturbs Kerrigan. "Why in the holy hell doesn't somebody open up?" he whispers. "Playing Little-Bo-Peep in this jungle is apt to wreck a man's nerves."

"You're still as trigger-happy as voters at a Kentucky election."

"I'm still alive."

"You won't be if you keep sticking your head up."

"I'll be here when your dog tags part."

We slide around a boulder and directly to our left discover a machine-gun nest. It lies downhill from us; and five men make up the crew. One kraut lies behind the gun with his finger on the trigger. Another holds the ammunition belt. Two more are stretched out with rifles. A sergeant, in a prone position fifteen feet away, peers through binoculars.

"The pleasure is yours," I say. "Pick them off, deadeye."

"No. I pass you the honor."

"Shoot the gunner. The others may surrender."

"Would you suggest that I plug him right behind the ear?"

"If you can get under his helmet."

"Better make it the temple."

"Make it anywhere but shoot; I'll cover the others."

"Okay. Here we go for bingo." He lifts his rifle and takes careful aim. The carbine cracks. The kraut with the binoculars lets out a yell. Kerrigan, ordinarily a crack shot, has completely missed the gunner and hit the sergeant in the foot.

Five furious, desperate Germans whirl upon us. The sergeant, spotting us first, rises to his knees, whips out a Luger and begins firing. The bullets go wild. I hurl a grenade, but it strikes a tree, bounces, and explodes harmlessly. The machine gunner jerks his barrel toward us, Kerrigan rises to one knee and shoots him in the face. He slumps over the gun. Another kraut kicks the body aside and grabs the trigger. I pump two bullets into him; and Kerrigan follows with a grenade. The sergeant is knocked backwards by the blast; and I take no chances with him. Before he can stir again, I empty my gun into his body.

It is all over within five minues, but the noise we made seems to have touched off the battle fuse. The rain-drenched hill roars with screams, curses, and clattering guns.

Kerrigan and I wipe the water off our faces and lean against the rocks to get our breath.

"What was wrong, Bo-Peep?" I finally say. "Have you got a kink in your gun barrel?"

The Irishman spits wrathfully. "The water got in my eye," he says.

"The water got in your blood."

"That was a nice little throw you made with the grenade. Like to have you on my ball team."

"My hand was wet. It slipped."

"You damn near slipped us into eternity. To think they wanted to make you an officer on Anzio."

"Why not?"

"You couldn't make out a morning report with a staff of stenographers."

"You're crazy. I've got a fine brain for figures."

"Yeah. Female, that is." He pauses thoughtfully. "An officer!" he snorts. "If you ever take a commission, I hope you get your ass shot off."

"Thanks for the good will."

"You're welcome."

He gets up and peers around the rocks. "We'd better get out of this firetrap before the krauts get too curious about what happened to their machine-gun crew."

"You want to do some more fighting?"

"Might as well. What else is there to do on a rainy day?"

Up the slope we find two dead men in a shell crater. They lean against the bank of the hole with their helmets pulled down over their eyes. About both of the mouths is the curious ghost of a smile. The mortar shell which landed in the large crater must have caught them in the middle of a laugh.

"They say lightning never strikes twice in the same place," observes Kerrigan. "Maybe these guys believed it."

"Do you know them?"

"No. They must be new men. Funny thing. When I was a kid, I ran away from home to keep from going to my grandpa's funeral. Couldn't bear the thought of seeing anybody dead. Do you think that tommy gun's in working condition?"

"Looks all right."

Sliding into the hole, he picks up the weapon and checks the mechanism.

"It's okay," he says. In the ammo pouch, he finds several clips of ammunition. He straightens up and glances at the faces of the two soldiers. "Did you ever notice that when they're dead, they all look alike?" he asks.

"Yeah."

"Oh, well," he shrugs, "it's just a matter of time. The worms crawl in and the worms crawl out. The worms crawl through your mouth and snout. How does that song go?"

"I don't know, but it sounds beautiful."

"It tells the truth."

"You sure you can handle that tommy gun?"

"Don't talk like a moron. I can knock a gnat's eye out with it. That carbine's barrel was as crooked as the long road home."

"I'd feel safer if you let me do the shooting and you just throw rocks."

"Oh, go to hell."

Again the fury of combat closes about us.

17

TWO days later Kerrigan is hit by a mortar-shell fragment, but his luck holds to the end. The sharp, steel splinter simply clipped off half of his right hand. The wound is sufficient to remove him from combat permanently, but in time it will not greatly affect his ability to hoist a bottle.

I do not see him before he is taken to the hospital. These are extremely busy days and nights; and every man is required to give his utmost. We are driving into the Vosges mountain chain, which is the chief obstacle lying between us and the Rhine. Speed is most important. The rain still falls; the coldness increases. Soon snow and ice will take over the rugged hills, increasing the difficulty of our advance immeasurably.

The terrain is perfect for defense. The thick forests, hiding innumerable snipers and machine-gun emplacements, must often be cleared by tree-to-tree fighting. The enemy has dug in high upon the steep craggy slopes, from which they pour artillery and mortar fire into our ranks. At night the fog closes in. Under its cover, the Germans infiltrate our lines; and hand-to-hand fighting becomes commonplace. I whet my bayonet until it is razor-sharp and keep it always handy.

Our immediate objective is a quarry near Cleurie. It is only a pin-point on a very large map, but in the memory of the men who fought there, it looms like King's Mountain in the Revolutionary War.

Lying high upon a rocky, wooded, almost perpendicular slope, the quarry is the anchorage point in the German lines, dominating a long section of roadway essential to our advance. Cut from solid rock, its numerous tunnels protect its defenders from our artillery and mortars. Every approach is covered by machine guns set up for cross-fire. Enemy cannon and mortars have the slopes zeroed-in. And a large detachment of sharp-shooters with telescopic sights on their rifles has been added for extra insurance.

The German command, knowing the importance of the position, has ordered it to be held as long as one man can pull a trigger. We have received counterorders to take it. Several times we try to drive head-on up the slope, but we are driven back with heavy losses by a hellish storm of enemy fire.

We dig in and wait for command to figure out shrewder strategy. Our command post and kitchen have been established in a house that stands at the base of a knoll which hides us from the big guns in the quarry area. Beyond the knoll is another rise which lies between us and the enemy-held hill. That is usually no-man's land.

In the darkness, units of the enemy slip down the slope to establish forward positions. Often less than a hundred yards separates us from their lines. We hear them talking back and forth; and their bloody excursions into our own positions are nightly occurrences.

Today the fighting has been unusually heavy. We have been probing with patrols to find a weak link in the enemy chain and have taken a severe battering for our efforts. Now the dusk closes in; the fog rolls over the trees; and it is time to start posting our watches for the night.

I scan the men available. Most of them have been under fire since morning and are ready to collapse from strain and weariness. Knowing what I am after, they lower their eyes and keep silent while waiting for their names to be called. It is the same look that we developed as rookies when a noncom entered the barracks to tap men for an unpleasant detail.

Then I spot a fresh face. It belongs to a bulky redheaded man who looks as though he could handle a BAR.

"What's your name?" I ask.

"Barnes."

"How'd you like to pull a little guard duty?"

"Sahgent," he drawls, "I ain't lost nothin' out there. But if you tag me, I guess I'm it."

"You know how to use a BAR?"

"I've shot one on the range."

"Any combat experience?"

"None but what I've read about in the *Stars and Stripes*. I just got here today."

"Well, you've got to get started sometime. Come on."

We go up a woodland trail to a point near the crest of the knoll. I find a position that offers clear fire space for covering the trail and a tree that will protect the sentry on one side.

"Maybe you've been told before that this is the real thing," I say. "But make no mistake; this is it. Keep on the alert for the slightest sound. The krauts are as tricky as Indians. If you're caught off guard, you'll be the first to get it."

"I don't aim to do much sleepin'."

"Good. If anybody, anything moves over the top of that hill, shoot and shoot fast."

"What if it's one of our own men?"

"It won't be. We'll come up the hill only, and we'll identify ourselves if we do."

"But, sahgent."

"Yeah."

"I ain't never shot nobody. I don't know whether my nerve will stand up."

"Everybody feels like that the first time. Now get this straight in your head. If a man comes over that hill, he'll be a German. One of you is going to get killed. The man that shoots first will be the one that lives. So don't let that civilian conscience get in your way. Draw your bead and pull that trigger fast. You'll feel all right in a bit."

"I feel like a hen at a hawks' convention."

"Good night and good luck."

I turn to leave.

"Sahgent."

"Yeah."

"You got a drink of water?"

"You've got your canteen."

" 'Y god, so I have; so I have."

On the way down the hill, I halt to check a group of men posted in a series of foxholes.

"Is everything all right?" I ask.

Bergman sticks his head above the ground. "Can you get me a new grave mate? Compton's been snoring so loud I can't keep my mind on women."

"Cover his head up with dirt."

"He's been dead so long he wouldn't know the difference. How do things look for the night?" •

"You can't tell. I've put a new man up the hill, and he might freeze if the krauts hit. Watch out for him."

"I'm froze already."

"You'll probably be in a warm spot by morning."

"I hope I'm not in hell."

At the command post the company noncoms have assembled for briefing on the next day's operations. Captain Hogan is pointing out details of terrain and enemy positions on charts when I hear the rattle of the BAR.

I leap to my feet. "Excuse me, sir. That shooting is in my sector."

"Better check it."

I dart through the door and up the hill. The sound of a groaning, threshing body sounds in the darkness. Barnes is shaking like a nude in a blizzard.

"G-g-goddam," he stutters, "I sh-shot somebody."

"Shoot him again. He's still alive."

"G-g-god, no. I've already shot him once."

"Give me your gun."

"It's j-j-jammed."

"You'd better get it un-jammed toute-de-suite. You've got the outpost here; and those krauts never travel alone."

"You going to leave me here by myself?"

"I've got to get back to a meeting."

"I can't stand hearing that man groaning."

"Just be glad it's not yourself. Remember he's your enemy. And he'll likely die in a litle bit. Brace yourself."

"Good g-g-god," he says wonderingly, "to think I was brought up in a Christian home."

"All of us were. Don't get the idea that you've got a special case in this man's army."

"I couldn't kill a chicken."

"The chickens didn't try to kill you."

As I pass the secondary defenses, Bergman asks, "What's the matter?"

"The guy killed his first kraut and is about to cry over it."

"Put me up there. I left my conscience at the repple depple."

"No. Let's leave him alone. If he don't go nuts, he'll be a veteran by morning."

"Yeah. I guess it's better that way. I can rest better with a nervous guy up ahead. He'll blast or squawk if even a rabbit hops."

As I enter the command post, Captain Hogan turns his worried red eyes upon me. "What's up?"

"It was a kraut. Barnes got him at the top of the hill. But I think we'd better get back to our men. Looks like an attack."

"Don't those sonsabitches ever get tired?" His question is addressed to the thin air, and nobody replies.

"Well, briefly, here's the situation. To the right of the quarry near this big rock, we know—"

Brrrrp. The captain pauses. Rat-ta-ta-ta. One of our machine guns answers. A grease gun whirrs. The bullets plop into the walls of the house. It seems but a matter of seconds before the whole area is swept with fire.

The captain folds his map. "Get to your men," he says quietly, "and remember that every foot of land you yield tonight will have to be retaken tomorrow."

We scramble to our feet. I grab a carbine and a full case of grenades. The light of the gasoline lantern is put out; and we dive through the door.

Outside strings of white tracer bullets slice through the darkness. I drop to my knees, gauge the height of the lead; then I get to my feet and dash crouching up the hill. The Germans lower their angle of fire; and before I reach Barnes I am crawling.

He lies flat on the earth so silent and motionless that at first I think he is dead.

"Barnes."

His head pops up.

"Are you all right?"

"Wh-what goes on?"

"It's an attack. Did you fix your gun?"

"G-g-good god, let's get out of here."

"We can't." Breaking open the case of grenades, I shove it between us. "If you want to live, don't let anything get over that hill. You know how to use a grenade?"

"Pull the key and heave 'em?"

"That's it. Give yourself time; watch for the trees."

From over the crest comes a mutter in German. A shiver shoots up my spine. I twist to my side and lob the grenade. The explosion is followed by a scream.

Barnes becomes suddenly energetic, tossing the grenades with the frenzy of a mad man.

"Take it easy. We don't want to run out of ammunition."

"I'll take it easy." He soon learns that a man does not necessarily die because a machine gun sputters and that the enemy is not merely a being with warm flesh and blood. He is part of a wall of menace that expresses itself in the snapping of a branch, a roll of gravel, or a shadowy bulk that looms in the night. In the heat, Barnes learns coolness and calm fury. He becomes a valuable man.

Dawn finds us clinging to most of our positions. The bulk of the Germans have retreated. But the little patch of real estate, known to us as "the ridge," came high. Beneath the trees the slain lie thick; and this morning many a man is sporting a bloody bandage.

A young private, his dirty face marked with tear streaks, approaches me. "Is it all right if I go back up the hill, sergeant?" he asks.

"Why?"

"I left a buddy up there."

"Wounded?"

"I think he's dead."

"What makes you think so?"

"I heard him fall. He groaned a little while. Then he got quiet. Before I could get to him, the krauts hit my position; and I had to give ground."

"Well, you can't do him any good now. If he's alive, the medics have got him."

"But we'd been together since basic." His voice pleads.

"Stay off that hill."

"But the medics could've missed him."

"This is an order. Stay off that hill."

So many men have come and gone that I can no longer keep track of them. Since Kerrigan got his, I have isolated myself as much as possible, desiring only to do my work and be left alone. I feel burnt out, emotionally and physically exhausted. Let the hill be strewn with corpses so long as I do not have to turn over the bodies and find the familiar face of a friend. It is with the living that I must concern myself, juggling them as numbers to fit the mathematics of battle.

The battalion commander and executive officer visit the front lines. They want to see with their own eyes what is holding up our advance. They would like a peek into the quarry itself. Excellent and courageous leaders, they pick only four men to escort them up the treacherous hillside.

It is another dreary, gray day. The lines are quiet, but I cannot sleep. And I am bored with the lack of activity, which breeds the thinking that I try to avoid. Picking up several hand grenades and a carbine, I trail the patrol up the hill.

As I prepare to round a huge boulder, two enemy grenades explode. A machine gun ripples. Silence returns. My scalp tingles as the hair starts rising. That machine gun is only a few yards away.

I pause, pull the pin from a grenade, and peer around the rock. The Germans have not been overly clever with their ambush. Instead of picking off the officers first, they threw the grenades at the four men, knocking out two and machine-gunning one of them as he writhed upon the ground.

That was their mistake. Before the gunner could swing his weapon, the officers had tumbled into a shallow hole, where they now lie pinned. The krauts, evidently not considering a rear guard, have become downright careless with their concealment as they attempt to slaughter the officers.

Grasping the carbine in my left hand and a grenade in my right, I step suddenly from behind the rock. The Germans spot me instantly. The gunner spins the tip of his weapon toward me. But the barrel catches in a limb, and the burst whizzes to my right.

I lob the grenade and grab the carbine trigger with one movement. Before the grenade has time to burst, two krauts fall with carbine slugs in their bellies. I quickly lob two more grenades into the position. Four of the eight Germans are killed; three are put out of action by wounds.

The eighth, a squat, fat man, tries to escape. He dashes down the hill with a waddling gait, like a duck being chased by an ax-man. I line my sights upon his helmet, but hesitate in pulling the trigger. How can one shoot such a ridiculous figure. It is like killing a clown.

But the clown has a gun and is, therefore, dangerous. I squeeze the trigger. The helmet jumps. The man falls as if struck in the head with a club.

I snap the safety lock on my carbine and turn to the battalion commander. He is as cool as the October morning. "Those grenades are not a bad idea. Next time I'll bring my own," says he, brushing the dirt off his clothes.

We pick up our wounded and start down the hill. A single feeling possesses me. It is one of complete and utter weariness.

Shortly after dusk, we are called into action again. But we are hit only by a kraut patrol that has been trapped in our lines on the left flank. The skirmish lasts but a few minutes; and quietness returns as the exhausted men on both sides settle down for the night, content for the moment to live and let live.

Before midnight my jumpy nerves kick me to wakefulness. A jeep is chugging up the road that leads through the forest. Eyes snap open. The men turn to one another doubtfully. That stretch of road is covered by both our guns and the Germans'. Traveling on it by stealth is dangerous enough. And to telegraph one's position with a clattering vehicle seems the ultimate in foolhardiness.

All ears turn toward the sound.

"It's the medics," a voice decides.

"Not up that road. The litter bearers would hoof it through that area."

"Maybe it's the krauts taking a ride in a captured jeep."

"They wouldn't be that crazy."

The spit and crackle of an enemy rifle grenade comes through the night. The jeep engine dies with a cough. I take off through the trees bordering the road.

"Lieutenant Mack!" I call, as I scuttle to a new position.

"Murphy."

"It's me. Come quickly in this direction."

As he crawls through the trees, his bald head shows dimly.

"Are you hurt?"

"Most humiliating," he replies. "The bastahds have injured my dignity, not to mention my posterior. I think I collected a few splinters."

When he stands I see that he is armed only with his familiar leather riding crop.

"What were you figuring on doing? Straddling a kraut and galloping him to death?"

"The uncouth barbarians didn't even give a warning."

"When you come up to the lines, you better bring a gun. Those krauts are totally unimpressed by a horse whip."

"It was such a wondrous night, I was quoting Shelley to my driver."

"Where is your driver?"

"When you hear through these lovely forests a zip like the hounds of hell on winter's traces, that'll be the driver. We've been in these circumstances before."

"I know."

Lieutenant Mack is our supply officer, who has maintained an elegance of speech and manner through the months of combat. We have affectionately nicknamed him "the governor." Precise and meticulous in habit and dress, he has a weird streak in his personality that scoffs at personal danger.

"How is the company?"

"Pretty dog-eared and beat-up. We've been going at a steady grind."

"Are you eating all right?"

211

"When our supply officer gets the grub to us. How are things in the rear echelons?"

"Devastating. Perfectly devastating. I went back to Besançon the other day. The brothels there are being put off limits; and the town is already drained of cognac. The boys are now bitching for overnight passes to extend Operation *Amour.*"

"We could use a few of them up here."

"Impossible. They'd need a pro-station; and a trailer could never make that road."

"They'd get it up here all right, but without kisses."

"I know. War is most outrageously inconvenient."

Two men in the heavy weapons platoon are shot by a sniper. The bullets pierce the center of their foreheads; and they fall on the slope near the spot where the Germans attempted the ambush. I do not know the men, but the news of their slaughter irritates me. Perhaps, it is just that I am tired of cowering in a mud hole while waiting for the enemy to strike. I need a release from taut nerves.

It is mid-afternoon. Rays of sunlight filter though the clouds. The light is all right. Before reporting to company headquarters, I carefully clean my carbine.

"I want to go up and try to get that sniper," I say.

Captain Hogan pinches his chin with two fingers. "Take a patrol. The kraut's evidently well hidden; and we can't risk having another man killed right now."

"Wouldn't a patrol be a giveaway? Don't you think the sniper would fire into a group?"

"He may."

"I think it would be safer to go alone. I'll keep my head down."

"Take along a couple of men. You may need them. I'll telephone batt to hold up our mortar fire for an hour in your area. Don't overstay your time; or one of our own guns may get you." He glances at his wrist watch. "I'll try to halt the mortars at

1300. But wait until you hear them let up before proceeding."

"Yessir."

"And Murphy. Don't get too damned close to that quarry."

"You couldn't drag me there with a mule train."

I call for two volunteers to accompany me. Owl, a smoky-eyed Cherokee Indian, picks up his gun.

"Where to?" he asks.

"Up toward the quarry to look for that sniper."

"Count me in."

Barker slips a fresh clip of cartridges into his Garand.

"No, not you," I say.

"Why not? Am I a stepchild?"

"Maybe you'd better stay with the men."

"Don't be silly. Nothing will happen before dark. Let's go."

The men turn their heads toward Barker. We all know he is up for rotation. On any day he may get the order that will send him back to America on a furlough.

"Well, what's so funny about me?" he asks, becoming conscious of the stare of the men. "Am I wearing red ribbons in my hair? Is my fly open?"

"You shouldn't take the risk," I say.

"Who should? The hell with it. Let's go."

We cross the ridge, stepping as warily as though we were walking on thin ice. There is no indication of the enemy in the area. A breeze moves in the trees. The wooded hill is a peaceful checkerboard of light and shade. A frightened bird darts from the ground with a thrum of wings.

We halt at the edge of a small clearing. Owl points to the spot where our two men were killed. The brown stain of their blood is still on the ground. We study the terrain to determine the source of the accurate sniper fire.

"If he's at his old post, he can't be far away," says Owl. "He couldn't get much range through the trees."

"I'd say he was uphill," adds Barker. "Those guys were shot

right after they stepped into the open. If the kraut had been on either side, he would have waited until they got further into the clearing."

Directly ahead is the huge rock around which I stepped to throw the grenades at the machine-gun nest. It gives me an idea. The Germans, knowing we have come up that trail before, perhaps think we will repeat the performance. So the sniper has been posted in the vicinity as a safeguard.

I take off my helmet and check my weapons. "Wait here until I look around," I say.

"The hell you say. I'm going along," declares Barker.

"No. It was my idea; so it's my party. One will have a better chance than three."

Owl shrugs and removes his helmet. "There's always time to get shot. Why hurry?"

"If nothing happens in fifteen minutes, I'm starting up," says Barker.

"Come ahead."

Keeping under cover of the brush, I skirt the clearing and move toward the boulder. An acute sense of loneliness comes over me. I and my enemy, it seems, are the last two men on earth. I pause; and fear makes my body grow limp. I look at the hills and sky. A shaft of sunlight pierces the clouds, making the wet leaves of the trees glisten goldenly. Life becomes infinitely desirable.

The hill now becomes infested with a thousand eyes peering through telescopic sights, with cross-hairs on the center of my head. Terror grows. I crash my fist to my forehead. The fantasy passes. I inch forward.

At the boulder I stop. My straining ear can catch no sound. I get to my feet and with my left hand against the rock for support step into the open. It happens like a flash of lightning. There is a rustle. My eyes snap forward. The branches of a bush move. I drop to one knee. We see each other simultaneously.

His face is as black as a rotting corpse; and his cold eyes are filled with evil. As he frantically reaches for the safety on his rifle, I fire twice. He crashes backwards. I throw two hand grenades to take care of any companions lurking in the area. Then I wilt.

When Owl and Barker reach the scene, I am mopping the cold sweat off my forehead.

The sniper is sprawled on the ground just beyond the old machine-gun position. The two bullet holes are in the center of the forehead; and one of the grenades has torn off an arm.

Owl's nimble fingers rummage through the pockets.

"A batch of papers. Looks like letters."

"Keep them. They may have information we can use."

"Money." The Indian holds up a thick roll of francs and looks at us doubtfully.

"Keep it," says Barker. "Or some lousy kraut will get it."

"Okay. We'll buy a drink with it."

I suddenly feel like vomiting.

The Indian picks up a handful of leaves and wipes the blood off the gun. "It's better than ours," says he appraisingly. "Who wants it?"

"You can have it."

"It has a good sight."

"I've heard they're the best."

"If I get home, maybe I can fit it on a rifle for deer."

I check my watch. It is 1350. We have ten minutes to get back to our lines.

On the way down the hill, I notice that the Germans killed in the machine-gun nest are still unburied. The soggy corpses have taken on a wooden appearance. Again my stomach retches.

At headquarters I make my report. Then I go to the room that serves as a kitchen, take my carbine apart, and start cleaning it.

18

THE TROUBLESOME spot is finally recognized for what it is: a point, consisting of a few acres of ground, so strategically located and fanatically defended that nothing short of a full-scale assault can eliminate it. While we hold the lines, phases of the attack are co-ordinated by tired, worried officials of the division.

Our armor pours five hundred rounds of high explosives into the quarry. At the same time a saturation mortar barrage is laid on the area. When the fire lifts, we drive up the slopes and are again hit hard by the fanatical enemy.

A battalion, heavily supported by artillery, tries a flanking movement while we remain in a blocking position. For a whole afternoon and night, the battle rages. The next day my company gets its orders to jump off. Under a creeping mortar barrage, we scramble up the hill, by-pass the quarry proper, and go over the crest. The ugly job of cleaning out the quarry has been assigned to other units.

But the Germans are full of surprises. Before night, my company is pinned to a hillside. The krauts, who usually choose elevations for defensive stands, have fooled us in this instance. They have dug in by a dry stream bed at the base of the slope. Trees, cut and arranged in haphazard crisscross patterns, completely conceal their positions. They let us move over the hilltop, and then tear into our ranks with rifle and machine-gun fire.

Mist gathers in the lowland, further hindering visibility. Crawling over the slope on our bellies, we try to pry out the enemy locations. But the camouflage is perfect. There is but one thing to do. I borrow a walkie-talkie radio and start maneuvering a patrol down the hill.

A tense silence comes over the area. Phantomlike, we slip through the trees with senses alert for an ambush. Brrrrrp. A man carrying two cases of machine-gun ammo is hit in the side. He lets out a scream and collapses. The metal cases clatter on the rocky ground.

Immediately our position is swept with fire from five machine guns. The bullets zip three feet from the ground. We lie on our backs, seize our trench shovels, and frantically start scooping holes in the stony soil.

The Germans lower their angle of fire. A man is hit in the chest. Pieces of his lungs spatter the ground. His flesh quivers; and he gurgles, "Oh God, oh God." Two men rip off his shirt. A blast catches them. They sink over the wounded man and are still.

Dragging the radio, I inch my way toward Owl.

"Cover me; I'm going down," I say.

"I'll cover you." He raises his carbine with his left hand. The barrel shakes. It is then that I see his right arm is shattered.

I patch up his arm as best I can with a compress and bandage. The Indian lies on his back, with his dark eyes staring at the sky; and no sound comes from his lips.

"Don't move, or you may draw more fire," I say.

He rolls over on his stomach and again attempts to steady his weapon.

"It's no use. You're too weak. Keep quiet until the medics get here."

He buries his face in the crook of his good arm.

I move down the slope like a lizard. The machine guns pick me up, but miraculously they all miss. The tip of a helmet appears over a log. I draw a bead on its center and wait. Slowly the head rises. When the bare forehead shows, I squeeze the trigger. The head snaps backwards as if caught in a hangman's noose.

The guns find my old position as I scuttle to a new one and press the "talk" button on my radio.

"Red Three calling Red Six. Red Three calling Red Six."

"Come in, Red Three."

"Chemical mortars should do the trick. Try co-ordinates . . ."

"Repeat, Red Three. I cannot hear you."

"Chemical mortars. Co-ordinates: 75.6 – 50.3."

"Speak up, Red Three. Static . . ."

The voice fades.

"Red Three calling Red Six."

"Come in, Red Three."

"Chemical mortars. Co-ordinates: 75.6 – 50.3."

"Right. 75.6 – 50.3."

The first shell flutters over the enemy lines and crumps into the hill beyond. I check the map again.

"Red Six. Red Three calling Red Six. Over 100 – right 30."

"Repeat, Red Three. You must have a rat in your radio."

"Over 100 – right 30."

The second shell falls a little short.

"Red Six. Red Six. Over 10 – right 10."

"You're not coming through, Red Three."

A German, dug in behind a huge oak tree, peers around the trunk. I drop the radio and grab my carbine. As he raises his rifle, my bullet tags him in the throat. His mouth jumps open. The second bullet crashes into his face.

"Red Six. Red Six."

"Come in. What happened?"

"Over 10 – right 10, and fire for effect."

The third shell bursts in the middle of the krauts.

"Red Six calling Red Three. How's the range?"

"Dead center. Send some medics down. Several men are badly hurt."

The game of hide-and-go-seek is over for the Germans. They were adequately protected from horizontal fire, but the mortar shells dig through the tree limbs before exploding. Shrieks of rage and agony come from the krauts. Against the barrage their guns remain impotent and silent. A German staggers blindly through the smoke, holding his arm before his eyes. Three rifles crack almost simultaneously, knocking him backwards.

Owl has moved. I spot him further down the slope. He is crawling feebly, dragging his carbine by the sling.

At my touch, he turns glazed eyes upon me.

"Where you going?" I ask.

"Shoot 'em. Filthy bastards tear my arm off."

"Take it easy. We'll have help in a few minutes.'

"I'll shoot 'em. I'll—I'll blow their guts out."

"It's all over but the shouting. Lie still."

"I shoot 'em. Tear their heads off." He begins pulling himself to his knees, but crumples. A merciful faint has blacked him out.

The man shot in the chest is dead. The two who went to his aid are still alive, but badly wounded. They have been dragged to the cover of a tree. One with a bloody bandage around his head gasps for breath through a wide-open mouth. The other is trying to light a cigarette with a trembling hand. I grasp the fingers and touch the flame to the tobacco.

"Thanks."

"Are you hurting?"

"I hurt like hell. Seems like a red-hot iron is buried in my shoulder."

"You'll get help soon; then a nice, long rest in the hospital."

"I don't want to go back. I just got into action this week."

"You've done your part."

"I haven't done anything but stop some lead. I swore I'd get me some krauts. They killed my brother in Italy."

"Oh."

"He was just two years older than me."

"We all lose somebody."

"He was the best pitcher you ever saw. People said he was big-league stuff. Had a curve that would break a mile."

"He's still big-league stuff."

"Will I lose my arm?"

"No. You'll be all right."

"I'm coming back up."

"You'll be back up."

A moan comes from the man who was hit in the side.

"He's alive," says the shoulder casualty. "He's been so quiet I thought he was dead."

The fallen trees now turn into obstacles for the krauts. Caught in the net of mortar fire, they emerge from their holes, blinded and choking. As they flounder in the branches, we bore into them with our rifles.

The company moves down the hill. We mop up the enemy strongpoint hole by hole. Then we sling our weapons on our shoulders and climb the slope beyond.

Now the Germans begin their characteristic slow retreat. Over the thickly wooded countryside, they give ground stubbornly, bitterly. They batter our ranks with artillery and mortars; and in the forests units lie like coiled snakes, striking suddenly and viciously.

The weather turns cold. In the mornings the ground is white with frost; snow is already on the mountaintops. The earth freezes and thaws, turning the terrain into an ocean of mud through which we must wallow toward our objectives. At night we shiver and sleep fitfully.

While we pause for two days to reorganize, three of us are called to regimental headquarters. A colonel pins gold bars on our shoulders and pats us on the back.

"You are now *gentlemen* by act of Congress," he says, smiling at our muddy uniforms and bearded faces. "Shave, take a bath, and get the hell back into the lines."

We are moving without opposition through a dense forest when we come upon signs of the enemy. The tracks are fresh and unmistakable. I shift my BAR men forward. Our march becomes a stalk.

We are braced for the artillery barrage, but not covered. At the first crash we fall and start a withdrawal. Tree bursts rip the area. Three machine guns chatter. Sniper bullets snap overhead. We fall back to an area beyond a trail that winds through the forest. The fire ceases as suddenly as it began; and the forest appears as peaceful as a park.

As we lie on the ground waiting for orders, a lieutenant from another company strolls by. He wears a leather air corps jacket, but no helmet. And for weapons he has only a revolver.

"Where do you think you're going?" I ask.

"After rations. I'm looking for a short cut for my jeep."

"Not up that trail. It's a short cut to hell."

He fingers a small mustache and addresses me sarcastically. "Did you just get up, lieutenant?"

"We just got shoved back. I'm telling you this area's swarming with jerries."

"Thanks. I'll keep an eye open for them."

"Not for long, if you stick to that path."

He laughs and shakes his head.

"I've been at the front for some little time, and I think I know my way around."

"Okay. Okay."

He does not get over fifty yards up the trail before a sniper drills him through the brain. He drops and dies with scarcely a wiggle.

We are ordered to dig in for the night.

Paderwicz starts scooping us a hole while I post the guards. Our rations are skimpy; and the irritated men lie in their holes and listen to the growling of their stomachs.

"Right now," says Paderwicz, "what had you rather have than a woman?"

"One night of sound sleep."

"I'd take duck's blood puddin'."

"You and your duck's blood pudding. That's all you've talked about for weeks."

"There ain't nothin' nicer."

"I'll try some after the war."

"I wish I had some now."

"Right now, I'd settle for a hunk of cold corn bread."

"Corn bread? What in the hell is that?"

"Kind of bread we make out of corn meal in the South."

"Corn meal?"

"Yeah. The corn is ground up. That's meal."

"You call that fit for a civilized man?"

"We like it."

"How come you don't eat duck's blood puddin'?"

"Don't remember ever seeing any."

"What kind of place do you live in anyhow?"

"A small town."

"You give me your address, and I'll send you some real chow when we get home."

"Fine. I'll give you the address tomorrow."

"Corn bread. Jeez, that's a good one."

He is still talking when I drop off to sleep.

"Lieutenant."

My eyes pop open. "Yeah. Who's that?"

"Chelson. I'm at the outpost; and there's a German keeps wandering around our place hollering, 'Walter.' What'll we do?"

"Shoot him."

"Yessir."

I am still awake when he returns.

"Lieutenant."

"Yeah."

"How we going to shoot the German when we can't see him? It's too dark."

"You've got hand grenades. Throw them; and don't bother me any more tonight. I've got to get some rest."

"Yessir. How many grenades?"

"Just how long have you been with this outfit?"

"Only a few days. I'm plumb new at this business."

"A couple grenades ought to do the trick. If they don't put a muffler on the guy, chuck some more."

"Yessir. I sure thank you."

I can now hear the wailing voice of the German. He is evidently lost and terrified. The two grenades explode. The kraut quits hollering.

Paderwicz stirs sleepily. "What goes on? Can't a guy have no peace a-tall?"

"It was a jerry wandering around in the woods and calling a buddy. Probably thought he was in his own lines."

"All that commotion over one damned German?"

"Our guard got rattled. He's new."

"Seems like we got nothin' left but new guys."

"Yeah. They come and go."

Toward morning the tree by our hole is struck by a phosphorous shell. The blast deafens us. The evergreen lights up like a Christmas tree, as the hot, gleaming phosphorous rolls over its branches.

Paderwicz screws his fingers in his ears. "Are you hurt?"

"No. I'm all right. And you?"

"I'm okay. If there's any way a guy can get any sleep in this man's army, I've never figured it out. I ain't had one night's sleep since the day I was inducted. If it's not one thing, I'll be a sonofabitch, if it ain't three."

Shortly after dawn we begin our attack under a walking barrage of our artillery. When we pass the body of the lieutenant, frost is glistening on his uniform.

"If his mama could only see him now," says Paderwicz,

casually adjusting the carrying strap of his walkie-talkie. "His kind never learns."

"He was a fool."

"His men are probably wondering what happened to their rations."

We leave the trail and push directly through the woods. Except for sporadic mortar fire, the enemy is quiet, too quiet to suit me.

Crack!

Paderwicz is dead before his body thuds against the ground. The sniper's bullet got him just above the left eye. I leap behind a tree.

Crack!

It is like being struck with a ball bat. The ricocheting bullet digs a channel through my hip and knocks me flat. The sniper throws his camouflage cape back to get a better view and drills my helmet. That is the last mistake he ever makes. My head is not in the helmet.

I raise my carbine and with my right hand fire pistol-fashion. The bullet spatters between the German's eyes. It was his brain or nothing. He would not have missed the second time.

I try to get up, but cannot. My right leg seems paralyzed.

"Are you hurt bad, Murph?" It is Barker, who bends over me.

"I don't know. I don't think so."

"Let's have a look."

"Whew!" says he, examining the wound. "It's long and deep, but the bone's not hurt. If all goes well, you should be able to sit down in a month or so."

"Kerrigan would get a kick out of this."

"Kerrigan?"

"He always said if I took a commission, he hoped I got my ass shot off."

"Well, you did; and you have."

"You'd better catch up with the rest of the platoon. I'll send somebody up to take over my spot."

"It's been a long time since North Africa. You know, I leave on rotation tomorrow."

"I didn't know, but I'm glad."

"Yep. Papers came through. In a couple of weeks I'll be back in the States."

"Good. Forget this whole mess, and enjoy yourself."

"I won't be forgetting you fellows. I sort of feel like a dog for running out on you at a time like this."

"Don't be silly. You're lucky."

"By the way, you won't be needing that lucky carbine of yours any time soon?"

"I don't think so."

"Then can I take it. I need some luck. The next twenty-four hours is going to be one long sweat."

"Sure. The gun's yours. You'd better get Paderwicz' radio too."

"Somebody already picked it up."

"Fine. You'll likely need it."

When we reach the road, the medics place my stretcher across a jeep hood. The third battalion is in the area, waiting for orders to move into battle. The men peer at me, but not from dumb curiosity. I have done the same thing many times. We all want to know whether the body beneath the bloody blankets is that of a friend.

I catch the eye of a freckled-faced youngster. We had our basic training together, but I cannot remember his name.

"Hello, Indiana."

"Why it's Texas. You hurt bad?"

"No, I'll be back in a couple of weeks."

"That's good. You take it easy, Texas."

At the aid station, I wait for a long time before receiving medical attention. My hip feels as though a white-hot brand had been raked across it; and I feel sick in mind and body.

As if he had never seen a wounded man before, a doctor

stares at me bewilderedly. He is perhaps half-dead with fatigue, but I am too ill to know or care.

"Well, goddammit, do *something*. Don't stand there with egg on your face."

"You're in no position to talk like that, lieutenant."

"I'm in no position to do anything but wait until you lousy sawbones take a notion to do a little work."

"We'll get to you as soon as we can."

"Don't knock yourself out."

He blows up like a turkey gobbler.

That night practically my whole platoon is wiped out. Among those killed were Marsh, who so dearly loved to sing, and Barker, to whom my lucky carbine was not much good.

Because of the rain and mud, we cannot be evacuated for three days. We lie on cots, six to a pyramidal tent, while the fever spreads through our flesh. Delirious men moan and curse. Water patters against the canvas.

When I reach the hospital, a doctor strips the bandage from my wound. From the corner of my eye, I see him shake his head.

"Is it gangrene?" I ask.

"It's probably just infected," a nurse replies.

"It's gangrene. I know damned well it's gangrene."

"An infection. You'll be all right before long."

But it is gangrene. For nearly a month, the doctors pump me full of penicillin and whittle away dead and poisoned flesh. More weeks pass before I can walk again.

When I regain the use of my leg, I catch a ride to another hospital twenty miles away. I have learned that Kerrigan is there.

His back is to me when I enter the ward. For a moment I watch as he awkwardly shuffles a deck of cards with his bandaged hand.

"Is this the venereal ward?" I ask loudly.

"Nosir," says a white-faced youngster with his arm missing. "This is casualty. Convalescent."

"Then what is that syphilitic sergeant doing here? Kerrigan, I mean."

The ward becomes as silent as an empty church. Kerrigan turns slowly, shaking his head in disbelief.

"Why you mule-headed, rattle-brained, scrambled-eyed whore of a lieutenant!"

Mouths drop open.

"You crawling, creeping crap from Texas. You battle-happy sonofabitch!"

"He never did show the proper respect for officers," I explain to the other men.

"Respect!" he spits. "Why—why, you beagle-eared bastard, what are you doing in the rear area?"

"You'll be tickled to know that I got shot. Yeah. Lost a hunk of my hip."

"Oh, Lord, to think I missed that. Brother, am I glad to see you. You haven't changed a bit."

"And you're uglier than ever."

The ward relaxes.

19

WHEN I return to the front in January, the division, fighting under terrible conditions of terrain and weather, has completed its push through the Vosges, cracked the enemy's "winter line," and reached the Rhine at Strasbourg. On the opposite side of the river lies Germany itself. But many weeks must pass and many men die before we can attempt a crossing.

During these cold, cloudy days, the whole front is restless.

Far to the north the Battle of the Bulge is coming to an end. A number of our units have entered Germany and are jockeying for solid footholds on enemy soil. Over the wintry roads of France and Belgium streams of men and supplies pour into reserve. Our forces are maneuvering for positions to launch the all-out assault on Germany in the early spring.

We do not realize the vastness of the operation. The minds and energies of the men are concentrated on the tasks at hand. In these days my division is engaged in one of the toughest assignments in its history: eliminating the Colmar Pocket, a heavily fortified area rolling south from our lines toward the Swiss border.

In effect, it is a huge and dangerous bridgehead thrusting west of the Rhine like an iron fist. Fed with men and materiel from across the river, it is a constant threat to our right flank; and potentially it is a perfect springboard from which the enemy could start a powerful counterattack.

The division has clipped the fringes of the pocket and is poised near the town of Guémar for an attack on the hard core itself. The area, swept by icy winds from the Vosges, favors the enemy defensive. It is composed of patches of forests, flat fields, and meadows, and numerous villages which have been converted into German strongholds.

The enemy is well supplied with armor. Tanks, concealed in the forests, dominate the open plains over which we have to advance. The temperature, even at mid-day, seldom rises above fourteen degrees. Snow is almost knee-deep. Even without the harassment of enemy fire, the nights are one long hell in which it is our full-time concern to keep from freezing.

Two rivers, the Fecht and the Ill, flow between us and the enemy. Two sister regiments, the 7th and the 30th, steal across the Fecht at night after making a thousand-yard breach in the German lines. The 7th whips down the river to hit an enemy strongpoint at Ostheim. The 30th proceeds southeast, clearing a forest and capturing a small bridge over the Ill.

That slim wooden track spanning the river is to make history. The 30th's foot soldiers move across it and deploy over the snowy plains in preparation for an attack on two tiny villages, Holtzwihr and Riedwihr, between which stretches a tract of woodland.

Now with the infantry ready, a tank starts crossing the bridge. The structure trembles. The tank pauses. The engineers wave it forward. With a crash the bridge collapses. The tank settles at the edge of the water; and for the time being that is the end of effective armor support for the infantry.

The 30th cannot wait. Its attack has been timed to co-ordinate with a drive by the French on the left and a similar push by the 7th on the right. So the 30th foot soldiers, encountering but light resistance, plunge across the fields to the outskirts of the two villages and capture a section of the forest.

Meanwhile, both the French and 7th have been held up by fierce enemy stands. The 30th, with its two flanks exposed and fronted by a powerful foe, could hardly be in a worse position tactically.

At four-thirty in the afternoon, disaster strikes. In the vicinity of Holtzwihr, the third battalion is hit by ten enemy tanks and tank destroyers. Against the armor our men have no defense. They might as well be tackling crazed elephants with their bare hands.

The armor slices the battalion into small pockets and methodically rakes them with machine-gun fire. Even had they time to dig in, our men could hardly make a dent in the frozen ground. They are completely without cover when hit from three sides.

An hour later, the blow falls on the first battalion near Riedwihr. It is cut to pieces in a similar manner. The men who can escape begin a bloody withdrawal. When they reach the Ill, many swim or ford the stream. In a short while their clothes are dripping with icicles.

My regiment, which has been held in divisional reserve, is

ordered into the attack. The third battalion, assigned to establish a bridgehead across the Ill, jumps off at three in the morning. It makes good progress until an enemy counterattack supported by four tanks batters it back to the river. The German fire is extremely accurate. Three tanks, supporting the third battalion's attack from stationary positions on our side of the Ill, are knocked out a few minutes after their guns are unlimbered.

It is now obvious that, without the help of rolling armor, we are ramming our heads into a stone wall. But the infantry attacks, regardless of cost, must continue. The Germans cannot be allowed to shift their power strategically. With a concentration of force and swift armor maneuvers, they may destroy our units one by one.

Meanwhile our frantic engineers are trying to get a bridge across the river. It is our task to keep the enemy at bay until the job is completed.

When the third battalion, mauled and exhausted, reels back, we move through their position and fan out over the plains. It is our turn to move up and take a beating. As we dog-trot through the snow, no smile appears on a face, no lip murmurs the customary wisecrack. As we move through an area littered with dead men and abandoned equipment, the soldiers mutter curses and speak bitterly of suicide missions.

We reach the edge of the woods near Riedwihr before the Germans unleash their cyclone of tank and artillery fire. We fall back and crawl into holes dug by the cannon shells.

Why the krauts do not follow up with a counterattack is inexplicable. Against their heavy tanks we are virtually defenseless as we cower in the frozen earth.

Elleridge, the ex-schoolteacher, shares a hole with me. His teeth chatter; and his face is blue from the cold. Not since D-Day in southern France has he mentioned the advantages of military travel.

The shadows lengthen; the wind rises; and clouds sweep

---

lower over the earth. We remove our shoes and massage our numbed feet.

"Well, professor, what does the tourist guide book say about this section of France?"

His lips crack into a game but freakish smile. "It says the weather is cool; the reception, warm; food is scarce; and the present tourists are bitterly anti-American. Their chief occupation is the slinging of lead. It says one of the most interesting aspects of the countryside is the complete absence of allied armor. It says that here life is real; life is earnest; and the grave is not the goal. I wish the man that wrote *that* was with us in this hole. I am not selfish. I wish a lot of people were here to enjoy the wintry charms of Alsace. Take a post card: Dear friends, having a wonderful time. Wish you were here—and I were in San Diego."

"If we get out of here alive, you'll have something to tell your pupils."

"Oh, yes. There we were, children, burning with patriotism and eagerness to get at the throat of the enemy. As the sun set on that glorious day, we were not like slaves harried to their dungeons. But wrapping the draperies of our earthen couches about us, we lay down to pleasant dreams. I think my goddamned feet are frozen. I still haven't stirred up any circulation."

"Why should you worry? You're making history."

"Yeah. Why don't somebody write it right? Why don't somebody put it so everybody can see men cringing in the snow like miserable, frightened and frozen rats, wondering whether the krauts or the cold will get them first."

"Why don't you write it? You were an English teacher."

"I can't. Nobody can. You've got to live it. That damned shoe dubbing is no good. It stops up the pores in the leather. When you walk, your feet sweat; your socks get wet; and it's like putting your feet on cold storage. How's our ammunition?"

"We've got enough if the krauts don't bring their tanks out."

"What I wouldn't give for a bazooka. If the Germans hit us with their armor—"

"We won't have to worry about a bazooka. We won't have to worry about anything. It'll all be over."

"You get so tired, you don't care. It doesn't matter. Nothing matters. You stand up and do the best you can, and then to hell with it."

"Speaking of hell—"

"I've been thinking about that too. And it doesn't worry me either. If I go there, I'll spend the first forty years thawing out."

"Your morale's slipping."

"Yeah. What I need is a good USO show to cheer me up. I can see it now. The master of ceremonies with the double-breasted coat dripping down to his knees. 'Ladies and gentlemen'—you're supposed to laugh, because there ain't no ladies present."

"And there ain't no gentlemen."

"Ha! Ha! As the kraut said to the G.I. facing a Mark IV tank, 'This is going to kill you.'"

During the night, we take turns at staying on watch. I fall asleep. My hair freezes to the ground. A gun cracks. I jerk awake, leaving patches of my hair in the ice.

By morning, the bridge over the Ill has been completed sufficiently to permit the crossing of a few tanks. Three of them join us. The presence of armor is most cheering, but it also means that we are not to retreat.

As we line up for another attack, the quiet woods seem to explode. A mortar barrage is thrown on us; machine guns crackle; and rifle bullets snap through the air. Again we scramble for cover. I see the two lieutenants who were commissioned with me leap into the same hole. A mortar shell trails them in. It is over in an instant. Black smoke rolls from the hole, covering the bloody hulks that a moment ago were two living men.

A blast knocks me down. I roll into a hole and jerk up my

trouser legs. From the knees down the flesh is peppered with tiny steel fragments. But the luck of the Irish is with me. The wounds are all superficial.

Our armor pulls ahead of us with gun barrels traversing. From the woodland comes a crash of shells. Two of the tanks burst into flames. Their escape hatches open; and the still living members of the crew bail out. Blazing like torches and scream- ing horribly, they roll in the snow. Bullets spit around the agonized bodies as enemy riflemen crack down.

The third tank is also in trouble. Its gun refuses to work. The hatch opens. The tank commander, a quiet Jewish lieu- tenant, peers out. He gives an order. The crippled tank moves forward toward what appears to be certain destruction.

Shells explode all about it. Lead spatters against the armor. But the tank never pauses until it reaches a spot directly be- tween the burning men and the forest. There the driver takes the supreme chance. He turns the tank's side to the enemy, thus using it as a shield for the wounded, but presenting a broad and stationary target to the Germans. The crew clambers out and stacks the smoldering bodies on top.

As the tank crawls back toward us with its ghastly cargo, it is swept by small-arms fire. But it is impossible to tell if any of the men are hit. They are too near death to react. The tank passes within a few feet of my hole; and the stench of burning flesh stifles me. The white bones drip like icicles from what is left of one man's foot.

Under heavy fire we withdraw from the position. More armor is moving up, but a small creek separates us from it. Since the tanks cannot reach us, we must get to them. Circling a jutting neck of the woodland, we join the armor and strike again.

As we advance, the fighting develops into individual duels. Once I am pinned behind a tree by a stubborn kraut using a huge pine for cover. Only a few yards separate us. We snipe at one another, but neither of us scores a hit.

I spot Kohl hugging another tree trunk to my right.

"Bust him one from your side," I yell.

"I can't see him."

"Go ahead. Shoot. Let him know where you are."

"That's exactly what I don't want him to know."

"Well, he knows my address; so here goes. Be ready to pick him up if he jumps your way."

I inch my head around the tree trunk, remembering the times that I have had my own sights set on a helmet while waiting for temple or forehead to appear.

Crack!

I flinch and recover. It is Kohl's rifle that fired. The back of the German's recoiling body flashes past the tree, and I nail him in the side. As he drops to his knees, I finish emptying the ammo clip into his body. He lies, curled in the snow like a tired child at the end of a busy day.

Six hundred yards deep in the forest, we have to halt our advance. Our ammunition is low, and we must wait for fresh supplies to be brought up before continuing.

Night has fallen. Wind whistles through the barren tree limbs. Few words are spoken. The company, which started the attack at almost full strength, has been slashed to pieces. Huddling in the snow, we open cans of greasy rations and attempt to eat.

Through a rift in the clouds, a star winks calmly. In a hut, taken over for a command post, the staff officers check their maps. Men stamp their frozen feet on the earth in an effort to knock the numbness from them. A tired voice says, "I'm going to grab me some sleep. Wake me up at Judgment Day."

Around one o'clock in the morning our ammunition and several replacements arrive. One of the newcomers is Candler, who has just returned from America on a rotation furlough.

"How was the trip?" I ask.

"Not like you'd think. I had the crazy notion that I could leave the war behind. But I couldn't."

"Brother, just give me a chance at it," says a voice.

"That's what you think. You try to forget, but nobody will let you. They're so goddamned nice they lay their sympathy on with a trowel. Some drunk asking you about your ribbons. Some brave woman crying about a son in an army camp two hundred miles away. Some vet from the last war patting you on the back and telling you what a great job you're doing. 'Wished I was young enough to get in again myself. How's them women in Paris?' "

"How's the women back home?" a voice asks.

"Everything's in a mess. Busiest people after this shindig will be the divorce lawyers. Wait and see."

"Did you get warm?"

"No. I come from Colorado. How's the company?"

"You won't know it. Practically everybody's new."

"Who's been killed?"

"There've been so many I can't remember. You remember Paderwicz?"

"Yeah. The Polack."

"A sniper got him. Then Barker. He was supposed to leave on rotation the next day."

"No."

"Smith and Kerrigan were wounded. Brandon was killed a long time ago."

"Yeah. I remember that. How's our set-up here?"

"It's rough. Have you had any sleep?"

"I've had enough. When do we move out?"

"At two o'clock."

"Wonder if I could get a carbine. I don't like an M-1 for this woods fighting."

"You can probably find one in the field in the morning."

I report to the command post for orders. Our company is to drive to the edge of the woods facing Holtzwihr, dig in, and hold. Another unit will move through our lines and continue the attack at dawn. I get my bearings from a field map and return to the men.

"All right, everybody. Let's go."

The command is followed by a creaking of gear and a mumble of curses.

"Lieutenant."

"Yeah."

"There's a man sitting against that big tree crying."

"What's wrong with him?"

"I don't know. He won't talk."

I go over and shake him by the shoulder. "Come on. Let's go."

"I can't take it any more, lieutenant."

"What's come over you?"

"I don't know. I got the shakes."

"You can't make it."

"If I could, I would. I'm not fooling."

"Stick around the C.P. The krauts may hit this spot."

"Yessir. I'm ashamed, but I can't help it."

"Have you got something on your mind?"

"Nosir. I just started shaking."

"Can you sleep?"

"I haven't slept in a week."

"You better report to the medics."

His head goes back to his knees, and the sobbing starts again.

"What's wrong with that joe? Battle-happy?" asks Candler.

"Looks like he's taken about all he can."

"I know how he feels. Many's the time I've just wanted to sit down and cry about the whole damned mess."

As we stumble through the dark forest, a man trips and accidentally jerks the trigger of his carbine. The bullet plows into the fellow just ahead of him.

"Oh, excuse me," says the first soldier.

"Now, if that ain't what I call military courtesy."

"Are you hurt badly?"

"No, just had my hip shot off. What's the matter with that tanglefoot?"

"I tripped, and—"

"Kohl, get him back to the C.P.; and check on that guy with the crying jag."

"What you want me to do with weeping Willie?"

"Tickle him under the chin," says a voice.

We reach the edge of the forest. For two hours the night is filled with the clump, clump of pick and shovel gnawing at the rock-hard earth. The efforts are futile, but the exercise keeps us from freezing. When we finally give up trying to chew holes in the ground, we stamp up and down a narrow road winding through the woods to stir up heat in our bodies.

As the dirty, gray light of dawn spreads over the terrain, a tension grips us. To the infantryman, daybreak is the critical hour. It is the customary time for attacking or being attacked. Our support has not yet arrived.

I contact battalion headquarters.

"Any change in orders for Company B?"

"No. Hold on to your position. Our attack is going to be delayed."

I hang up the receiver and study the landscape tactically. We are at the butt-end of a rough U, whose sides are formed by fingerlike extensions of the woods stretching toward Holtzwihr. Directly before us are flat open fields beyond which I can see a church steeple and housetops in the village, a mile away. The narrow road over which we have been pounding our feet leads from the woods to the town. A drainage ditch flanks its right side. Underbrush near the forest edge has been cleared away to furnish fire breaks for the enemy.

During the night, two tank destroyers have moved up to our position. They have parked on the road; and most of the crew members are asleep. Rousing the lieutenant in charge, I say,

"You'd better get your TD's under cover. They're like ducks sitting in the road."

He climbs out through the turret, yawning.

"If we get off, we'll get stuck."

"You've got no cover there."

"If the krauts attack, we can see them coming."

"Okay, it's your funeral."

Just across the road, the platoon machine-gun squad has set up its weapon under a tree.

"What's happened to the attack?" the squad sergeant asks.

"It's been held up."

He whistles and shakes his head. "How long do you think this beat-up outfit could stand off a counterattack?"

"I don't know. How's your ammunition?"

"We've got about four hundred rounds."

"Make it all count, if we are attacked."

"I don't aim to do any practicing."

Checking the other men, I find that our right flank is exposed. Some unit failed to get up on schedule.

The morning drags by. A forward artillery observer with a radio joins us. The icy tree branches rattle in the wind.

Again I contact headquarters.

"What about orders?"

"No change. Hold your position."

At two o'clock in the afternoon, I see the Germans lining up for an attack. Six tanks rumble to the outskirts of Holtzwihr, split into groups of threes, and fan out toward either side of the clearing. Obviously they intend an encircling movement, using the fingers of trees for cover. I yell to my men to get ready.

Then wave after wave of white dots, barely discernible against the background of snow, start across the field. They are enemy infantrymen, wearing snowcapes and advancing in a staggered skirmish formation.

One of our tank destroyers starts its engine and maneuvers for a firing position. It slides into a ditch at an angle that leaves the turret guns completely useless. The driver steps on the gas; the tank wallows further into the ditch; the engine dies. The crew bails out and takes off for the rear.

"I'm trying to contact headquarters," shouts the artillery observer.

I had forgotten about him. We cannot afford to have the radio captured.

"Get to the rear," I holler. "I'll get the artillery by phone."

"I don't want to leave you."

"Get going. You can't do any good. Just take care of that radio."

I grab a map, estimate the enemy's position, and seize the field telephone.

"Battalion," cheerfully answers a headquarters lieutenant.

"This is Murphy. We're being attacked. Get me the artillery."

"Coming up."

"I want a round of smoke at co-ordinates 30.5 – 60; and tell those joes to shake the lead out."

"How many krauts?"

"Six tanks that I can see, and maybe a couple hundred foot soldiers supporting."

"Good god! How close?"

"Close enough. Give me that artillery."

I hang up the receiver and grab my carbine just as the enemy's preliminary barrage hits. It is murderous. A single tree burst knocks out our machine-gun squad. The second tank destroyer is hit flush, and three of its crew are killed. The remainder, coughing and half-blinded, climb from the smoking turret and sprint down the road to the rear. At that moment I know that we are lost.

The smoke shell whizzes over, landing beyond the oncoming Germans.

200 right; 200 over. And fire for effect.

Our counterbarrage is on the nose. A line of enemy infantry-men disappear in a cloud of smoke and snow. But others keep coming.

The telephone rings.

"How close are they?"

"50 over, and keep firing for effect." That artillery curtain must be kept between us and the enemy.

The tanks are now close enough to rake our position with machine-gun fire. Of the hundred and twenty-eight men that began the drive, not over forty remain. And I am the last of seven officers. Trying to stop the armor with our small arms is useless. I yell to the men to start pulling out.

"What about you?" shouts Kohl.

"I'm staying up with the phone as long as I can. Get the men back, and keep them grouped. Candler will help you."

"Candler's dead."

The telephone rings.

"How close are they?"

"50 over, and keep blasting. The company's pulling back."

I raise my eyes and see that the men are hesitating. Clapping down the receiver, I yell, "Get the hell out of here. That's an order!"

Kohl says something, but his words are lost in a shell burst. He shrugs his shoulders, beckons with his thumb, and the men stumble through the woods, casting worried glances backward.

I seize my carbine and start sniping. The advance wave of infantrymen is within two hundred yards of my position.

The telephone rings.

"How close are they?"

"50 over. Keep it coming."

Dropping the receiver, I grab the carbine and fire until I give out of ammunition. As I turn to run, I notice the burning tank destroyer. On its turret is a perfectly good machine gun and several cases of ammunition. The German tanks have sud-denly veered to the left.

I change my plans and drag the telephone to the top of the tank destroyer. The body of the lieutenant with whom I talked early in the morning is sprawled over the edge of the hatch. His throat has been cut; a small river of blood streams down the side of the tank destroyer. I finish dragging the body out and dump it into the snow.

The telephone rings.

"How close are they?"

"50 over, and keep firing for effect."

"How close are they to your position?"

"Just hold the phone and I'll let you talk to one of the bastards."

Hastily checking the machine gun, I find that it has not been damaged. When I press the trigger, the chatter of the gun is like sweet music. Three krauts stagger and crumple in the snow.

Crash! The tank destroyer shudders violently. Vaguely I put two and two together and conclude that the TD has received another direct hit.

The telephone rings.

"This is Sergeant Bowes. Are you still alive, lieutenant?"

"Momentarily." I spread the map on my left palm. "Correct fire: —"

Crash! I am conscious of a flash and explosion. I reel back with the map and telephone receiver in my hands.

"Lieutenant. Lieutenant. Can you hear me? Are you still alive, lieutenant?"

"I think so. Correct fire: 50 over, and keep the line open."

I feed another belt of cartridges into the machine gun and seize the trigger again. The smoke is so thick that I can barely see through it; and the smell of smoldering flesh is again in my nostrils. But when the wind blows the smoke aside, I bore into any object that stirs.

The gun has thrown the krauts into confusion. Evidently they cannot locate its position. Later I am told that the burning tank destroyer, loaded with gasoline and ammunition, was expected to blow up any minute. That was why the enemy tanks gave it a wide berth and the infantrymen could not conceive of a man's using it for cover.

I do not know about that. For the time being my imagination is gone; and my numbed brain is intent only on destroying. I am conscious only that the smoke and the turret afford a good screen, and that, for the first time in three days, my feet are warm.

Now the Germans try a new tactic. A gust of wind whips the smoke aside; and I see an enemy sergeant in the roadside ditch not thirty yards from my position. He peers cautiously about, then turns his head and motions his squad forward. As I spin my gun barrel upon him, a billow of smoke comes betweeen us.

For a minute or so I wait. The tree branches overhead stir stiffly in the gust, the smoke column folds to one side. The twelve Germans, huddled like partridges in the ditch, are discussing something, perhaps my possible location. I press the trigger and slowly traverse the barrel. The twelve bodies slump in a stack position. I give them another methodically thorough burst, and pick up the phone.

"Correct fire, battalion. 50 over."

"Are you all right, lieutenant?"

"I'm all right, sergeant. What are *your* postwar plans?"

The barrage lands within fifty yards of the tank destroyer. The shouting, screaming Germans caught in it are silent now. The enemy tanks, reluctant to advance further without infantry support, lumber back toward Holtzwihr.

I snatch the telephone receiver. "Sergeant. Sergeant Bowes. Correct fire: 50 over; and keep firing for effect. This is my last change."

"50 over? That's your own position."

"I don't give a damn. 50 over."

Concussion from the enemy barrage almost knocks me from the tank destroyer. For a moment I am stunned; and then I see the telephone receiver in my hand.

"Sergeant Bowes. Battalion. Sergeant." There is no answer. The telephone line has been knocked out.

My cloudy brain slowly directs my actions. Carefully I fold the field map and notice that it has been riddled with shell fragments. I examine my hands and arms. They are unscratched.

A dull pain throbs in my right leg. Looking down, I see that the trouser leg is bloody. That does not matter.

As if under the influence of some drug, I slide off the tank destroyer and, without once looking back, walk down the road through the forest. If the Germans want to shoot me, let them. I am too weak from fear and exhaustion to care.

20

EXCEPT for a vague pain in my leg, I feel nothing: no sense of triumph; no exhilaration at being alive. Even the weariness seems to have passed. Existence has taken on the quality of a dream in which I am detached from all that is present. I hear the shells bursting among the trees, see the dead scattered on the ground; but I do not connect them with anything that particularly concerns me.

I reach an outpost held by a small group of men from another company. A corporal, with a blond, bristling beard, pokes his head out of an old German foxhole dug by the roadside.

"They ain't headed this way, lieutenant?"

"I don't think so. Not right now, at least. Where's your officer?"

"Officer? The last'n I seen got knocked off last night."

"Well, you'd better keep your eyes open. The krauts are all over hell and half of Georgia."

"Sure, sure, lieutenant. We keep on a double alert plus tree."

Gradually the shock passes. The fog clears from my brain. The sky seems to have become lighter; and the air, uncommonly cold. Weariness returns to my flesh, and my knees tremble. I am now aware of the battle roar on my left. I hear the drone and whine of fighter bombers. Air support. That is good.

Again I begin to think in terms of strategy. The Germans, deserted by their armor and slashed by our artillery, are weak and off balance in my sector. We must hit them before they can consolidate their gains or bring up reinforcements.

I find my men.

"What happened?" asks Kohl.

"The artillery cut them to pieces. But some got through. We've got to go back up before they get set."

"Is this a private war? Or can we expect a little help?"

"What happened to that outfit that was supposed to attack this morning?" asks Elleridge. "Did they forget to wind their watches?"

"I don't know. I don't know anything, except we've got to get back up, and quickly."

"Anything to git out of this place," says a tall, lanky private slinging his gun on his shoulder. "My mama said there'd be days like this."

"But she didn't say they would come in bunches like grapes," adds a squat, swarthy man who has a sprig of pine sticking like a plume from his helmet net. "Has anybody got some adhesive tape? I got a blister on my heel as big as a saucer."

"This is a fine time to think of that. Why didn't you fix your feet when you were resting?"

"It don't hurt unless I walk."

"You won't be walking long; you'll be running. Let's get it over with," says the tall soldier.

"Now is everybody all right? Has everybody got plenty of ammo?"

"If they ain't, they're welcome to mine," drawls a voice. "I'd just love to stay here and do the dishes."

"I got no grenades, lieutenant."

"Somebody give the guy a couple of grenades."

"Have I got time for a crap, lieutenant?"

"No. What in hell have you men been doing?"

"I just felt the urge a minute ago."

"Hold it. I don't know what we're going to find up ahead. But be prepared for the worst."

"I hoid de whole kraut division broke troo."

"That's a lot of boloney."

"That's what I hoid."

"You heard wrong. Any more questions?"

"How about the tanks?"

"They were on the run, but they may be back."

"How far are we going?"

"I'd like to know the answer to that one myself."

"Are we going to get any chow tonight?"

"You'll probably get rations after dark."

"Any sign of mines yet?"

"I haven't seen them if there are."

"If we take the town, can I take my crap?"

"So long as you don't expose your flanks."

"Haw! Haw! That's a good'n."

"So long as he don't expose his flanks."

"Any more questions?" Final drags are taken from cigarettes, and the butts are flipped to the snow in silence. "All right, let's go."

We stick to the road until we reach the outpost.

"You back again, lieutenant?" asks the corporal.

"Have you seen anything of the krauts yet?"

"We ain't seen nuttin'; and we ain't heard nuttin' except big stuff fallin' around. You not goin' back up?"

"We're going to try."

"Hot damn, 'at puts us in the rear area again." He turns with a broad grin at his comrades. "How you rear echelon lice feel now?"

"Don't be too happy. We may come barreling back this way any minute."

We leave the road, spread out through the forest, and resume the advance in a ragged skirmish formation. A rifle cracks. We leap behind trees and hug their trunks. Within a minute we are in the middle of a furious fire fight.

The man who caught the first bullet is still in the open. He is bent double, evidently from a stomach wound. Suddenly he sits down. Another bullet flips his head back. He rolls over with jerking muscles.

The krauts are firing from behind a small knoll, and getting at them is a difficult proposition. I slip to the earth and start crawling. A bullet kicks snow into my face. I squirm back to the tree.

The squat soldier with the blistered foot slithers over the snow on his belly with a hand grenade in each hand. I see him flinch and pause as a bullet finds his left shoulder. The tall soldier who was ribbing him but a short while ago rises to one knee and lays a blast of fire over the prone body. Again the squat man slides forward. His grenade hits the top of the mound; skids over. Knowing the krauts will be occupied with the grenade, we dash forward in a rough semicircle.

By the time the explosion dies, most of us are in new positions. Doubtless the krauts think we intend to rush them. Three helmets pop up over the mound. A volley of rifle fire smashes into them.

The squat man throws his second grenade. Its blast is followed by silence.

We charge the knoll and on its slope find seven more Germans who have given their all for *Der Führer.*

The rest of the afternoon is spent in battling such pockets of resistance. In one brief but brutal assault after another we push the enemy from our sector. And that night we lie among the bodies of our comrades who fell at the edge of the forest in the early afternoon.

Before dawn, the 30th, reinforced and reorganized, moves up to take the ball. By-passing our lines, its units smash through fields and woodland, building its drive like a steam roller that has lost its brakes on a grade. Two companies move toward Holtzwihr. One is hit by a tank. It falls back, regroups, and stabs again. By ten o'clock in the morning the ruined village is cleared of its last German; and the pressure is taken off us.

We have not long to lie around and lick our wounds, however. The big attack is on. Every man, every gun is needed. Replacements come up to fatten the company; and a few old men are to be sent to the rear with frozen feet and shattered nerves.

Elleridge is among those who are waiting to be evacuated. His feet are in such bad shape that he cannot stand; and he is dreadfully afraid that they will have to be amputated.

"I had a lot of postwar plans for my feet," says he. "If I lose them, I want to be buried in some veteran's hospital and spend the rest of my life cheating blind men at poker."

"Don't take it so seriously. When you get thawed out, you'll be all right."

"Yeah. I'll be all right. You can talk to me straight."

"You don't have to use your feet teaching school."

"Evidently you don't have to use your head either. Or your heart. It's a game. Jeezus. Grow old along with me. The best is yet to be."

"What are you talking about?"

"It's part of a poem that I used to feed to the kids. You want to hear the rest of it?"

"No. You want some coffee?"

"Can't you imagine old crutches stumping into the school room with a big smile on his face and his insides like a patch of woods that a fire has eaten through."

"I said do you want some coffee?"

"I'm up to my ears in coffee. It does no good. I'm still cold."

"We ought to get some mail. I'm expecting a couple dozen letters from nobody."

"I don't want to hear from anybody. I tell you I'm burnt out."

"You talk more like a schoolteacher by the minute."

"Do I? I'll get over it." He grins suddenly. "I'm feeling mighty sorry for myself."

"You sure as hell are."

"Skip me. They used to say I was a sensitive soul back in college; and maybe I caught too much before I could get the guards up."

"Who didn't?"

"That's right. Who didn't?"

"You want some coffee?"

"Sure. I could use some java."

As we sip the coffee, Kohl approaches. "A new batch of cannon fodder just came in," says he. "What do you want done with them?"

"How do they look?"

"As cheerful as a graveyard. Part of them are greenhorns; and the rest are reclaimed casualties. The repple depples must be scraping the bottom of the barrel."

"Are they pleasingly plump?" asks Elleridge. "Are their teeth sound? I hope none of them have the hoof and mouth disease."

"Where'd you leave them?"

"Lieutenant Anders came up with them. He's got them in charge."

"Anders? What's he doing back?"

"Ask him. He probably don't know either."

"He's a good man, with guts to spare. I'm glad he's back."

"I saw him get hit," says Elleridge. "It happened somewhere in the Vosges. He was leading a platoon through the woods when a tree burst got him. He was knocked down; and I thought he was dead. But he got up and kept on fighting until he passed out."

"He's still white as a ghost," says Kohl.

"This nice fresh air will put color back into his cheeks," says Elleridge. "Spend your winters in beautiful Pneumonia Valley, where you'll find all the peace and quiet of hell on a holiday."

"I'd better go give them the once-over. Take it easy, Elleridge. If I don't see you again, good luck."

"I'm sorry I conked out. I know you need men badly."

"We'll get them."

"I'm sorry too that I acted like an ass. Who the hell am I to complain? I'm still alive."

"You'll be okay. Don't worry about those feet. They'll be all right."

"Don't worry about them? I didn't even know I had any left till they started thawing. Well, so long. They say there's nothing so bitter as a dreamer whose dreams go sour. Guess that's me."

"Don't pat any nurses on the fanny," says Kohl. "I had a pal who tried it and bruised his hand on a corset stave."

The replacements are huddled together in the room of a half-demolished building. A glance is all that is needed to distinguish between the rookies and the ex-casualties. The latter are still pale from hospitalization; and their attitude is calm and indifferent. On some bloody field and bed of pain they have learned resignation. The new men are more peevish and defiant.

"I wish I could give you a pep talk," I say. "But I'm fresh out of pep. I don't have to tell the old men what to do. To you new men, I say, follow instructions. And use your heads, or you won't have any heads left to use. This company specializes in killing; and we haven't got time to take care of a bunch of wounded krauts. If they want to give up, take them. If they don't, kill them. As far as I'm concerned, you're all able men until you prove yourself otherwise. Any questions?"

"Sir, can I swap my carbine for a tommy gun?" asks a man with a scar-streaked cheek.

"What you want with a tommy gun?"

"I hear there's going to be a lot of house-to-house stuff."

"Who told you that?"

"I heard it on the way up."

"You still believe what you hear?"

"After three years in this man's army, I'd believe that Santa Claus wore green whiskers."

"Kohl, see if you can find him a tommy. Any more questions?"

"Will our mail follow us, lieutenant?"

"Yes. But there's no telling when it'll catch up."

"What have the krauts been using mostly?"

"Everything in the book, including a lot of armor."

"Will we need bayonets?"

"You'll never know what you'll need. Keep your bayonets handy."

"I've lost mine."

"That's just T.S. You should take care of your equipment. Any more questions? Okay. Get ready for an inspection. And don't anybody leave this area."

They bustle out the door, but one man lingers.

"Sir, I think something's wrong with me."

"What is it?"

"I—I think I've got the crabs."

"What gives you that idea?"

"It ain't an idea. I know so."

"Where in hell did you pick them up in this neck of the woods?"

"At the replacement depot. On toilet seats I think."

"Yeah, I know. Well, what do you want me to do? Mark you a latrine casualty and send you to the rear? Or do you think we ought to open up a pro-station in the front lines?"

"I don't know—I mean nosir."

"Look around. You'll find some gasoline. Try dousing yourself with it."

"Yessir."

"And leave your pants down until the gas dries, or you're liable to wind up with a blister."

"Yessir."

"And if that don't work, just leave your pants down a little longer and freeze them."

As he walks meekly away, Anders shakes his head. "The same old army," he says. "You have to see these things to believe them."

"How're you feeling?"

"Washed up. The wound's about well, but my nerves are jumping around like frogs."

"They shouldn't have sent you back up."

"I asked for it."

"Yeah."

"How's it been?"

"Rough as I've ever seen it. We've lost two-thirds of the company in the past four days."

"Whew! When do we go up?"

"Probably tonight. I'm dead on my feet. Will you look over the men's equipment?"

"Yeah. Sure."

"See that they've got dry socks; and don't let them throw away their galoshes."

"Okay."

"Did you have any fun while you were gone?"

"Yeah. I met a nice little dish in the hospital."

"Yeah?"

"A blonde from Houston."

"That's my territory."

"That's what you think. Had a date with her the night I had to pull out."

"Yeah?"

"I didn't get to see her. Left her a note."

"The poor girl. I can just see her pining away for the lack of somebody to make a pass at her."

"Aw, Murph. The trouble with staying up in the lines is that you get so damned cynical. She was a nice babe."

"Yeah. I've been so good I dreamed I went to heaven."

"No kidding?"

"Yeah. Got into a fur-lined foxhole."

"You must've been all wet."

"Right. When I woke up I was."

"This girl of mine—"

"I met me a nurse, too."

"Yeah?"

"Brunette with a figure that'd knock your eye out."

"No? Probably shacking up with some med corps colonel."

"She wouldn't do that with me."

"The hell she wouldn't."

21

ON the following afternoon, we move into the front lines. As we plod up the icy road, a wind, whipping across the plains, occasionally lifts a cloud of powdery snow and drives it into our faces. The flesh stings as though pricked with hundreds of needles; and our feet, despite all precaution, grow wet and numb.

Behind me, I hear the rhythm of slogging footsteps; the heavy breathing and swearing of men who think they have reached the limit of endurance and exasperation. But they have not. Before night our situation will have changed infinitely for

TO HELL AND BACK

the worse. We will be under fire and the temperature will have dropped even lower.

Bergman, with his peculiar sense of humor, is a great help when the going is rough. Sensing the mood, he now shouts, "Nobody can say we're not moving into action as cool as cucumbers."

Instantly his remark brings a chorus of responses.

"Aw, who's de wise guy?"

"Throw him in the snow."

"Feed him beans. Feed him beans."

"If you freeze," says the Swede, "you get stacked up like wood and tawed out wit a flame trower."

"Aw, shadup."

"Save yoh bret."

"You ain't seen nothing yet," declares the Swede cheerfully. "Wait'll we swim that river."

"Never will I forgive that draft board," says a voice bitterly. "I wish I had the whole damned bunch right here."

"You didn't get drafted. You volunteered."

"Who volunteered?"

"Aw, nuts! Save yoh bret. Save yoh bret."

I understand their mood, but have no sympathy for it. We are all moving up together and must take our chances with fortune. Right now I am concerned with the individual only as a fighting unit. If his feet freeze, I will turn him over to the medics. If his nerves crack, I will send him to the rear. If he is hit, I will see that his wound is treated. Otherwise, I look upon him as a unit whom I must get to the front and in battle position on schedule.

At the whistle of a solitary shell, the company halts abruptly. From the sound, I know that the projectile is going wide of us. We are in no danger. I wheel about. Part of the men follow the noise with an experienced ear; some have dropped to their bellies; others, as if hypnotized by the sound, stand gaping stupidly.

253

The shell crashes into a field on our right. The staring men flop to the earth. I walk back through the ranks.

"For those of you who've never heard it before, that was a sample of German artillery. The time to duck is when you hear a shell coming, not after it explodes. All right, on your feet, everybody. Platoon leaders, spread your men out more. Let's go."

One man fails to rise.

"Okay, what's wrong with you, soldier? You heard the order. Get off your rear-end."

"Yessir. I didn't know we was ready."

As I turn, I hear loud snickers.

"What's wrong with you, Rusty? Think your number was up?"

"Aw, save yoh bret."

"That was the guy who claimed he fought in the ring."

"Yeah. Ring-around-roses."

"Aw, choke de chatter. Save yoh bret."

The Colmar Canal is a fifty-foot-wide ribbon of water that stretches across the plains between the Rhine and the city whose name it bears. On the military map it looks as formidable as the river Ill. Flanked by banks twelve feet high, the slowly moving water has not been frozen. Crossing it may prove to be a costly and bloody task. But we must get over. The plan of action is now obvious. We are to by-pass Colmar, knife south, and cut the highways and railroad feeding the pocket from Germany.

Under the cover of darkness, we move toward the north bank of the canal. The earth trembles from our growling, rumbling artillery; and ahead we can see streams of tracer bullets slicing the darkness. Later I learn that an entire antiaircraft battalion has turned its weapons against ground targets. Within three hours it pumps twenty two thousand rounds of ammunition across the canal.

We eat on the move, dipping our spoons into cans of a revolting mixture that passes for vegetable stew. The wind has increased in intensity. Explosions rip the earth before us. The artillery flashes dance weirdly over the faces of the men. We look like a phantom body of troops doing a forced march through hell.

I step to one side of the road to let the company pass. A man turns his head aside and vomits.

"What's wrong there, soldier?"

"That goddam horse meat. It's made me sick before."

"Can you carry on?"

"I'll carry on as long as there's a gut left in my body."

"That's the spirit. What's wrong with you there, soldier?"

"I don't know. I'm just freezing."

"Brace up, and cut out the crying. We're all here together."

"And you ain't seen nothing yet." Bergman is still in there pitching.

"Are you all right, men?"

"I ain't never been more unright."

"What's the matter with you?"

"Muh pack's all screwed up."

"Fall out and get it unscrewed. Then get back into position on the double."

"If your feet fall off, what're you supposed to do?"

"Pick them up and carry them. What's that, soldier?"

"Nobody said nuthin'."

"Go ahead and bitch, but keep moving."

"Got any enlistment blanks, lieutenant? Rusty just decided to be a thirty-year man."

"Aw, guzzle the gas."

"How much further, lieutenant?"

"I don't know. We'll find out when we get there."

"Gittin' shot's gonna be a pleasure after this here hoofin'."

"What's wrong with you stragglers? Come on. Catch up."

"You walking too fast, lieutenant."

"If the rest of the company can do it, so can you. Come on. Pick them up."

"Man back here sick, lieutenant."

"What's wrong with him?"

"He got overheated."

"Jeezus! Now I've hoid everything. Eskimo wit da fever."

"Are you really sick, soldier?"

"I can still navigate, lieutenant."

"The man is just out of the hospital."

"You want to fall out?"

"Nosir."

"Da guy's nuts. Jus' as' me if I wanta get out, lieutenant."

"Okay. Let's step it up. We'll probably get a break at the assembly area."

"We'll probably get broke in two."

"And you ain't just a-birdin', son. You ain't birdin' a-tall."

Because of the mass of our weapons and the shrewd planning of our strategists, the canal crossing is accomplished with ease. The terrific preparatory barrage has knocked the Germans punch-drunk. Before they can reorganize, units of our assault troops paddle over the water in rubber boats and establish bridgeheads. Engineers shove over footbridges. By midnight two infantry regiments are on the south bank of the canal.

For the next two days, we slash across the countryside, battering down points of resistance and mopping up areas of thinly scattered troops. The whole strategy now seems to hinge on speed. We must hit the enemy before he can get to his feet.

Sleep is not among our rations. The snow has turned to slush; and we slog from objective to objective on leaden feet. There is little need for personal camouflage. Our clothes are so muddy that, except for the shape of our helmets, we can scarcely be distinguished from the Germans.

One night, however, it looks as though we may get a breathing spell. We have cleared a section of woods southwest of the embattled town of Urschenheim and settled down. The exhausted men sit in mud, lean their backs against trees, and sleep. Despite the power of our offensive, the enemy has slugged back hard; and the company strength has again been whittled alarmingly.

I am about to doze when the order comes. Urschenheim has fallen; and our battalion is to make a dash for the Rhone-Rhine canal and attempt to capture a bridge on the outskirts of Kunheim. It is a race against enemy demolition. The Germans have considerable men and armor on this side of the canal; so the bridge will likely be left standing until it becomes too risky.

The orders say that I must assemble my men directly back of Urschenheim. To this I object. I contact headquarters with my argument.

"I want a change of orders," I say.

"A what?"

"A change of orders. Let my company skirt Urschenheim and join the battalion on the road northeast of the town."

"Why?"

"The krauts are sure to turn their artillery on Urschenheim, and some of the shells are coming over into the area where we're supposed to assemble."

"What makes you think that?"

"Think it! For godsake, don't they always shell a town after pulling out; and don't some of the shells always go wild?"

"That's right. But there's nothing I can do about it. The orders came from higher up."

"You want me to get my men killed?"

"Easy, lieutenant. I'm not running this army."

"Can't you get the orders changed?"

"You know damned well I can't. This is a rush, and you'd better get moving. Good luck."

That is all that I can do. This is the army; and orders are orders. I wake Anders and tell him to get the men ready to move.

"Gawdalmighty," he blinks. "What now?"

"An attack."

"We're being attacked?"

"No, we're doing the attacking. Seems there's a little bridge over the canal we're supposed to take before morning."

"Damn, I hate to do this. All right, men, you've had your beauty sleep. Let's get ready to shove off."

The men are too tired to protest. Like dumb brutes feeling the dig of a spur, they reach for their weapons and pull themselves to their feet.

When the company is assembled, I say, "This is not my idea. I'm as tired as the rest of you. But this attack is important; and we've got to go."

Still there is remarkably little grumbling. I would feel better if I heard a few strong oaths.

"We may get some artillery; so keep on your toes."

"And save yoh bret," says the unmistakable voice of Rusty. "Save yoh bret."

Before we have had time to regroup for instructions, the shells fall into our midst. Eight men are knocked out; and Anders cracks up. It is not his fault. He has courage to spare, but body and nerves have taken all they can stand. He has heard one explosion too many; seen one man too many die.

As we check the dead and wounded, his voice goes thick. I grab him by the shoulder. He shudders and begins to shake violently.

"What's the matter?"

"I've gone all to pieces."

"Stay here and wait for the medics. You shouldn't have come back up."

"N-no. No. No."

"You're no good in that shape."

"I'll come out of it."

"The hell you will. You can't let the men see you in that condition."

"I'll be quiet. I won't say anything."

"You're going to tell it to the doctor."

"If you think so, maybe I should. Maybe I should."

He rejoins us the next day. I curse him heartily, but he only grins. When we come under heavy artillery fire, that grin is quickly erased. His nerves collapse again. His mouth sags; his speech becomes jerky; and his hands shake so that he can hardly insert an ammunition clip into his carbine. Whether or not he knows or wants it, he is through. Finished. This time when I send him to the rear, I also send the colonel word to keep him there.

A group of Germans surrenders to my company. A sad, muddy lot, they throw their helmets down and stand with raised hands while we shake them down. Their eyes are dead and indifferent. They seem more exhausted than we.

We are sprawling on the ground together when we hear the tanks. It is too late to run. I glance at the prisoners. Most of them sit with bowed heads, giving no indication that they are aware of the situation.

I grab a German helmet and clap it on my head. Other men do likewise. Three tanks, accompanied by a sprinkling of infantrymen, pass within thirty yards of us. We wave at the krauts; and they return the greeting. For the next ten minutes, I scarcely breathe. If one prisoner shouts, if one German eye examines the dirty uniforms beneath our helmets, it is the end for us.

The tanks speed around a bend in the road; and the forest swallows them. I wipe the cold sweat from my forehead and thank God for mud and exhaustion.

In a few minutes we take up the pursuit. The bridge is in sight. One of the enemy tanks races across it to temporary security. Then with a thunderous explosion, the bridge heaves and falls into wreckage. Enemy demolition has beaten us to it.

As we crash toward Biesheim in the final phase of the assault, the fighting increases in ferocity. The krauts are fully aware of their plight. If we get through Biesheim and take the communications center of Neuf-Brisach, their supply lines will be cut and the pocket sealed, making it strategically useless.

On the approach to Biesheim, forward elements of the 7th fall into ambush. In the darkness, they unknowingly pass through the enemy lines. The Germans wait in silence until a number of men have got through; then they turn a concentration of mortar and machine-gun fire upon them.

The trapped men leap into a ditch, but find it already occupied by enemy infantrymen. While rifle butts crush skulls, a lone soldier races through a hail of small-arms fire to the rear. He secures two light tanks and climbs upon the hull of the lead one to guide it through the darkness.

As it reaches the ditch where our men are fighting, the tank receives a direct hit. The soldier on top is killed; the tank, set afire. But the flames give the rear units their marker. They rush forward, guided by its light, and close in with the Germans.

Fearing such an ambush ourselves, we creep as stealthily as mice through the strange territory. A brick wall rears before us. We pause, listening intently for the clink of metal, the guttural whisper, or the scrape of a boot. But, except for the sighing of the wind through the trees, there is no sound.

I roll over the wall and find myself in a cemetery. Some of the graves are covered with mica; and they glitter with the light of a sinking moon. We are in luck. The wall extends entirely around the place; and in case of an attack, the tombstones and grave mounds will be handy as cover.

I signal the men; and they clamber over the wall. Though

dog tired and miserable with cold, they cannot overlook the irony of the situation.

"Jeezus! The graveyard company finally gets home."

"Move over friends. You got some company."

"Be funny to wake up here in the middle of the night."

"Think nuttin' of it. Just say, 'Resurrection morning; and I'm the first one up.'"

"We workin' in cahoots with the G.R.O.?"

"Keep your voices down."

"I been tellin' 'em, lieutenant. If dey choke de chatter, dey save der bret."

With entrenching picks, we knock holes in the wall for our machine-gun barrels. I post the guards and take the watch on the gate for myself. I dare not sit down for fear of falling asleep. Leaning against a tombstone, I face the gate.

Once I risk closing my eyes and immediately drop off to sleep. I awake with a jerk. I cannot take that chance again. Removing my pistol from its holster, I hold it at my waist with both hands. The next time I doze the gun slips from my fingers, strikes my feet, and brings me back to consciousness.

Day is just breaking when Bergman calls me.

"This is a set-up right out of the books," says he.

I peer through the hole in the wall. In an open field directly before us, a German sergeant is yawning and stretching himself. Then he barks something that is evidently a command. From slit trenches, his sleepy men arise.

Bergman gauges the range and lines his sights. "Dying at reveille is going to be easy," says he. "They can just turn over and go back to sleep forever."

One of the krauts gets tripped in his blanket. He stumbles and falls while his comrades laugh loud and jeeringly.

"Okay?" asks Bergman.

"I count twenty men."

"You think that's all of them?"

"Must be. Okay, let them have it."

The machine gun rattles. Four of the Germans crumple. The others stare wildly about, seeking the direction of the fire. Again the gun clatters. Two more krauts fall. The others throw up their hands.

"Just like something from the books," repeats Bergman.

"Yeah. Okay, men, go out and get them."

Another day has begun.

With the fall of Neuf-Brisach, German resistance crumbles. After the pocket has been completely cleared, we are sent to a rest camp. In seven weeks the division has suffered over forty-five hundred casualties.

22

THE SNOW melts; the streams rise; and the earth turns into an endless bog as the winter closes. Our training program has been intense. A putting together of the maneuvers and maps gives us an easy tip-off on the forthcoming action. The emphasis has been on street fighting, river crossings, and the reducing of permanent fortifications. That can mean but one thing. We are preparing for the big jump-off into Germany itself.

One day the leaf buds appear again on the trees; and in the rear area, where we have been stationed since the fall of the Colmar Pocket, French villagers begin spading their gardens. The men grow restless. With an uneasy eye, they watch the coming of spring. They see the fields drying in the warm winds and know that the ground will soon be ready to support armor.

Hope and fear walk hand in hand. We can see the end now,

but we are going back up. And always in a man's mind is that one lead pill, that one splinter of steel that can lose him the race with the finish line in sight.

We argue a great deal over the attitude the Germans will take about fighting on their own soil. Some believe that resistance will collapse once we have crossed the Rhine; others think the enemy will make a last ditch stand, fighting increasingly harder as we drive into his homeland.

There are rumors that Germany, pounded by bombings and attacked from all sides, is tottering. It is rotten internally and cannot hold out, once the crust of its defense is broken. Equally strong rumors say that the entire country is a fortress similar to the Colmar Pocket. It must be ground down slowly and agonizingly before the final victory.

News has suddenly become important. The men cluster around radios and newspapers. Each bit of information is discussed, analyzed, and applied to our situation. With the vast pattern of strategy now clear, we no longer feel like an isolated group fighting on a lost front. Each movement of the British, the French, or the Russians, directly affects our own destiny.

The phrase, "If I live," becomes less common. The early March sun hangs overhead; and beneath it, men, carefully cleaning their weapons, again talk of home.

I have seen too much to grow optimistic. The road across Germany is a long one; and each mile of it must be bought with somebody's blood. Why not mine? My luck has been extraordinary, but there is an end even to the extraordinary. So until the last shot is fired, I will go on living from day to day, making no postwar plans.

Then the unexpected happens. Captain Hogan, returning from a special assignment, resumes command of the company. I am transferred to liaison duty, which virtually removes me from combat.

There will be small dangers, of course, and moments of

minor terror. With nerves schooled to uncertainty, the hair will still rise and the flesh creep as I sense the presence of the enemy in the ruins of his defeated towns. But the constant peril of the front lines is temporarily over.

I receive the gift of life without inward emotion. I am so much a part of the war now that it does not matter. There will be other days and other orders. Eventually I feel that I will go back up; and somewhere, sometime, the bullet bearing my name will find me.

Meanwhile, my job is to serve as contact man between the units of the division. When we begin the attack, I have a jeep, a driver, an interpreter—and a violent distrust of anything German. My duties should not take me to the front, but I have learned to prepare for the worst.

In battle, lines often change swiftly. And those in the immediate rear are suddenly at the immediate front. To the 50-caliber machine gun mounted on the jeep, I add a few rifles, two German machine guns, and a case of grenades.

The forward elements of the division move up at night. Crossing the German frontier, they reach an area that is heavily mined; and enemy armor crashes out to meet them in a counterattack. By daylight, the familiar roar of battle is rolling over the earth.

At regimental headquarters, where I wait for orders, the phones jangle constantly. Staff officers grab messages, anxiously scan them, and turn to their maps. Soon we all know that part of the division has met major resistance at a point considerably east of the Siegfried Line.

Outside an armored battalion rolls up the highway. From the open turrets of the tanks poke the worn, greasy faces of men. A column of infantrymen falls out by the side of the road to let the armor pass. The soldiers huddle together in groups. I know the feeling. The loneliness of battle is already closing in.

At noon my regiment jumps off. Within a few days, the division has smashed through to the Siegfried Line.

At headquarters, I learn of Captain Hogan's death. He was in a captured pillbox when a mortar shell got one of his men. Badly wounded, the man tried dragging himself back to cover. The captain crawled out to give him a hand. Another shell landed, sending a piece of steel into the captain. A lieutenant went after him. The third shell landed with pin-point accuracy; and the three men died together.

The remainder of the company reached a deserted enemy fire trench at the edge of the Siegfried Line. From the security of concrete pillboxes, the Germans zeroed-in the trench with rapid firing mortar guns. The company was pinned. Anyone attempting to leave the trench lived but a few seconds.

For two days I brooded over the news while running official errands in the rear. But finally I could take it no longer. I had been with the company since North Africa; and it had become a part of my life's blood. Its lot was my lot; and to hell with regulations.

At headquarters I casually check on the position, fixing the location firmly in mind. There can be no mistake, but I must not arouse suspicion. Officially I am going up toward the front to check a telephone line.

My communications sergeant drives the jeep; and he guesses my intention.

"If you don't come back," he says glumly, "what kind of a spot will it put me in?"

"I'll be back."

"But if you don't make it, lieutenant?"

"You were acting under orders, my orders. Nobody can do anything to you."

"Okay. But I still don't like it."

"Just consider it none of your business; and don't act like you're driving a hearse. You're not going to be in any danger."

"I'm not afraid. I was thinking about you."

"Why? I'm asking for it."

"Okay. So you ask for it."

"Don't you ever break any rules?"

"I've broken about every rule in the book."

"So have I. One more won't matter."

On reaching a point from which we can see the famed "dragon teeth," I halt the jeep and crawl out. The terrain ahead is composed of barren, rolling hills and offers little cover. I check a field map to get my bearings. The sergeant is still worried.

"You taking nothing but a carbine, lieutenant?"

"That's all I'll need."

"Jeezus! What I wouldn't give for a picture of this. A guy tackling the Siegfried Line with a pea-shooter."

"What would you take?"

"I'd take off."

"That's exactly what I intend to do. If the Siegfried Line isn't already busted, some track records soon will be."

Able to see for hundreds of yards, I walk upright and in the open. If krauts are in the area, I want to draw their fire from a distance. The odds are in favor of their missing the first time.

But nothing happens. I may as well be strolling through a desert. No sign of life appears about the zigzagged trench or the pillboxes beyond. Then my heart seems to jump from my chest as the idea strikes me. What if the entire company has been captured or wiped out? Dear God, no. I stumble forward.

They do not see me as I stand above them. Bearded, filthy, and listless, they sprawl on the bottom of the trench, looking like warmed-over death. The sunlight glistens on a red thatch of hair.

"Bergman, what the hell are you doing down there?"

He casts a blank glance upward.

"Come on. Let's get out of there."

"For Christ's sweet sake, how did you get up there?"

266

"I just walked up. Come on now. Let's quit playing ground hog."

A shell screams overhead and crashes into one of the pillboxes. The men cower.

"Nothing to be afraid of. It's one of our own tanks."

"We got no tanks."

"We got plenty of stuff left. Now off those fat fannies. Let's move across Germany."

I walk on down the trench.

"All right, Rusty. What's the matter?"

"Dey done battered hell out of us, lieutenant."

"Well, let's batter them back."

"Dey done trow everting over but deh gun barrels." His voice sounds like that of a child who has been wrongfully punished.

"Come on there, man. Quit saving the bret."

"Fix it up so I can get a court-marcher. De stockade would be a pleashuh."

"I'll speak to the general about it."

Another shell passes over. Rusty cringes as it explodes against a second pillbox.

"Dey be trowin' Hitler in poisern over in a minute. Dey done trow everting else."

"It's our own tanks."

"Well, tank 'em for nuttin. We done got hell beat out'n us."

"It's all in your mind. Come on, Rusty. Save the bret."

I continue along the edge of the trench, insulting and pleading. Of the officers, only a second lieutenant remains. He is very young; and his eyes are staring and haunted. I can see that he is in as bad shape as his men.

"We've got to get out of here while the gettin's good," I say.

"To the rear?"

"No. You've got to go forward."

"I don't know whether the men can take any more."

"They can take it. Can you?"

"I can take it."

We coax the sergeants out of the trenches; and one by one the men follow. I have never seen a more thorough psychological beating. They glance anxiously about the terrain; and their movements are shaky and uncertain. It looks like a mass collapse of nerves. I would like to pull them back for a rest, but I cannot. They have to move forward.

When the tanks drew no response from the pillboxes, I rightly assumed the Germans had abandoned them. We march straight through the Siegfried Line; and not a shot is fired at us. Nobody remembers when the krauts left. Under the terrible punishment, reality had been replaced by a phantom. But in the minds of the strained and exhausted men, that phantom was real—a common occurrence in combat.

I get the men under cover and tell the lieutenant to keep them there until contacted by other units. Then, retracing my steps through the maze of silent fortifications, I return to headquarters, where I find that I have not been missed.

Beyond the Siegfried Line, our forces consolidate; and the drive becomes like a great river pushing against a series of rotting dams. A dam breaks; and the torrent lashes onward until it hits another obstruction. Between the major points of resistance lie gaps protected by lines so thinly held that locating the actual front is often difficult.

After we cross the Rhine, the dike crumbles; and a flood of men and arms pours over Germany. Even the most fanatical Nazis must now see that the game is up, but they still dupe the people with the promise that further resistance will bring a negotiated peace, rather than an unconditional surrender.

If they still want war, they can have it. With victory in our grasp, we do not soften. Our artillery levels whole sections of towns. Flames lick over burning buildings. Infantry and armor prowl rubble-strewn streets, and blood flows needlessly in the gutters.

After the battle lines roll on, windows drip with white flags. If a house fails to show the surrender token, we do not knock on the door and say, "Please." We simply rip its windows with machine-gun fire to point out the oversight. The method is most effective.

Near Munich my jeep pulls up to a prison camp. I step through the gate with pistol drawn and come face to face with a German guard. He flinches; but before I can pull the trigger, an American yells, "Don't shoot. Don't shoot, lieutenant. He's a good joe."

"Have you gone soft in the head or the heart?"

"No. No. I've been here more than a year; and he's always treated us decently."

A good joe? Maybe he is. I cannot see men any more. I only see uniforms. I return the pistol to its holster.

"Tell him to turn himself in to the American authorities," I say to the interpreter.

There follows a brisk conversation in German. "He's afraid to go out on the streets," the interpreter explains. "He thinks he'll be shot. He wants to know if the prisoners will testify that he never mistreated them."

"That's up to the prisoners."

"He was okay," the newly liberated prisoner insists. "I'll testify to it if necessary."

"Tell him to relax and wait here then. Nobody's going to hurt him, at least not yet."

The interpreter translates. The German mumbles something and stumbles toward a pair of steps.

There is something pathetically human about his odd, hobbled walk. What it is I do not know. Perhaps it is the knowledge that we carry in our hearts that nobody ultimately wins. Somewhere we all go down. Force used tyrannically is our common enemy. Why align ourselves with it in whatever shape or fashion.

Now comes the picture of mass defeat, the most awesome spectacle of the war. It is in the bent bodies of old women who poke among ruins seeking some miserable object that will link their lives with the old days. It is in the shamed, darting eyes of the defeated. It is in the faces of the little boys who regard our triumphant columns with fear and fascination. And above all it is in the thousands of beaten, dusty soldiers who stream along the roads toward the stockades. Their feet clump wearily, mechanically, hopelessly on the still endless road of war. They move as haggard, gray masses, in which the individual has neither life nor meaning. It is impossible to see in these men the quality that made them stand up and fight like demons out of hell a few short months ago.

Except for tying up the bag with formalities, the war is over. A number of us are granted rest leaves. The train on which we ride clackety-clacks toward the French Riviera. Early in the morning, it halts in a little town; and above the wheezing of the engine, I hear the ringing of church bells and strains of accordion music.

Wiping the sleep from my eyes, I go to a station-side window. On the platform is a group of American artillerymen, wearing faded ODs and muddy combat boots. They wait with the patience of cows. A red-faced sergeant, leaning on a Garand, draws imaginary patterns with the toe of his shoe.

"What's all the noise about?" I ask.

He shrugs. "Guess it's the news of the German surrender."

"It's official?"

"Yessir. Haven't you heard the radio?"

"No. I've been riding since yesterday."

"We've been on the move for a week. Looks like the South Pacific. That's the big rumor anyhow."

"Maybe you're going back to the States."

"Oh, no. We've just been over nine months. Where you headed?"

"For a leave on the Riviera."

"No kiddin'! That's where all them beautiful babes are supposed to be, ain't it?"

"So I've heard."

"Well, if you find an extra blonde, give her my address. General Delivery, South Pacific."

"I'll do that."

"And slug one down for me, lieutenant. If you can't find a scotch and soda, I'll settle for some of the shellack that passes for booze in this country."

"Well, take it easy."

"I couldn't take it easier."

As the train pulls out, I return to my compartment.

"Where are we?" asks a yawning infantry lieutenant.

"Somewhere in France."

"I've been somewhere in France till I'm sick of it."

"Yeah."

"What goes on outside?"

"It's VE-Day."

"Well, I'll be damned. Somebody ought to holler," says a pudgy quartermaster captain. "I haven't got the energy."

"You shouldn't have from the way you've been snoring. Has anybody got an eye-opener?"

"You shouldn't drink before breakfast. Ruin your stomach."

"Who's got a stomach left? We ought to do something to celebrate."

"Why? I don't feel any joy bells ringing in my heart."

"We want to sit here like a bunch of clucks with the war over and everything?"

"We've still got Japan."

"So what? How about some poker? Anybody like to pick up some easy change?"

"I never play poker before breakfast. Bad luck."

"Where the hell did you get that idea?"

"From a one-armed madame in South Bend. She lost her life

savings to a traveling salesman. Had her cards before her coffee. I tell you it's bad luck."

"Speaking of women," says a graying engineers captain.

Clackety-clackety-clack. The train races onward.

In the Cannes hotel, I crawl into a tub of hot water and wallow around like a seal. Knotted muscles snap loose; and my eyes droop.

"Hey, there. You want to drown yourself?" My roommate, the restless lieutenant on the train, pauses in the middle of his shaving. "If you want to drown yourself, do it with champagne."

"I didn't know a body could get so tired."

"I'm out on my feet too. But a few snorts will fix that up."

"Yeah?"

"I'm going to take this town apart. You want to come along?"

"No, I'm going to hit the sack."

"Well, get out of the tub, bub. We've got a couple beds with sheets and everything, you know."

"I'll see you later."

"Okay. But remember, this burg's loaded with soldiers. If you want a dame, you'll have to hustle."

When I awake from the nap, it is mid-afternoon. From my window I can see the gulls wheeling over the Mediterranean and white breakers lapping the beaches. A hum comes up from the crowded city streets; and somewhere an orchestra is playing "Lili Marlene."

Turning to my pack in search of a necktie, I spy my service pistol. Automatically I pick it up, remove the clip, and check the mechanism. It works with buttered smoothness. I weigh the weapon in my hand and admire the cold, blue glint of its steel. It is more beautiful than a flower; more faithful than most friends.

The bells in a nearby cathedral start ringing. I toss the gun back into the pack and seize my necktie.

In the streets, crowded with merrymakers, I feel only a vague irritation. I want company, and I want to be alone. I want to talk, and I want to be silent. I want to sit, and I want to walk. There is VE-Day without, but no peace within.

Like a horror film run backwards, images of the war flicker through my brain. The tank in the snow with smoldering bodies on top. The smell of burning flesh. Of rotting flesh too. Novak rotting in a grave on Anzio. Horse-Face. Knowed an old girl once. The girl, red-eyed and shivering, in the Naples dawn. And Kerrigan. Kerrigan shuffling cards with half a hand. He was far luckier than Antonio. Yes, Antonio, trying to stand on the stumps of his legs with the machine gun ripping his body. And Brandon dead under the cork tree. Deer daddy, I'm in school. "I'll never enter another schoolroom," says Elleridge.

He was right. It is as though a fire had roared through this human house, leaving only the charred hulk of something that once was green.

Within a couple of hours, I have had enough. I return to my room. But I cannot sleep. My mind still whirls. When I was a child, I was told that men were branded by war. Has the brand been put on me? Have the years of blood and ruin stripped me of all decency? Of all belief?

Not of all belief. I believe in the force of a hand grenade, the power of artillery, the accuracy of a Garand. I believe in hitting before you get hit, and that dead men do not look noble.

But I also believe in men like Brandon and Novak and Swope and Kerrigan; and all the men who stood up against the enemy, taking their beatings without whimper and their triumphs without boasting. The men who went and would go again to hell and back to preserve what our country thinks right and decent.

My country. America! That is it. We have been so intent on death that we have forgotten life. And now suddenly life faces us. I swear to myself that I will measure up to it. I may be branded by war, but I will not be defeated by it.

Gradually it becomes clear. I will go back. I will find the kind of girl of whom I once dreamed. I will learn to look at life through uncynical eyes, to have faith, to know love. I will learn to work in peace as in war. And finally—finally, like countless others, I will learn to live again.

About the Author

AUDIE MURPHY was the most decorated American soldier during World War II. He went on to a long film career, starring in *The Red Badge of Courage*, *The Quiet American*, and his own *To Hell and Back*. He was killed in a plane crash in 1971 at age forty-six.